PRENTICE HALL

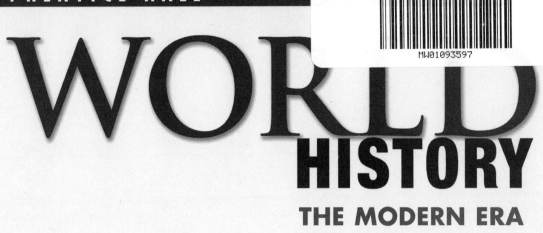

WORLD HISTORY
THE MODERN ERA

Reading and Note Taking Study Guide

PEARSON

Upper Saddle River, New Jersey • Boston, Massachusetts • Chandler, Arizona • Glenview, Illinois

13-digit ISBN: 978-0-13-372428-8
10-digit ISBN: 0-13-372428-X

11 12 13 14 15 V031 14 15 16

Contents

How to Use This Book

The **Reading and Note Taking Study Guide** will help you better understand the content of *Prentice Hall World History*. This book will also develop your reading, vocabulary, and note taking skills.

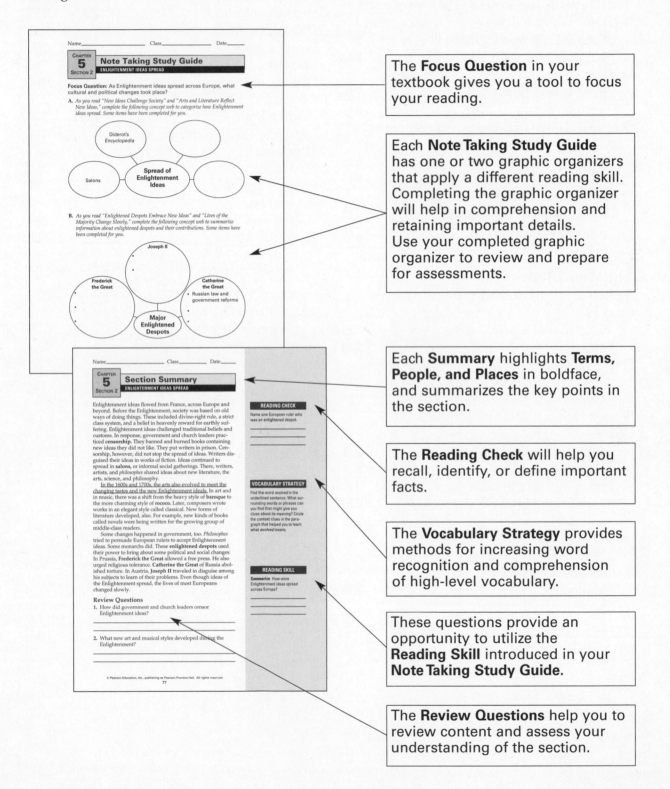

The **Focus Question** in your textbook gives you a tool to focus your reading.

Each **Note Taking Study Guide** has one or two graphic organizers that apply a different reading skill. Completing the graphic organizer will help in comprehension and retaining important details. Use your completed graphic organizer to review and prepare for assessments.

Each **Summary** highlights **Terms, People, and Places** in boldface, and summarizes the key points in the section.

The **Reading Check** will help you recall, identify, or define important facts.

The **Vocabulary Strategy** provides methods for increasing word recognition and comprehension of high-level vocabulary.

These questions provide an opportunity to utilize the **Reading Skill** introduced in your **Note Taking Study Guide**.

The **Review Questions** help you to review content and assess your understanding of the section.

The **Concept Connector Journal** supports the **Concept Connector** features and the **Concept Connector Essential Question Review** found in each chapter of your text, as well as the **Concept Connector Handbook** found at the end of your textbook. These journal sheets will help you to compare key concepts and events and to see patterns and make connections across time.

Each journal worksheet covers one of the 18 concepts you will be tracking throughout your course.

The **Essential Question** helps you think about the impact of the concept throughout history.

Complete the **WARM-UP** to help you understand the concept.

Turn to the **Concept Connector Essential Question Review** in your text before you begin answering the questions. Information to help you answer the questions can be found in the chapters, the **Concept Connector Handbook,** and the **Concept Connector** features in your textbook.

The WebQuest is an important part of building understanding of the Essential Question. Go online at **PHSchool.com** and input the Web Code to find the directions for completing a WebQuest on each Concept Connector topic. In your journal, write a brief explanation of how the WebQuest affected your response to the Essential Question.

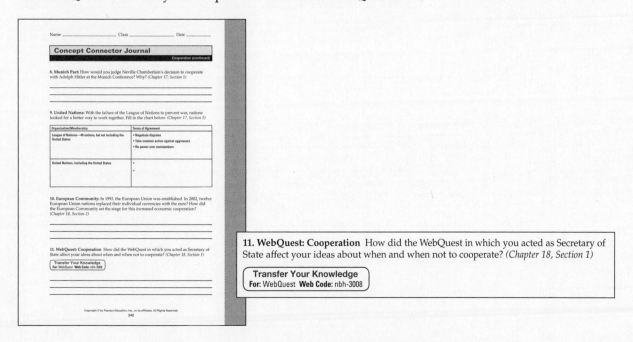

11. WebQuest: Cooperation How did the WebQuest in which you acted as Secretary of State affect your ideas about when and when not to cooperate? *(Chapter 18, Section 1)*

Transfer Your Knowledge
For: WebQuest **Web Code:** nbh-3008

PART
1.1

Note Taking Study Guide

TOWARD CIVILIZATION

As you read this section in your textbook, complete the outline below to summarize information about the periods of early human history and the development of civilizations.

I. Old Stone Age/Paleolithic Period

   A. From time of first stone toolmakers to about 10,000 B.C.

   B. Nomadic way of life

      1. Hunting and gathering bands of 20 to 30 people

      2. Made simple tools and weapons

      3. _____

      4. _____

      5. _____

II. _____

   A. _____

   B. _____

      1. _____

      2. _____

      3. _____

      4. _____

III. _____

   A. _____

   B. _____

   C. _____

      1. _____

      2. _____

   D. _____

      1. _____

      2. _____

   E. _____

      1. _____

      2. _____

PART 1.1 Section Summary
TOWARD CIVILIZATION

The period from the time of the first stone toolmakers to about 10,000 B.C. is known as the **Old Stone Age,** or the Paleolithic Period. Paleolithic people were **nomads,** or people who move from place to place to hunt for animals and edible plants. They lived in bands of 20 to 30 people and made simple tools and weapons. They developed spoken language, invented clothing made from animal skins, and learned to build fires.

About 10,000 years ago, nomadic bands learned to farm. This allowed them to remain in one place, which ushered in the **New Stone Age,** or Neolithic Age. Neolithic people established permanent villages and learned to tame animals. Village life reshaped the roles of men and women. During times of want, warfare increased. <u>Success in battle enabled some men to gain status as warriors, which gave them power over both women and other men.</u> The status of women declined.

About 5,000 years ago, the advances made by early farming communities led to the rise of civilizations. Historians have identified seven basic features common to most early civilizations: well-organized central governments, complex religions, job specialization, social classes, arts and architecture, public works, and writing.

Food surpluses in the river valleys of Africa and Asia helped populations to expand. As populations increased, some villages grew into cities. The challenge of farming in a river valley contributed to the development of city governments. Projects to control flooding and channel waters to fields required organization. Over time, city governments became more complex, and government **bureaucracies** grew.

Social organization also became more complex. People were ranked according to their jobs. Priests and nobles were usually at the top, followed by merchants and **artisans,** or skilled craftworkers. Below them were the peasant farmers and slaves at the very bottom. Priests developed writing to record information. Early writing was made up of **pictographs,** or simple drawings that represented ideas.

As ancient rulers gained more and more power, they conquered territories beyond their cities. Some conquered many cities and villages, creating **empires,** or groups of states, territories, and peoples ruled by one person.

Review Questions

1. Why did city governments develop in river valleys?

_____

_____

2. How were people ranked socially in early civilizations?

_____

_____

READING CHECK

Who are nomads?

_____

_____

_____

VOCABULARY STRATEGY

What does the word *status* mean in the underlined sentence? Note that the word *status* is repeated in the next sentence. As men gained *status* as warriors, the *status* of women declined. How does this help you understand the meaning of the word *status*?

READING SKILL

Identify Causes and Effects
Create a 4-step flowchart to show how the development of farming led to the growth of cities in river valleys. Begin your flowchart with "Nomadic bands learned to farm."

```
┌─────────────────────┐
│                     │
└─────────────────────┘
          ↓
┌─────────────────────┐
│                     │
└─────────────────────┘
          ↓
┌─────────────────────┐
│                     │
└─────────────────────┘
          ↓
┌─────────────────────┐
│                     │
└─────────────────────┘
```

Name_____ Class_____ Date_____

Note Taking Study Guide
FIRST CIVILIZATIONS: AFRICA AND ASIA

As you read this section in your textbook, complete the outline below to summarize information about the first civilizations in North Africa and the Middle East.

I. Ancient Kingdoms of the Nile
   A. Villages in Nile River valley joined into two kingdoms.
   B. _____
   C. Old Kingdom (about 2575–2130 B.C.)
   D. _____
   E. _____
II. _____
   A. _____
   B. _____
III. _____
   A. _____
   B. _____
     1. _____
     2. _____
     3. _____
   C. _____
     1. _____
     2. _____
IV. _____
   A. _____
   B. _____
   C. _____
   D. _____
V. _____
   A. _____
   B. _____
   C. _____
   D. _____
   E. _____

PART 1.2 Section Summary
FIRST CIVILIZATIONS: AFRICA AND ASIA

<u>The first civilizations emerged in river valleys and developed complex ways of life.</u> In the **Nile River** valley in Egypt, villages joined together into two kingdoms. These kingdoms were later united under King Menes.

The history of ancient Egypt after King Menes is divided into three periods, the Old, Middle, and New Kingdoms. During the Old Kingdom, the Egyptian rulers, or **pharaohs,** organized a strong central government and built pyramids as tombs. During the Middle and New Kingdoms, trade and warfare brought Egypt into contact with other civilizations, which led to **cultural diffusion.**

Egyptians worshiped many gods and goddesses and built tombs to preserve their bodies for the afterlife. Egyptian society was organized into classes. At the top was the pharaoh, who was considered both a king and a god.

Another civilization, the **city-states** of Sumer, developed along the Tigris and Euphrates rivers. This area was called **Mesopotamia,** and was located in the **Fertile Crescent.** The city-states often fought for control of land and water. War leaders eventually became rulers, and a social **hierarchy** emerged. The Sumerians built dikes, irrigation ditches, and **ziggurats,** or pyramid-temples. They also invented the earliest form of writing, called **cuneiform,** which **scribes** learned how to read and write.

About 2300 B.C., Sargon, the ruler of Akkad, conquered the city-states of Sumer. He built the world's first empire. About 1790 B.C., Hammurabi, king of Babylon, conquered much of Mesopotamia. His law code was the first major collection of laws in history.

About 2000 B.C., the **Hebrews** migrated from Mesopotamia to Canaan. They developed Judaism, a **monotheistic** religion based on the belief in one God. They recorded events and laws in the Torah, their most sacred text. **Prophets** preached a strong code of **ethics** and urged the Hebrews to obey God's law. The Hebrews established the kingdom of Israel, which eventually split into two parts. Invading armies captured the Hebrews, who later became known as Jews. About 2,000 years ago, many Jews were forced to leave their homeland. This scattering of the Jewish people is known as the **diaspora.**

Review Questions

1. Why did Egyptian rulers build pyramids?

_____

_____

2. Who invented the earliest form of writing, and what was it called?

_____

_____

READING CHECK

What was the diaspora?

_____

_____

_____

VOCABULARY STRATEGY

Find the word *complex* in the underlined sentence. What do you think it means? The word *simple* is an antonym of the word *complex*. Use this clue to help you figure out the meaning of *complex*.

READING SKILL

Compare and Contrast Compare and contrast the geography of civilizations in Egypt and in Sumer.

_____

_____

_____

PART 1.3 Note Taking Study Guide
EARLY CIVILIZATIONS IN INDIA AND CHINA

As you read this section in your textbook, complete the outline below to summarize information about early civilizations in India and China.

I. Cities of the Indus Valley

    A. India's first civilization arose in Indus River valley about 2600 B.C.

    B. Two main cities were Mohenjo-Daro and Harappa.

    C. _____

II. _____

    A. _____

        1. _____

        2. _____

    B. _____

        1. _____

        2. _____

    C. _____

        1. _____

        2. _____

        3. _____

III. _____

    A. _____

        1. _____

        2. _____

    B. _____

        1. _____

        2. _____

    C. _____

        1. _____

        2. _____

        3. _____

    D. _____

        1. _____

        2. _____

        3. _____

PART 1.3 Section Summary
EARLY CIVILIZATIONS IN INDIA AND CHINA

India's first civilization emerged in the Indus River valley about 2500 B.C. This civilization flourished for 800 years and covered the largest area of any in ancient times. Its two main cities, **Mohenjo-Daro** and Harappa were carefully planned, with plumbing systems and underground sewers. By 1700 B.C., though, most of these cities were abandoned, perhaps because of floods or earthquakes.

Meanwhile, herders from Central Asia moved into northern India and intermarried with its people. Their descendants, called **Aryans,** spread eastward to the Ganges River basin. By 500 B.C., a new Indian civilization, with many rival kingdoms, had emerged.

Most of what we know about the Aryans comes from the **Vedas,** a collection of religious teachings. The Aryans divided themselves into social groups based on occupation. Over time, these divisions grew into a system of **castes.** These are social groups into which people are born and cannot leave. The Aryans were **polytheistic,** or believed in many gods. They eventually came to believe that a single spiritual power, called **brahman,** existed in all things. Some Aryans became **mystics,** who devoted their lives to seeking spiritual truth.

The ancient Chinese believed that China was at the center of Earth and the sole source of civilization. <u>Physical barriers, including mountains and deserts, separated China from the rest of the world and contributed to this belief.</u>

Chinese civilization began in the Huang He valley. About 1650 B.C., a Chinese people called the Shang came to power in northern China. In 1027 B.C., the **Zhou** people overthrew the Shang. The Zhou **dynasty,** or ruling family, lasted until 256 B.C. They promoted the idea of the Mandate of Heaven, or the divine right to rule. This idea was later used to explain the **dynastic cycle,** or the rise and fall of dynasties.

The Chinese prayed to many gods and nature spirits. Over time, these religious practices came to center on respect for ancestors. The Chinese also believed that the universe reflected a balance between two forces, yin and yang. They studied the planets and eclipses and created an accurate calendar. They also developed bronzemaking and silkmaking and made the first books.

Review Questions

1. When and where did India's first civilization emerge?

_____

_____

2. Name three achievements of the ancient Chinese.

_____

READING CHECK

What are castes?

_____

_____

_____

VOCABULARY STRATEGY

What does the word *barriers* mean in the underlined sentence? Two examples of physical *barriers* are given in the sentence. How do these examples help you understand the meaning of *barriers*?

READING SKILL

Identify Main Ideas List four main ideas about the Aryans from the second paragraph of the Summary.

_____

_____

_____

_____

PART 2.1

Note Taking Study Guide

EMPIRES OF INDIA AND CHINA

As you read this section in your textbook, complete the outline below to summarize information about the religions and empires of India and China.

I. Hinduism and Buddhism

   A. Both developed in ancient India.

   B. Hinduism

      1. _____

      2. _____

   C. _____

      1. _____

      2. _____

II. _____

   A. _____

      1. _____

      2. _____

   B. _____

   C. _____

      1. _____

      2. _____

III. _____

   A. _____

      1. _____

      2. _____

   B. _____

      1. _____

      2. _____

   C. _____

      1. _____

      2. _____

IV. _____

   A. _____

   B. _____

      1. _____

      2. _____

Name_____ Class_____ Date_____

Hinduism and Buddhism both developed in ancient India. Hinduism has no single founder and no single sacred text. Hindus believe that everything is part of the spiritual force called brahman. The rebirth of the soul in another body, or **reincarnation,** allows people to work toward the goal of union with brahman.

Unlike Hinduism, Buddhism had a single founder, **Siddhartha Gautama,** known as the Buddha. Buddhism urges people to seek enlightenment through meditation, rather than through the priests, rituals, and many gods of Hinduism. The goal of Buddhism is **nirvana,** or union with the universe and release from the cycle of reincarnation.

In 321 B.C., Chandragupta Maurya forged the first great Indian empire. The Maurya dynasty eventually conquered much of India. Asoka, Chandragupta's grandson, converted to Buddhism, and his policies brought peace and wealth. After his death, rivals battled for power.

About 500 years after the Mauryas, the Gupta dynasty reunited much of India. Under the Guptas, India enjoyed a golden age of peace and achievement. Most Indians of that period were village peasants. The village and the family maintained order, and caste rules governed every part of life.

Important philosophies and religions in ancient China also developed. China's most influential philosopher, **Confucius,** was born in 551 B.C. He was concerned with social order and good government. He put **filial piety,** or respect for parents, above all other duties. His ideas came to influence every area of Chinese life. Another Chinese philosopher, Hanfeizi, insisted that strict laws and harsh punishments were needed to maintain order. Hanfeizi's teachings came to be known as Legalism. A third philosophy, Daoism, arose around the same time. Daoists sought to live in harmony with nature and viewed government as unnatural.

When the Zhou dynasty weakened, a new ruler, **Shi Huangdi,** rose to unify all of China. He built a strong government, as well as the Great Wall. After his death, a new dynasty, the **Han,** was founded. Under the Han, the Chinese made huge advances in trade, government, technology, and the arts. Under the Han, the Silk Road linked China to the Fertile Crescent.

Review Questions

1. According to Hindus, what is the purpose of reincarnation?

_____

_____

2. Name three philosophies that developed in ancient China.

_____

_____

READING CHECK

What major building project took place under Shi Huangdi?

_____

_____

_____

VOCABULARY STRATEGY

What does the word *converted* mean in the underlined sentence? The verb *convert* comes from the Latin word *vertere,* which means "to turn." The verb *convert* is often used to describe a religious experience. Use these clues to help you understand the meaning of *converted.*

READING SKILL

Contrast List some main differences between Hinduism and Buddhism.

_____

_____

_____

Name_____ Class_____ Date_____

As you read this section in your textbook, complete the outline below to summarize the information about ancient Greece.

I. Early People of the Aegean

  A. Minoans

    1. Traders on the island of Crete

    2. _____

  B. _____

    1. _____

    2. _____

II. _____

  A. _____

  B. _____

    1. _____

    2. _____

  C. _____

    1. _____

    2. _____

    3. _____

  D. _____

    1. _____

    2. _____

  E. _____

    1. _____

    2. _____

III. _____

  A. _____

  B. _____

  C. _____

IV. _____

  A. _____

  B. _____

PART 2.2 Section Summary
ANCIENT GREECE

The Minoans created the earliest civilization in the Aegean region. They were traders from the island of Crete who adapted Egyptian and Mesopotamian ideas to their own culture. Minoan civilization reached its height between about 1600 and 1500 B.C., but had vanished by 1400 B.C. The Mycenaeans, another civilization of sea traders, soon dominated Crete and the Greek mainland. They are best remembered for their part in the Trojan War, which was described by **Homer** in the *Iliad* and the *Odyssey*.

After Mycenaean civilization declined, the Greeks lived in small, isolated farming villages. Eventually, they began to build many small city-states. They often warred among themselves, but they shared a common culture, including their language, religion, and festivals. The Greeks evolved a unique version of the city-state, called the **polis.** Their cities often had two levels. They built temples on the **acropolis,** or high city, above the main city. At first, the ruler of the polis was a king. This type of government is called a **monarchy.** Power slowly shifted to a landholding elite, or **aristocracy.** Wealthy merchants, farmers, and artisans came to rule some city-states. The result was a form of government called an **oligarchy,** or rule by a small, powerful elite.

Two of the most important Greek city-states were Sparta and Athens. Sparta was a warrior society. Athens was a **democracy,** or government by the people. When the Persians threatened the Greeks, the city-states joined together to defend themselves. <u>After the Persian Wars, Athens thrived.</u> Under the leadership of **Pericles,** Athenian culture flourished. Athens also developed a **direct democracy,** in which a large number of citizens took part in day-to-day government.

Philosophers like Socrates, Plato, and Aristotle developed new ideas about truth, reason, and government. They used observation and reason to find causes for events. Greeks also developed new styles of art, architecture, poetry, and drama.

Greece was eventually controlled by King Philip of Macedonia. After his death, his son **Alexander** the Great conquered a vast area and spread Greek civilization. Greek culture blended with Persian, Egyptian, and Indian cultures to create the Hellenistic civilization.

Review Questions

1. For what event are the Mycenaeans best remembered?

_____

_____

2. How did Greek philosophers find causes for events?

_____

_____

READING CHECK

What civilization resulted from the blending of Greek, Persian, Egyptian, and Indian cultures under Alexander the Great?

_____

_____

_____

VOCABULARY STRATEGY

Find the word *thrived* in the underlined sentence. What does it mean? The sentence that follows the underlined sentence contains a synonym for the word *thrived.* What is that synonym?

READING SKILL

Categorize In which of the following categories does Athenian government under Pericles belong? Circle all that are correct.

city-state

warrior society

monarchy

aristocracy

oligarchy

democracy

Name_____ Class_____ Date_____

As you read this section in the textbook, complete the outline below to summarize information about ancient Rome and the rise of Christianity.

I. The Roman World Takes Shape

  A. Rome began as a small city-state in Italy.

  B. Romans overthrew Etruscan king and set up a republic.

    1. At first, patricians controlled the government.

    2. _____

  C. _____

II. _____

  A. _____

  B. _____

    1. _____

    2. _____

    3. _____

III. _____

  A. _____

  B. _____

  C. _____

IV. _____

  A. _____

    1. _____

    2. _____

    3. _____

  B. _____

    1. _____

    2. _____

    3. _____

V. _____

  A. _____

  B. _____

    1. _____

    2. _____

    3. _____

Section Summary
ANCIENT ROME AND THE RISE OF CHRISTIANITY

Rome began as a small city-state in Italy. In 509 B.C., the Romans overthrew the Etruscan king who ruled their area. They set up a **republic,** a government in which the people choose the officials. At first, **patricians,** or members of the upper class, controlled the government. Eventually, commoners, or **plebeians,** were elected to the Roman senate. Meanwhile, Rome's armies expanded Roman control until it reached from Spain to Egypt.

Rome's conquests made it very wealthy, but this wealth led to corruption. Rome faced many civil wars. Eventually, a Roman general named Octavian restored order and took the name **Augustus.** He exercised absolute power, and his rule changed Rome from a republic to an empire. Roman emperors brought peace and order to the lands they controlled. As a result, the 200 years from Augustus to Marcus Aurelius are known as the *Pax Romana,* or "Roman Peace."

The Romans admired Greek culture and borrowed Greek ideas. Rome spread this blend of cultures, known as Greco-Roman civilization, to distant lands. Romans also excelled as engineers, building roads, bridges, and aqueducts. Probably the greatest legacy of Rome was its commitment to law and justice.

Early in the *Pax Romana,* Christianity began in the Middle East. A Jew named **Jesus** was born about 4 B.C. in Bethlehem. He called himself the Son of God and taught that his mission was to bring salvation and eternal life. Some people saw Jesus as a troublemaker. He was executed, but his disciples believed he had risen from the dead. Jews who believed that Jesus was the **messiah,** or savior sent by God, became the first Christians. For a while, Christianity remained a **sect** within Judaism. Then Paul spread Christianity to non-Jews. At first, Rome persecuted Christians, but later accepted Christian beliefs.

The Roman empire eventually split into two parts, east and west. In the west, corruption, poverty, and declining moral values contributed to the empire's decline. Germanic invaders finally conquered Rome in 476. However, the eastern Roman empire prospered and became known as the Byzantine empire.

Review Questions

1. In the Roman republic, what group originally controlled the government?

_____

_____

2. After Jesus was executed, what did his disciples believe happened?

_____

_____

READING CHECK

What was the *Pax Romana*?

_____

_____

_____

VOCABULARY STRATEGY

Find the word *exercised* in the underlined sentence. The word *exercise* often refers to physical activity or training, but it has a different meaning here. To help you understand the meaning of the word *exercised*, complete the sentence below, using a word other than *exercised*.

Augustus did not just have absolute power, he also _____ it.

READING SKILL

Recognize Multiple Causes
Name three causes that led to the decline of the western Roman empire.

_____

_____

_____

PART
2.4

Note Taking Study Guide

CIVILIZATIONS OF THE AMERICAS

As you read this section in the textbook, complete the outline below to summarize the information about the early civilizations in the Americas.

I. Olmecs, the First American Civilization

A. _____

B. _____

II. Civilizations of Middle America

A. First settlers were nomadic hunters.

   1. _____

   2. _____

B. _____

   1. _____

   2. _____

C. _____

   1. _____

   2. _____

III. _____

A. _____

B. _____

C. _____

   1. _____

   2. _____

D. _____

   1. _____

   2. _____

IV. _____

A. _____

   1. _____

   2. _____

B. _____

   1. _____

   2. _____

C. _____

D. _____

PART
2.4

Section Summary
CIVILIZATIONS OF THE AMERICAS

The first settlers in the Americas were nomads who probably migrated across a land bridge between Siberia and Alaska. They gradually spread throughout the Americas. The first American civilization, the **Olmec,** began along the Mexican Gulf Coast. It lasted from about 1500 to 500 B.C.

Later, other civilizations developed in Central and South America. The **Maya,** for example, built city-states in Mesoamerica. They created pyramid temples, a writing system, and an accurate calendar. Each city-state had its own ruling chief. Several hundred years after the Maya declined, the **Aztecs** conquered most of Mexico. The Aztec empire grew wealthy from **tribute,** or payment from conquered people. Conquered people were also the source of human sacrifices for Aztec religious rituals. The Aztecs developed a complex social structure with a single ruler, the emperor, at the top.

In the 1400s, the **Inca** came down from the Andes mountains of Peru. Led by Pachacuti, they conquered an empire 2,500 miles wide. The Inca emperor claimed to be divine and had absolute power. His officials kept records on quipus, or collections of knotted colored strings. The Inca united their empire by imposing their language and religion on the people they conquered. They also created one of the greatest road systems in history.

Before 1500, many different culture groups lived in North America. In the desert southwest, the **Ancestral Puebloans** built large villages, or pueblos, of stone and adobe brick. At the center of their village life was the **kiva,** a large underground chamber used for religious rituals. In the Mississippi and Ohio river valleys, farming cultures emerged as early as 1000 B.C. The Hopewell people left behind giant earthen mounds. Objects found in the mounds suggest that trade networks stretched from the Gulf of Mexico to the Great Lakes. Hopewell culture was replaced by the **Mississippians,** who built large towns and ceremonial centers.

Variations in climate and resources encouraged the development of different cultures in other parts of North America. In the far north, for example, the Inuits adapted to frozen terrain. In the Northeast, warring tribes eventually settled their differences and formed the Iroquois League.

Review Questions

1. How did the first settlers probably get to the Americas?

_____

_____

2. Why were there so many different culture groups in North America?

_____

_____

READING CHECK

What is tribute?

_____

_____

_____

VOCABULARY STRATEGY

What does the word *networks* mean in the underlined sentence? With what other *networks* are you familiar? What do *networks* have in common? This sentence refers to "trade" *networks.* Use your prior knowledge of other *networks* to help you understand what a trade *network* would be like.

READING SKILL

Compare and Contrast Compare and contrast the governments of the Maya, Aztecs, and Inca.

_____

_____

_____

_____

_____

_____

Name_____ Class_____ Date_____

As you read this section in the textbook, complete the outline below to summarize the information about Europe during the Middle Ages.

I. **Germanic Civilization**

   A. _____

   B. _____

II. **The Early Middle Ages**

   A. Charlemagne reunited much of Western Europe.

      1. _____

      2. _____

   B. _____

   C. _____

   D. _____

III. _____

   A. _____

      1. _____

      2. _____

      3. _____

   B. _____

      1. _____

      2. _____

         a. _____

         b. _____

IV. _____

   A. _____

   B. _____

      1. _____

      2. _____

V. _____

   A. _____

   B. _____

      1. _____

      2. _____

When **Germanic peoples** ended Roman rule in the West, they began to create a new civilization. They had no cities and no written laws. Instead, they lived in small communities ruled by elected kings. Europe became a fragmented region.

Around 800, **Charlemagne** reunited much of Europe. He revived learning and extended Christian civilization into northern Europe. He also set up a strong, efficient government. After Charlemagne's death, his grandsons divided his empire into three regions. Muslims, Magyars, and Vikings all attacked these regions. A new system, called **feudalism,** evolved in response to the need for protection from the invaders.

Under feudalism, powerful lords gave land to lesser lords, or **vassals.** A lord granted his vassal a **fief,** or estate, which included the peasants who worked the land. In exchange for land and protection, vassals pledged service and loyalty to the greater lord. Because feudal lords battled constantly, many nobles trained as **knights,** or mounted warriors. They adopted a code of conduct called **chivalry,** which required them to be brave, loyal, and true to their word.

The **manor,** or lord's estate, was the heart of the medieval economy. Most manors included one or more villages and surrounding lands. Most of the peasants on a manor were **serfs.** They could not be sold like enslaved people, but they spent their lives working for the lord of the manor. In return, the lord gave them protection and the right to farm some land for themselves.

After the fall of Rome, the Christian Church split into an eastern and a western church. The western church, headed by the pope, became known as the **Roman Catholic Church.** As the Church grew stronger and wealthier, it became the most powerful **secular,** or worldly, force in medieval Europe. Because the Church administered the sacraments, it also had absolute power in religious matters.

By the 1000s, advances in agriculture and commerce spurred economic revival in Europe. Farming was improved by new iron plows and the three-field system. New trade routes and goods also increased wealth. Merchant **guilds,** or associations, came to dominate life in medieval towns.

Review Questions

1. Why did feudalism evolve?

_____

_____

2. Why did the Roman Catholic Church have absolute power in religious matters?

_____

_____

READING CHECK

What is chivalry?

_____

_____

_____

VOCABULARY STRATEGY

What does the word *efficient* mean in the underlined sentence? *Efficient* comes from the Latin word *efficere,* which means "to bring to pass" or "accomplish." If a government is *efficient,* what would you expect it to be able to do? Use these clues to understand the meaning of *efficient* in this sentence.

READING SKILL

Identify Supporting Details
Identify the details in the Summary that support the following idea: By the 1000s, advances in agriculture and commerce spurred economic revival in Europe.

_____

_____

_____

PART
3.2
Note Taking Study Guide
THE HIGH AND LATE MIDDLE AGES

As you read this section in the textbook, complete the outline below to summarize the information about the High and Late Middle Ages.

I. Growth of Royal Power in England

   A. _____

   B. _____

   C. Evolving traditions

      1. Kings had conflicts with nobles and the Church.

      2. _____

   D. _____

      1. _____

      2. _____

II. _____

   A. _____

   B. _____

   C. _____

      1. _____

      2. _____

III. _____

   A. _____

      1. _____

      2. _____

      3. _____

   B. _____

      1. _____

      2. _____

IV. _____

   A. _____

   B. _____

   C. _____

V. _____

   A. _____

   B. _____

PART 3.2 Section Summary
THE HIGH AND LATE MIDDLE AGES

When William the Conqueror took the throne of England in 1066, he helped unify England and strengthen the monarchy. Other kings developed the basis for English **common law,** or law that is the same for all people. A jury system also developed. A **jury,** or group of men sworn to speak the truth, determined which cases should be brought to trial. In the early 1200s, a group of nobles forced England's King John to sign the **Magna Carta,** or Great Charter. The Magna Carta contained two basic ideas. First, it said that nobles had certain rights. Second, it made clear that the monarch must also obey the law.

The **Holy Roman Empire** arose from the many Germanic kingdoms that formed after the death of Charlemagne. When a single ruler united these kingdoms, the pope crowned him "emperor." His successors took the title "Holy Roman Emperor." Popes soon clashed with the Holy Roman emperors. Refusal to obey the Church could result in **excommunication.** This meant that someone could not receive the **sacraments,** or sacred rituals of the Church.

In the 1050s, Muslim Turks invaded the Byzantine empire. The Byzantine emperor asked the pope in Rome for help. Soon, thousands of Christian knights left for the Holy Land to fight **crusades,** or holy wars. The Crusades failed in their chief goal—the conquest of the Holy Land. Instead, they left behind a legacy of religious hatred. However, the Crusades increased European trade, papal power, and the power of monarchs. Contacts with the Muslim world also introduced Christians to regions they had not known existed.

A revival of learning took place in the High Middle Ages. Schools sprang up around cathedrals, eventually becoming the first universities. Ideas and texts from ancient Greece reached the universities through the works of Muslim scholars. New writings began to be produced in the **vernacular,** or everyday language of ordinary people.

In the late Middle Ages, bubonic plague, also called the **Black Death,** spread through Europe. One in three people died, and the plague brought social and economic upheaval. Famine and war added to the turmoil of the period.

Review Questions

1. How did nobles in the early 1200s limit the power of the English king?

_____

_____

2. What made excommunication such a serious punishment?

_____

_____

READING CHECK

What is the vernacular?

_____

_____

_____

VOCABULARY STRATEGY

What does the word *unify* mean in the underlined sentence? *Uni-* is a root word meaning "one" and *-fy* is a suffix meaning "make" or "cause to become." Use these word-part clues to figure out the meaning of *unify*.

READING SKILL

Understand Effects Name five effects of the Crusades.

_____

_____

_____

_____

Name_____ Class_____ Date_____

As you read this section in the textbook, complete the outline below to summarize the information about the Byzantine empire, Russia, and Eastern Europe.

I. The Byzantine Empire

    A. Roman emperor Constantine rebuilt Byzantium and renamed it Constantinople.

        1. Eastern Roman empire became known as Byzantine empire.

        2. _____

    B. _____

        1. _____

        2. _____

    C. _____

        1. _____

        2. _____

    D. _____

        1. _____

        2. _____

II. _____

    A. _____

    B. _____

    C. _____

    D. _____

    E. _____

    F. _____

        1. _____

        2. _____

        3. _____

III. _____

    A. _____

    B. _____

Name_____ Class_____ Date_____

By 330 A.D. the Roman emperor Constantine had rebuilt the city of Byzantium as his capital and renamed it **Constantinople**. The city thrived because of trade. The eastern Roman empire eventually became known as the Byzantine empire. The Byzantine emperor **Justinian** had the laws of ancient Rome organized into a collection, known as Justinian's Code. This code preserved and spread the heritage of Roman law.

In the Byzantine empire, the emperor controlled Church affairs, rejecting the pope's claim to authority over all Christians. By 1054, controversies caused a **schism,** or permanent split, between the Eastern (Greek) Orthodox and Roman Catholic churches.

Byzantine civilization blended Christian beliefs with Greek science, philosophy, and the arts. When the empire fell in the 1400s, Greek scholars took Greek manuscripts and their knowledge of Greek and Byzantine culture to the West.

During Roman times, a people called the Slavs lived in present-day Ukraine. In the 700s and 800s, Vikings began to trade with the Slavs. The city of **Kiev** became a trade center and the center of the first Russian state. Missionaries from Constantinople brought Christianity to Russia and developed an alphabet for the Slavic languages. In the early 1200s, the Mongols overran Russia. The absolute power of the Mongols served as a model for later Russian rulers. Eventually, the princes of Moscow gained power and defeated the Mongols. Between 1462 and 1505, **Ivan III,** or Ivan the Great, brought much of northern Russia under his control. He took the title **tsar,** the Russian word for *Caesar*. His grandson, known as Ivan the Terrible, introduced Russia to a tradition of absolute power.

Many ethnic groups, including Slavs, Asians, and Germanic peoples, settled in Eastern Europe. An **ethnic group** is a large group of people who share the same language and cultural heritage. Byzantine missionaries brought Eastern Orthodox Christianity and Byzantine culture to the Balkans. German knights and missionaries spread Roman Catholic Christianity to the area. In the late Middle Ages, many Jewish settlers came to Eastern Europe to escape persecution. Many kingdoms and small states arose in Eastern Europe, including Poland, Hungary, and Serbia.

Review Questions

1. Who controlled Church affairs in the Byzantine empire?

_____

_____

2. What two peoples came together to form the first Russian state?

_____

_____

READING CHECK

What is an ethnic group?

_____

_____

_____

VOCABULARY STRATEGY

What does the word *preserved* mean in the underlined sentence? An antonym of *preserved* is *destroyed*. Use this clue to help you understand the meaning of *preserved*.

READING SKILL

Recognize Sequence Number the following events from Russian history to show the correct sequence:

____ Kiev becomes the center of the first Russian state.

____ Mongols overrun Russia.

____ Slavs live in Ukraine.

____ Ivan the Great takes the title of tsar.

____ Princes of Moscow defeat the Mongols.

____ Ivan the Terrible reigns.

____ Vikings begin to trade with Slavs.

Name_____ Class_____ Date_____

As you read this section in the textbook, complete the outline below to summarize the information about the rise of Islam and Muslim civilizations.

I. Rise of Islam
  A. Muhammad
    1. Born in Mecca in western Arabia about 570
    2. _____
    3. _____
  B. _____
    1. _____
    2. _____
    3. _____
II. _____
  A. _____
  B. _____
  C. _____
III. _____
  A. _____
  B. _____
  C. _____
  D. _____
IV. _____
  A. _____
  B. _____
  C. _____
    1. _____
    2. _____
  D. _____
    1. _____
    2. _____
V. _____
  A. _____
    1. _____
    2. _____
  B. _____
    1. _____
    2. _____

PART 3.4 Section Summary
MUSLIM CIVILIZATIONS

Muhammad was born in Arabia about 570. According to Muslim belief, he was called in a vision to become God's messenger. He spent the rest of his life spreading Islam. Like Judaism and Christianity, Islam is a monotheistic religion. All Muslims accept five duties, known as the Five Pillars of Islam. These include belief in one God, daily prayer, charity to the poor, fasting, and the **hajj,** or pilgrimage to Mecca. Muslims believe that the Quran contains the word of God and is the final authority on all matters.

When Muhammad died, Abu Bakr was elected to be the first **caliph,** or successor to Muhammad. He was the first in a series of rulers who led military conquests that expanded Islam to the Atlantic and to the Indus Valley. Muslim merchants established a vast trading network that also spread Islamic ideas. Eventually, the Abbasid dynasty made **Baghdad** the capital of Islam, which became a great center of learning. Muslims pioneered the study of algebra and made advances in medicine and other fields. Islamic artists and architects created elaborate mosaics and beautiful **mosques,** or houses of worship.

In the late 1100s, a **sultan,** or Muslim ruler, defeated Hindu armies in India. His successors founded the Delhi sultanate. Muslim rule brought changes to India. Destruction of Buddhist monasteries led to the decline of Buddhism as a major religion in India. Many Hindus were killed. In 1526, Turkish and Mongol invaders, led by Babur, poured into India. They ended the Delhi sultanate and set up the **Mughal dynasty,** which ruled from 1526 to 1857.

In 1453, the Ottomans captured Constantinople and renamed it Istanbul. The **Ottoman empire** was a powerful force for 500 years. At its height, it stretched from Hungary to Arabia and across North Africa. Under Suleiman, who ruled from 1520 to 1566, the Ottoman empire enjoyed its golden age. <u>Ottoman poets adapted Persian and Arab models to produce works in the Turkish language.</u>

Another Muslim dynasty, the Safavid, united a strong empire in present-day Iran. Shah Abbas the Great ruled from 1588 to 1629 and revived the glory of ancient Persia.

Review Questions

1. What do Judaism, Christianity, and Islam have in common?

_____

_____

2. Name two ways in which Islam and Islamic ideas were spread.

_____

_____

READING CHECK

What is a sultan?

_____

_____

_____

VOCABULARY STRATEGY

What does the word *adapted* mean in the underlined sentence? *Adapt* comes from the Latin word *adaptare,* which means "to fit to." Use this word-origins clue to help you understand the meaning of *adapted* in this sentence.

READING SKILL

Identify Supporting Details
List two sentences from the Summary that support the following idea: Muslim rule brought changes to India.

_____

_____

_____

Name_____ Class_____ Date_____

Note Taking Study Guide
KINGDOMS AND TRADING STATES OF AFRICA

As you read this section in the textbook, complete the outline below to summarize the information about the kingdoms and trading states of Africa.

I. Bantu Migrations

II. Early Civilizations of Africa

    A. The Kingdom of Nubia

        1. _____

        2. _____

        3. _____

    B. _____

        1. _____

        2. _____

        3. _____

III. _____

    A. _____

    B. _____

    C. _____

        1. _____

        2. _____

        3. _____

    D. _____

        1. _____

        2. _____

    E. _____

        1. _____

        2. _____

IV. _____

    A. _____

    B. _____

V. _____

    A. _____

    B. _____

    C. _____

    D. _____

PART 3.5 Section Summary
KINGDOMS AND TRADING STATES OF AFRICA

Two important civilizations developed along the Nile River in Africa. One was Egypt. The other was **Nubia,** or Kush. Powerful kings ruled Nubia for thousands of years. The Egyptians sometimes conquered Nubia, and Nubians adopted many Egyptian traditions. About A.D. 350, armies from the kingdom of Axum overran Nubia.

Egypt and North Africa were ruled, for a time, by the Greeks and then the Romans. Linked to a global trade network, North African ports prospered. Camels that had been brought to North Africa from Asia revolutionized trade across the Sahara. Gold and salt were the main trade items. North Africans wanted gold to buy European goods. West Africans traded gold to North Africans in exchange for salt, which they needed to stay healthy.

By A.D. 800, the kingdom of **Ghana** had been formed in West Africa. The king controlled the gold-salt trade routes. Muslim merchants brought Islam to Ghana. Ghana declined in the late 1100s and was overtaken by the kingdom of Mali. Mali controlled both the gold-mining regions and the salt supplies of the Sahara. The greatest emperor of Mali was **Mansa Musa.** As Mali weakened in the 1400s, a new West African kingdom, Songhai, arose. Songhai was the largest state that had ever existed in West Africa. The kingdom controlled trade routes and wealthy cities like Timbuktu.

By the time **Axum** conquered Nubia, Axum had long been an important trading center. It linked trade routes from Africa, India, and the Mediterranean world. As Axum declined, other trading centers rose along the East African coast. By 1000, East African port cities were thriving from trade across the Indian Ocean.

Early African societies varied depending on geography, climate, and other factors. In some societies, the **nuclear family** was typical, while in other communities, the family included several generations. Religious beliefs were also varied. Some Africans followed traditional beliefs and were polytheistic. Others followed Christianity or Islam. **Griots,** or professional storytellers, preserved African values and history by reciting ancient stories. Migrations contributed to the diversity of cultures. The **Bantu migrations,** for example, spread Bantu languages throughout much of southern Africa.

Review Questions

1. Why did West Africans trade gold in exchange for salt?

_____

_____

2. What role did griots play in African society?

_____

_____

READING CHECK

What effect did camels have on trade in Africa?

_____

_____

_____

VOCABULARY STRATEGY

What does the word *global* mean in the underlined sentence? *Global* comes from the word *globe*. Use this word-family clue to help you understand the meaning of the word *global*.

READING SKILL

Identify Causes Why did cities along the East African coast thrive?

_____

_____

_____

Name_____ Class_____ Date_____

As you read this section in the textbook, complete the outline below to summarize the information about the civilizations in East Asia.

I. Sui Dynasty

   A. _____

   B. _____

II. Two Golden Ages of China

   A. Tang dynasty (618–907)

      1. _____

      2. _____

   B. _____

      1. _____

      2. _____

   C. _____

      1. _____

      2. _____

   D. _____

      1. _____

      2. _____

III. _____

   A. _____

   B. _____

   C. _____

      1. _____

      2. _____

IV. _____

   A. _____

   B. _____

V. _____

   A. _____

   B. _____

VI. _____

   A. _____

   B. _____

   C. _____

PART 3.6 Section Summary
SPREAD OF CIVILIZATIONS IN EAST ASIA

In the 500s, the Sui dynasty reunited China. Then a Sui general and his son, Tang Taizong, established their own dynasty, the **Tang.** Tang armies forced neighboring lands to become **tributary states.** These states remained independent, but had to send tribute to the Tang emperor. Tang emperors restored the bureaucracy and redistributed land to the peasants.

The Tang dynasty collapsed in 907, and the **Song** dynasty soon rose to take its place. The Song period was a golden age of wealth and culture. Under both the Tang and Song, China was a well-ordered society. The two main classes were the gentry and the peasantry. The gentry were wealthy landowners. Most scholar-officials came from this class. Painting and calligraphy became essential skills for the gentry.

In the 1200s, the **Mongols** invaded China and toppled the weakened Song dynasty. They established peace and order, and trade flourished along the Silk Road. In 1368, a rebel army drove the Mongols out of China. A new dynasty, the **Ming,** sought to reassert Chinese greatness. Under the Ming, Zheng He led a series of sea voyages into distant waters.

China influenced other peoples. Korea, for example, absorbed many Chinese traditions. Yet it maintained its own identity and even improved on a number of Chinese inventions, such as book printing and an alphabet. Japan also felt the influence of Chinese civilization. However, the surrounding seas protected and isolated Japan and allowed it to maintain its own distinct culture. However, in the early 600s, rulers of the Yamato dynasty sent young nobles to study in China. For a time, the Japanese modeled much of their society on Chinese ideas.

Japan eventually evolved into a feudal society. In theory, the emperor was at the top. In fact, he was a powerless, though revered, figurehead. The **shogun**, or supreme military commander, had the real power. He gave land to warrior lords who agreed to support him with their armies. These lords were called **daimyo.** They, in turn, gave land to lesser warriors called **samurai.** In 1603, Tokugawa Ieyasu founded the **Tokugawa** shogunate, which brought peace and stability to Japan.

Review Questions

1. How did Mongol rule affect trade?

_____

_____

2. What role did land play in the relationships between the shogun, daimyo, and samurai?

_____

_____

READING CHECK

What were tributary states?

_____

_____

_____

VOCABULARY STRATEGY

What does the word *revered* mean in the underlined sentence? *Revere* comes from the Latin word *revereri*, which means "to feel awe." Use this word-origins clue to help you understand the meaning of *revered*.

READING SKILL

Recognize Sequence Number the dynasties listed below to show the correct sequence.

____ Ming

____ Song

____ Sui

____ Mongol

____ Tang

CHAPTER 1 SECTION 1 — Note Taking Study Guide
THE RENAISSANCE IN ITALY

Focus Question: What were the ideals of the Renaissance, and how did Italian artists and writers reflect these ideals?

As you read this section in your textbook, complete the following outline to identify main ideas and supporting details about the Italian Renaissance.

I. **What was the Renaissance?**
   A. A changing worldview
      1. _____
      2. _____
   B. A spirit of adventure
      1. _____
      2. _____
   C. _____
      1. _____
      2. _____

II. _____
   A. _____
      1. _____
      2. _____
      3. _____
   B. _____
      1. _____
      2. _____

III. _____
   A. _____
      1. _____
      2. _____
   B. _____
      1. _____
      2. _____

(Outline continues on the next page.)

(Continued from page 34)

C. _____

    1. _____

    2. _____

D. _____

    1. _____

    2. _____

E. _____

    1. _____

    2. _____

F. _____

    1. _____

    2. _____

IV. _____

    A. _____

        1. _____

        2. _____

    B. _____

        1. _____

        2. _____

CHAPTER 1 SECTION 1	Section Summary
	THE RENAISSANCE IN ITALY

A new age called the Renaissance, meaning "rebirth," marked a great change in culture, politics, society, and economics. In Italy, it began in the 1300s and reached its peak around 1500. Instead of focusing on religion, as in the Middle Ages, the Renaissance explored the human experience. At the same time, there was a new emphasis on individual achievement. At the heart of the Renaissance was an intellectual movement called **humanism**. Renaissance humanists studied the classical culture of Greece and Rome to try to comprehend their own times. They wanted to broaden their understanding. They emphasized the **humanities**—subjects such as rhetoric, poetry, and history. Poet Francesco **Petrarch** was an early Renaissance humanist. He gathered a library of Greek and Roman manuscripts. This opened the works of Cicero, Homer, and Virgil to Western Europeans.

Italy was the birthplace of the Renaissance for many reasons. It had been the center of the Roman empire; remains of that ancient culture were all around. Rome was also the seat of the Roman Catholic Church, an important **patron** of the arts. Furthermore, Italy's location encouraged trade with markets on the Mediterranean, in Africa, and in Europe. Trade provided the wealth that fueled the Renaissance. In Italy's city-states, powerful merchant families, such as the Medici family of **Florence,** lent political and economic leadership and supported the arts.

Renaissance art reflected humanism. Renaissance painters returned to the realism of classical times by developing improved ways to represent humans and landscapes. For example, the discovery of **perspective** allowed artists to create realistic art and to paint scenes that appeared three-dimensional. The greatest of the Renaissance artists were **Leonardo** da Vinci, **Michelangelo,** and **Raphael.**

Some Italian writers wrote guidebooks to help ambitious people who wanted to rise in the Renaissance world. The most widely read of these was *The Book of the Courtier,* by **Baldassare Castiglione.** His ideal courtier was a well-educated, well-mannered aristocrat who mastered many fields. **Niccolò Machiavelli** wrote a guide for rulers, titled *The Prince,* on how to gain and maintain power.

Review Questions

1. How did the focus of study change between the Middle Ages and the Renaissance?

_____

_____

2. Identify two reasons why the Renaissance began in Italy.

_____

_____

Name_____ Class_____ Date_____

Focus Question: How did the Renaissance develop in northern Europe?

As you read this section in your textbook, complete the following chart to record the main ideas about the Renaissance in the North.

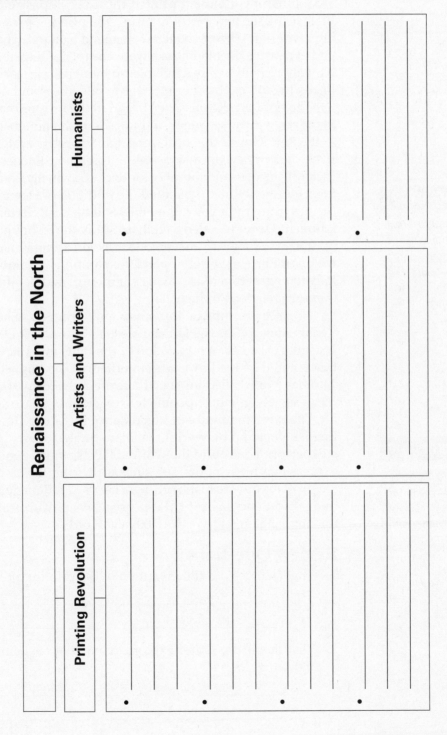

Section Summary

THE RENAISSANCE IN THE NORTH

By the 1400s, northern Europe began to enjoy the economic growth needed to develop its own Renaissance. An astounding invention—the printing press—helped to spread Renaissance ideas. In about 1455, **Johann Gutenberg** printed the first complete edition of the Bible using the new printing press. The printing press caused a printing revolution. Before, books were made by hand. They were rare and expensive. Printed books were cheaper and easier to produce. Now more books were available, so more people learned to read. Printed books exposed Europeans to new ideas and new places.

The northern Renaissance began in the prosperous cities of **Flanders,** a thriving center of trade. Flemish painters pursued realism in their art. One of the most important Flemish painters was Jan van Eyck. He portrayed townspeople and religious scenes in rich detail. Pieter Bruegel used vibrant color to portray lively scenes of peasant life. Peter Paul Rubens blended the tradition of Flemish realism with themes from mythology, the Bible, and history. German painter **Albrecht Dürer** traveled to Italy to study the techniques of the Italian masters. He soon became a pioneer in spreading Renaissance ideas to northern Europe. Dürer applied the painting techniques he learned in Italy to **engraving.** Many of his engravings and paintings portray the theme of religious upheaval.

Northern European humanists and writers also helped spread Renaissance ideas. The Dutch priest and humanist Desiderius **Erasmus** called for a translation of the Bible into the **vernacular** so that it could be read by a wider audience. The English humanist **Sir Thomas More** called for social reform in the form of a **utopian,** or ideal, society in which people live together in peace and harmony.

The towering figure of Renaissance literature, however, was the English poet and playwright William **Shakespeare.** His 37 plays are still performed around the world. Shakespeare's genius was in expressing universal themes, such as the complexity of the individual, in everyday, realistic settings. He used language that people understand and enjoy. Shakespeare's love of words also enriched the English language with 1,700 new words.

Review Questions

1. What changes did the invention of the printing press bring about?

_____

_____

2. What theme did Dürer explore in many of his paintings and engravings?

_____

_____

Note Taking Study Guide
THE PROTESTANT REFORMATION

Focus Question: How did revolts against the Roman Catholic Church affect northern European society?

As you read this section in your textbook, complete the following concept web to identify main ideas about the Protestant Reformation.

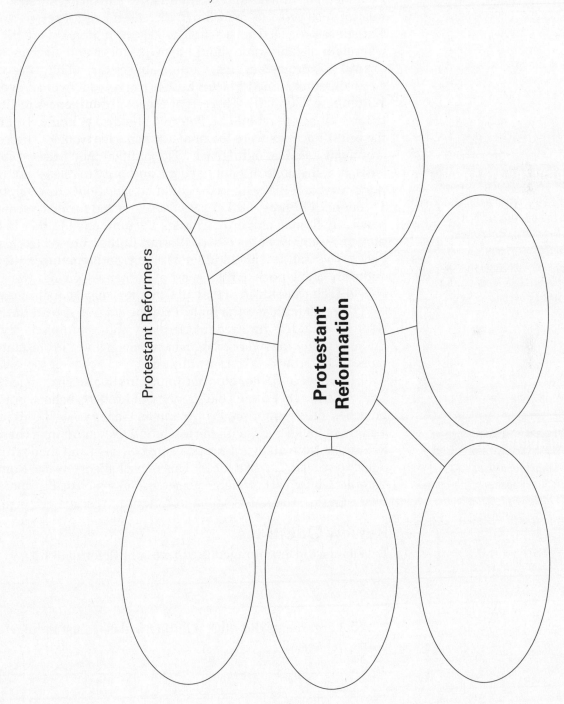

Name_____ Class_____ Date_____

CHAPTER 1 SECTION 3	Section Summary
	THE PROTESTANT REFORMATION

READING CHECK

Who was John Calvin?

_____

_____

_____

VOCABULARY STRATEGY

What does the word *doctrine* mean in the underlined sentence? The word comes from a Latin word that means "teaching" or "instruction." Use the word's origin to help you figure out what *doctrine* means.

READING SKILL

Identify Main Ideas What was one of the main beliefs at the heart of Luther's doctrines?

_____

_____

_____

In the 1500s, the Renaissance in northern Europe sparked a religious upheaval that affected Christians at all levels of society. This movement is known as the Protestant Reformation. In the late Middle Ages, the Catholic Church had become caught up in worldly affairs. Popes led lavish lives and hired artists to enhance churches. To finance such projects, the Church increased fees for services. Many Christians protested such acts. They also questioned why the Church in distant Rome should have power over their lives.

In 1517, protests against Church abuses turned into a revolt. A German monk named **Martin Luther** triggered it over an event in **Wittenberg,** Germany. There, a priest sold **indulgences** to Christians to raise money to rebuild St. Peter's Cathedral in Rome. To Luther, the priest's actions were the final outrage. He wrote 95 Theses, or arguments, against indulgences. He said that they had no biblical basis, that the pope did not have the authority to release souls from purgatory, and that Christians could be saved only through faith. Throughout Europe, Luther's 95 Theses stirred furious debate. The new Holy Roman emperor, **Charles V,** summoned Luther to the **diet,** or assembly, at the city of Worms. Luther refused to change his views. Thousands hailed Luther as a hero and renounced the authority of the pope. <u>At the heart of Luther's doctrines were several beliefs, including the idea that all Christians have equal access to God through faith and the Bible.</u> Printing presses spread Luther's writings and ideas throughout Germany and Scandinavia. By 1530, Luther's many followers were using a new name, "Protestants," for those who "protested" papal authority.

In Switzerland, the reformer **John Calvin** also challenged the Catholic Church. Calvin shared many of Luther's beliefs, but also preached **predestination.** Protestants in **Geneva** asked Calvin to lead them. In keeping with his teachings, Calvin set up a **theocracy.** Reformers from all over Europe visited Geneva and then returned home to spread Calvin's ideas. This new challenge to the Roman Catholic Church set off fierce wars of religion across Europe. In the 1600s, English Calvinists sailed to America to escape persecution.

Review Questions

1. What factors encouraged the Protestant Reformation?

_____

_____

2. What arguments did Martin Luther make against indulgences in the 95 Theses?

_____

_____

Focus Question: How did the Reformation bring about two different religious paths in Europe?

As you read this section in your textbook, complete the following flowchart to identify main ideas about the spread of the Protestant Reformation in Europe.

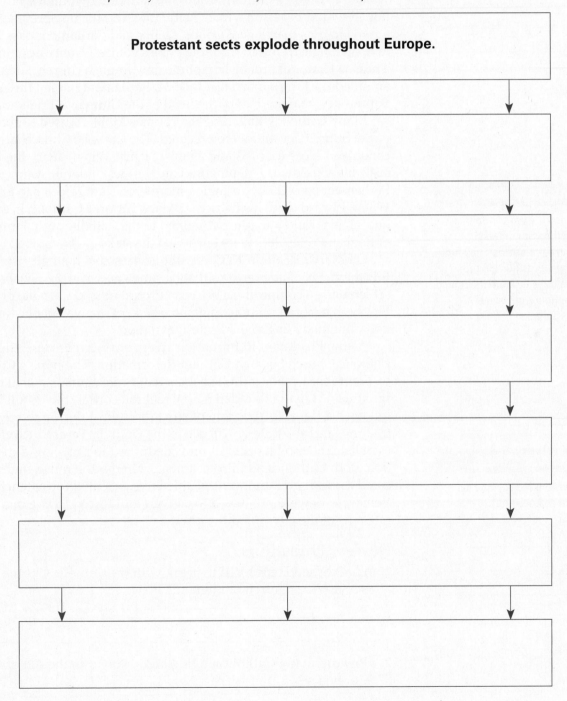

Protestant sects explode throughout Europe.

CHAPTER 1 SECTION 4

Section Summary
REFORMATION IDEAS SPREAD

As the Reformation continued, hundreds of new Protestant **sects** arose, influencing Protestant thinking in many countries. In England, the break with the Catholic Church came from **Henry VIII.** He and his wife, Catherine of Aragon, had one child, **Mary Tudor.** Henry wanted to divorce Catherine and marry another woman whom he hoped would bear him a male heir. However, the pope refused to annul Henry's marriage. Furious, Henry had Parliament pass laws to take the English church from the pope's control. Henry appointed **Thomas Cranmer** archbishop of the new English church. Cranmer annulled the king's marriage. In 1534, Parliament passed the Act of Supremacy, making Henry the head of the Church of England.

Many Catholics, including Sir Thomas More, refused to accept the Act of Supremacy and were executed. The Catholic Church later **canonized** More for his stand against Henry. When Henry died in 1547, his son Edward VI inherited the throne. Under Edward, Parliament passed laws bringing more Protestant reforms to England. When Edward died, his half-sister Mary Tudor, a Catholic, became queen. She wanted to return England to the Catholic faith. Hundreds of English Protestants were burned at the stake.

On Mary's death in 1558, the throne passed to her half-sister, **Elizabeth.** She made reforms that became known as the Elizabethan settlement—a **compromise** between Protestant and Catholic practices. Elizabeth restored unity to England; she kept many Catholic traditions, but made England a Protestant nation.

As the Protestant Reformation swept northern Europe, the Catholic Church began a Counter Reformation. The pope's **Council of Trent** reaffirmed Catholic beliefs that Protestants had challenged. **Ignatius of Loyola** founded a new religious order, the Jesuits. They followed a rigorous program of strict discipline, thorough religious training, and absolute obedience to the Church. **Teresa of Avila** established her own order of nuns dedicated to prayer and meditation. Both Catholics and Protestants fostered intolerance, and persecuted radical sects. Innocent people were executed for witchcraft. In Venice, Jews were pressured to convert and forced to live in a separate part of the city called the **ghetto.**

Review Questions

1. What caused Henry VIII to break with the Catholic Church and establish the Church of England?

_____

_____

2. How did many Catholics in England respond to the Act of Supremacy?

_____

_____

CHAPTER 1 SECTION 5

Note Taking Study Guide

THE SCIENTIFIC REVOLUTION

Focus Question: How did discoveries in science lead to a new way of thinking for Europeans?

As you read this section in your textbook, complete the following to identify main ideas about the Scientific Revolution in Europe.

Thinkers of the Scientific Revolution											
Nicolaus Copernicus	Developed sun-centered universe theory										

CHAPTER 1 SECTION 5	Section Summary
	THE SCIENTIFIC REVOLUTION

In the mid-1500s, a big shift in scientific thinking caused the Scientific Revolution. At the heart of this movement was the idea that mathematical laws governed nature and the universe. Before the Renaissance, Europeans thought that Earth was the center of everything in the heavens. In 1543, Polish scholar **Nicolaus Copernicus** proposed a **heliocentric,** or sun-centered, model of the solar system. In the late 1500s, the Danish astronomer **Tycho Brahe** provided evidence that supported Copernicus's theory. The German astronomer and mathematician **Johannes Kepler** used Brahe's data to calculate the orbits of the planets revolving around the sun. His calculations also supported Copernicus's heliocentric view.

Scientists from different lands built on the foundations laid by Copernicus and Kepler. In Italy, **Galileo** assembled a telescope and observed that the four moons of Jupiter move slowly around that planet. He realized that these moons moved the same way that Copernicus had said that Earth moves around the sun. Galileo's findings caused an uproar. Other scholars attacked him because his observations contradicted ancient views about the world. The Church condemned him because his ideas challenged the Christian teaching that the heavenly bodies were fixed in relation to Earth, and perfect.

Despite the opposition of the Church, a new approach to science had emerged, based upon observation and experimentation. To explain their data, scientists used reasoning to propose a logical **hypothesis,** or possible explanation. This process became known as the **scientific method.** The new scientific method was a revolution in thought. Two giants of this revolution were the Englishman **Francis Bacon** and the Frenchman **René Descartes.** Both were devoted to understanding how truth is determined, but they differed in their approaches. Bacon stressed experimentation and observation. Descartes focused on reasoning.

The 1500s and 1600s saw dramatic changes in many branches of science. English chemist **Robert Boyle** explained that matter is composed of particles that behave in knowable ways. **Isaac Newton** used mathematics to show that a single force keeps the planets in their orbits around the sun. He called this force **gravity.** To help explain his laws, Newton developed a branch of mathematics called **calculus.**

Review Questions

1. What assumption was at the heart of the Scientific Revolution?

_____

_____

2. Why did the Church condemn Galileo?

_____

_____

Name_____ Class_____ Date_____

Focus Question: How did the search for spices lead to global exploration?

As you read this section in your textbook, complete the following flowchart to identify causes and effects of European exploration.

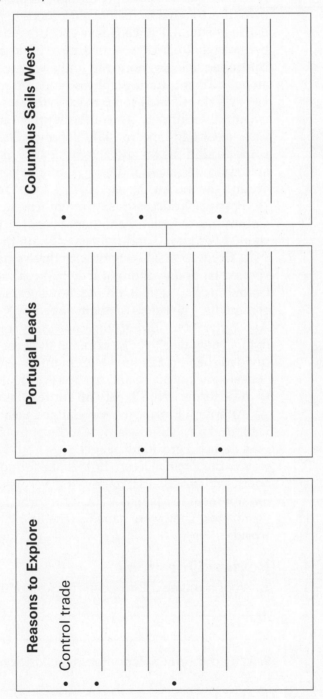

Columbus Sails West

Portugal Leads

Reasons to Explore

• Control trade

Name_____ Class_____ Date_____

CHAPTER
2
SECTION 1

Section Summary
THE SEARCH FOR SPICES

READING CHECK

What was the Line of Demarcation?

_____

_____

_____

VOCABULARY STRATEGY

What does the word *authority* mean in the underlined sentence? What context clues can you find in the surrounding words? Circle the words in the same sentence that could help you learn what *authority* means.

READING SKILL

Identify Causes and Effects

Identify one cause of European exploration.

_____

_____

Identify two effects of Prince Henry's encouragement of sea exploration.

_____

_____

_____

_____

By the 1400s, Europe's population and its demand for trade goods from Asia were growing. Especially desirable were spices. The chief source of spices was the **Moluccas,** an island chain in present-day Indonesia. Arab and Italian merchants controlled most trade between Asia and Europe. Europeans outside Italy wanted their own direct access to Asia's trade goods.

In Portugal, **Prince Henry** encouraged sea exploration. He believed that Africa was the source of the riches the Muslim traders controlled. He also hoped to find a way to reach Asia by sailing along the coast. **Cartographers** prepared maps for the voyages. Henry's ships sailed south to explore the western coast of Africa, eventually rounding the southern tip, which became known as the Cape of Good Hope. In 1497, **Vasco da Gama** led four Portuguese ships around the tip and across the Indian Ocean to reach the great spice port of Calicut in India. Soon, the Portuguese seized ports around the Indian Ocean, creating a vast trading empire.

Portugal's successes spurred others, including **Christopher Columbus,** to look for another sea route to Asia. Columbus persuaded Ferdinand and Isabella of Spain to finance his voyage. In 1492, Columbus sailed west with three small ships. When the crew spotted land, they thought they had reached the Indies. What Columbus had actually found, however, were previously unknown continents. The rulers of Spain appealed to the Spanish-born Pope Alexander VI to support their authority, or power, to claim the lands of this "new world." The pope set the **Line of Demarcation,** which divided the non-European world into two trading and exploration zones—one for Spain and one for Portugal. The two nations agreed to these terms in the **Treaty of Tordesillas.**

Although Europeans had claimed vast territories, they had not yet found a western sea route to Asia. In 1519, a Portuguese nobleman named **Ferdinand Magellan** set out west from Spain to find a way to the Pacific Ocean. In 1520, he found a passageway at the Southern tip of South America. Survivors of the long voyage, who did not include Magellan, finally returned to Spain nearly three years later. They were hailed as the first to **circumnavigate** the world.

Review Questions
1. What motivated Europeans to explore the seas?

_____

_____

2. Why did Prince Henry focus on Africa for his explorers' voyages?

_____

_____

Name_____ Class_____ Date_____

Focus Question: What effects did European exploration have on the people of Africa?

As you read this section in your textbook, complete the following chart to identify the effects of European exploration on Africa.

CHAPTER 2 SECTION 2

Section Summary

TURBULENT CENTURIES IN AFRICA

The Portuguese established footholds on the coast of West Africa, building small forts and trading posts. From West Africa, they sailed around the continent. They continued to establish forts and trading posts, but they also attacked coastal cities of East Africa, such as **Mombasa** and **Malindi,** which were hubs of international trade. They also took over the Arabs' thriving East African trade network.

Slavery had existed in Africa since ancient times. Europeans began to view slaves as the most important aspect of the African trade. By the 1500s, European participation had encouraged a much broader Atlantic slave trade, and it grew into a huge and profitable business to fill the need for cheap labor. They especially needed workers on their **plantations** in the Americas. Some African leaders tried to slow down or stop the transatlantic slave trade. The ruler of Kongo, **Affonso I,** who had been tutored by Portuguese **missionaries,** wanted to maintain contact with Europe but end the slave trade. The slave trade, however, continued.

The slave trade had major effects on African states. Because of the loss of countless numbers of young Africans, some small states disappeared forever. At the same time, new states arose, with ways of life that depended on the slave trade. The **Asante kingdom** emerged in the area occupied by present-day Ghana. In the late 1600s, an able military leader, **Osei Tutu,** won control of the trading city of Kumasi. <u>From there, he conquered neighboring peoples and unified the Asante kingdom.</u> Under Osei Tutu, the Asante kingdom held a **monopoly** over both gold mining and the slave trade.

The **Oyo empire** arose from successive waves of settlement by the Yoruba people in the region of present-day Nigeria. Its leaders used wealth gained from the slave trade to build a strong army.

By the 1600s, several other European powers had established forts along the west coast of Africa. In 1652, Dutch immigrants arrived at the southern tip of the continent. They built **Cape Town,** the first permanent European settlement in Africa, to supply ships sailing to or from the East Indies. Dutch farmers, called **Boers,** settled the lands around the port.

Review Questions

1. How did the Portuguese establish footholds on the coasts of Africa?

_____

_____

2. Who created the first permanent European settlement in Africa?

_____

_____

Note Taking Study Guide
EUROPEAN FOOTHOLDS IN SOUTH AND SOUTHEAST ASIA

Focus Question: How did European nations build empires in South and Southeast Asia?

As you read this section in your textbook, complete the flowchart below to identify causes and effects of European exploration in South and Southeast Asia.

Britain							
•		•					
Spain							
•		•					
Netherlands							
•		•					
Portugal							
•		•					

Name_____ Class_____ Date_____

Section Summary
EUROPEAN FOOTHOLDS IN SOUTH AND SOUTHEAST ASIA

What was the Dutch East India Company?

_____

_____

_____

What does the word *strategic* mean in the underlined sentence? Note that *strategic* is an adjective describing the settlement of Cape Town. The sentence following the underlined sentence gives you more information about Cape Town. Based on these context clues, what do you think *strategic* means?

Identify Causes and Effects
Identify one cause and one effect of the Mughal emperors' decision to grant trading rights to Europeans.

_____

_____

_____

After Vasco da Gama's voyage to India, the Portuguese, under the command of **Afonso de Albuquerque,** burst into the Indian Ocean. By then, Muslim rulers had established the **Mughal empire** throughout much of India. The Portuguese gained footholds in southern India, however, by promising local princes aid against other European rulers. In 1510, the Portuguese seized the island of **Goa** off the coast of India. Then, they took **Malacca.** In less than 50 years, the Portuguese built a trading empire with military and merchant **outposts.** For most of the 1500s, they controlled the spice trade between Europe and Asia.

The Dutch challenged Portuguese domination of Asian trade. In 1599, a Dutch fleet from Asia returned with a cargo of spices. Soon after, Dutch warships and trading vessels made the Netherlands a leader in European commerce. <u>The Dutch set up colonies and trading posts around the world, including their strategic settlement at Cape Town.</u> Cape Town's location gave the Dutch a secure presence in the region. In 1602, a group of wealthy Dutch merchants formed the **Dutch East India Company,** which had full **sovereign** powers. With its power to build armies, wage war, negotiate peace treaties, and govern overseas territory, the Dutch East India Company dominated Southeast Asia. Meanwhile, Spain took over the **Philippines,** which became a key link in Spain's colonial empire.

India was the center of the valuable spice trade. The Mughal empire was larger, richer, and more powerful than any kingdom in Europe. When Europeans sought trading rights, Mughal emperors saw no threat in granting them. The Portuguese—and later the Dutch, British, and French—were permitted to build forts and warehouses in coastal towns. Over time, the Mughal empire weakened, and French and British traders fought for power. Like the Dutch, both the British and the French had established East India companies. Each nation's trading company organized its own army of **sepoys,** or Indian troops. By the late 1700s, however, the British East India Company controlled most of India.

Review Questions

1. How did Portugal build a trading empire in South and Southeast Asia?

_____

_____

2. How did the Dutch come to dominate trade in Southeast Asia?

_____

_____

Name_____ Class_____ Date_____

Focus Question: How were European encounters in East Asia shaped by the worldviews of both Europeans and Asians?

As you read this section in your textbook, complete the following chart to understand the effects of European contacts in East Asia.

CHAPTER 2 SECTION 4

Section Summary

ENCOUNTERS IN EAST ASIA

Who conquered the Ming dynasty in 1644?

_____

_____

_____

What does the word *allegiance* mean in the underlined sentence? Think about your prior knowledge of this word. Ask yourself: To what do I owe my allegiance? Use your prior knowledge to help you figure out what *allegiance* means.

Identify Effects Describe the effect of the Japanese and Manchu invasions on Korea.

_____

_____

_____

When Portuguese traders reached China in 1514, they wanted Chinese silks and porcelains. The European textiles and metalwork they had to offer in exchange, however, were inferior to Chinese products. The Chinese, therefore, demanded payment in gold or silver. The Ming rulers eventually allowed the Portuguese and other Europeans a trading post at **Macao,** in present-day **Guangzhou.** With the traders came Portuguese missionaries and, later, the Jesuits. The brilliant Jesuit priest **Matteo Ricci** made a strong impression on the Chinese, who welcomed learning about Renaissance Europe.

By the early 1600s, the Ming dynasty was decaying. In 1644, the **Manchus,** who ruled Manchuria, succeeded in seizing Beijing and making it their capital. They set up a new dynasty called the **Qing.** Two rulers oversaw the most brilliant age of the Qing—Kangxi and his grandson **Qianlong.** Under both emperors, the Chinese economy expanded. Internal trade grew, as did the demand for Chinese goods from all over the world. The Qing maintained the Ming policy of restricting foreign traders, however. In 1793, **Lord Macartney** led a British diplomatic mission to China, but his attempt to negotiate for expanded trade failed.

Like China, Korea also restricted contacts with the outside world. In the 1590s, a Japanese invasion devastated Korea. Then in 1636, the Manchus conquered Korea. In response, the Koreans chose isolation, excluding all foreigners except the Chinese and a few Japanese. Korea became known in the West as the "Hermit Kingdom."

The Japanese at first welcomed Westerners. Traders arrived in Japan at a turbulent time, when warrior lords were struggling for power. The warrior lords quickly adopted Western firearms. Jesuit priests converted many Japanese to the Christian faith. <u>The Tokugawa shoguns, however, worried that Japanese Christians owed their allegiance to the pope rather than to Japanese leaders.</u> In response, the shoguns expelled foreign missionaries and barred all European merchants. To keep informed about world events, however, they permitted just one or two Dutch ships each year to trade at a small island in **Nagasaki** harbor. Japan remained isolated for more than 200 years.

Review Questions

1. Why did the Chinese demand that the Portuguese traders pay for Chinese silks and porcelain with gold or silver?

_____

_____

2. What suggests that the Ming were curious about Europe and wanted to gain knowledge about its culture?

_____

_____

CHAPTER 3 SECTION 1

Note Taking Study Guide

CONQUEST IN THE AMERICAS

Focus Question: How did a small number of Spanish conquistadors conquer huge Native American empires?

As you read this section of your textbook, fill in the chart below to help you record the sequence of events that led to European empires in the Americas.

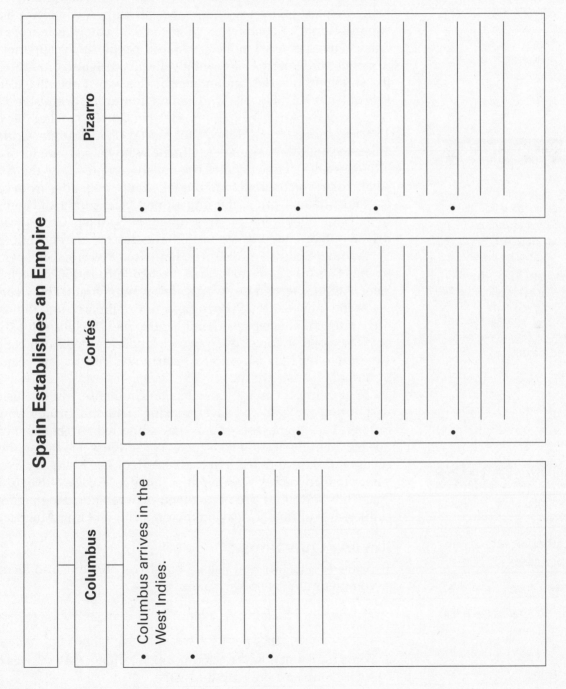

Spain Establishes an Empire

Pizarro

Cortés

Columbus

- Columbus arrives in the West Indies.

CHAPTER 3 SECTION 1

Section Summary
CONQUEST IN THE AMERICAS

VOCABULARY STRATEGY

Find the word *compelled* in the underlined sentence. What clues to its meaning can you find in the surrounding words, phrases, or sentences? For example, what does the phrase "relations grew strained" suggest about the relations between the two men? Circle other context clues in the paragraph that could help you figure out what *compelled* means.

READING SKILL

Recognize Sequence Sequence the following events:

_____ Spanish forces take over Inca lands.

_____ Pizarro arrives in Peru.

_____ Columbus takes the Taínos as prisoners.

_____ Cortés captures Tenochtitlán.

In 1492, Christopher Columbus reached the Caribbean islands now called the West Indies. Columbus' first meeting with Native Americans there began a recurring cycle of encounter, conquest, and death across the Western Hemisphere.

Columbus first encountered the Taíno people and claimed their land for Spain, taking prisoners back with him. A wave of Spanish **conquistadors,** or conquerors, followed. Ultimately, hundreds of Spanish overpowered millions of native people, using superior weapons and horses. Unknowingly, the Spanish also brought diseases like smallpox, measles, and influenza. This wiped out village after village of Native Americans, who had no **immunity,** or resistance.

One of the earliest explorers, **Hernán Cortés,** reached Mexico in 1519 and moved toward the Aztec capital, **Tenochtitlán.** Cortés was aided by an Indian woman, **Malinche,** who helped him form **alliances** with native peoples previously conquered by the Aztecs. Aztec ruler **Moctezuma** tried but failed to keep Cortés from coming to Tenochtitlán. <u>Cortés later imprisoned Moctezuma and compelled him to sign over lands and treasure to the Spanish.</u> Cortés was driven out, but he returned in 1521 and destroyed Tenochtitlán.

Another Spanish adventurer, **Francisco Pizarro,** sought riches from Peru's Inca empire. Pizarro reached Peru in 1532. The Inca ruler, Atahualpa, had just won a **civil war,** or conflict between people of the same nation. Pizarro captured Atahualpa and demanded a huge ransom. This was paid, but Pizarro had the Inca ruler killed anyway. Spanish forces overran Inca lands, adding much of South America to the Spanish empire. Pizarro was killed a few years later by a rival Spanish group.

Spain's impact on the Americas was immense. The Spanish took vast fortunes in gold and silver, making Spain the greatest power of Europe. They opened sea routes that connected two hemispheres and opened an exchange of goods, people, and ideas. However, they also brought disease and death to Native Americans. Many survivors converted to Christianity, seeking hope. Others, like the Maya, resisted Spanish influence by preserving their own religion, language, and culture, and ultimately leaving their imprint on Latin America.

Review Questions

1. Name two factors that helped hundreds of Spanish soldiers conquer millions of Native Americans.

_____

_____

2. Some native peoples resisted Spanish influence. What was one such group and how did it resist?

_____

_____

Name_____ Class_____ Date_____

Focus Question: How did Spain and Portugal build colonies in the Americas?

A. *As you read "Ruling the Spanish Empire," fill in the chart below to record the steps the Spanish took to establish an empire in America.*

Governing the empire	Catholic Church	Trade	Labor
• Viceroys • _____ _____ _____	• _____ _____ _____ • _____ _____ • _____ _____	• _____ _____ _____ • _____ _____ _____	• _____ _____ _____ • _____ _____ _____

B. *As you read "Colonial Society and Culture" and "Beyond the Spanish Empire," fill in the Venn diagram below to compare and contrast the Spanish and Portuguese empires.*

Spanish empire   Portuguese empire

CHAPTER 3 SECTION 2

Section Summary

SPANISH AND PORTUGUESE COLONIES IN THE AMERICAS

Spanish settlers and missionaries followed conquerors into the Americas. They built colonies and created a culture that blended European, Native American, and African traditions. By the mid-1500s, Spain's empire reached from modern California to South America.

The Spanish monarch appointed **viceroys,** or representatives who ruled in his name. They closely monitored Spanish colonies and managed their valuable raw materials. Conquistadors received **encomiendas,** or rights to demand work from Native Americans. Under this system, Native Americans were forced to work under brutal conditions. Disease, starvation, and cruel treatment caused a drastic decline in the Native American population. A priest, **Bartolomé de Las Casas,** begged the Spanish king to end the abuse, and laws were passed in 1542, banning enslavement and mistreatment. But Spain was too far away to enforce the laws. Some landlords forced people to become **peons,** paid workers who labored to repay impossibly high debts created by the landlord. To fill a labor shortage, colonists also brought in millions of Africans as slaves.

Blending of diverse cultures resulted. Native Americans contributed building styles, foods, and arts. The Spanish introduced Christianity and the use of animals, especially horses. Africans contributed farming methods, crops, and arts.

However, society in the colonies was strictly structured. **Peninsulares,** or people born in Spain, filled the highest positions. Next were **creoles,** or American-born descendants of Spanish settlers. Lower groups included **mestizos,** people of Native American and European descent, and **mulattoes,** people of African and European descent. At the bottom were Native Americans and African slaves.

Portugal, too, had an empire in South America, with colonies in Brazil. Portugal granted land to nobles, who sent settlers to develop the area. As in Spanish colonies, Native Americans in Brazil were nearly wiped out from disease. Brazil's rulers also used African slaves and forced Native American labor. A new culture emerged, blending European, Native American, and African traditions.

In the 1500s, wealth from the Americas made Spain and Portugal Europe's most wealthy and powerful countries. Pirates often attacked treasure ships from the colonies. Some pirates, called **privateers,** even did so with the support of their nations' monarchs.

Review Questions

1. What were encomiendas?

_____

_____

2. How were the Spanish and Portuguese colonies similar?

_____

_____

Name_____ Class_____ Date_____

Focus Question: How did European struggles for power shape the North American continent?

As you read this section of your textbook, complete the following timeline to show the sequence of events in the struggle for North America.

1763

1754

Late 1600s

1620

1608

1607

1534 — Cartier explores eastern Canada.

CHAPTER 3 SECTION 3

Section Summary

STRUGGLE FOR NORTH AMERICA

READING CHECK

What was the name of the agreement written by the Pilgrims to set the guidelines for governing their new colony?

_____

_____

_____

VOCABULARY STRATEGY

Find the word *prevailed* in the first underlined sentence. What do you think *prevailed* means? Read the second underlined sentence to see what happened after England *prevailed.* Use this information to help you come up with another definition, in your own words, for *prevailed.*

READING SKILL

Recognize Sequence What happened after the signing of the Treaty of Paris in 1763?

_____

_____

_____

In the 1600s, the French, Dutch, English, and Spanish competed for lands in North America. By 1700, France and England dominated large parts of the continent. Their colonies differed from one another in terms of language, government, resources, and society.

In 1534, Jacques Cartier explored and claimed for the French much of eastern Canada, called **New France.** Eventually, France's empire stretched from Quebec to the Great Lakes and down the Mississippi River to Louisiana. However, a permanent French settlement was not established until 1608 in Quebec. Harsh Canadian winters discouraged settlers, and many abandoned farming for more profitable fur trapping and fishing. In the late 1600s, the French king Louis XIV wanted greater **revenue,** or income from taxes. He appointed officials to manage economic activities in North America and sent soldiers and more settlers.

In the early 1700s, while New France's population remained small, English colonies expanded along the Atlantic coast. Jamestown in Virginia, the first permanent English colony, was established in 1607. In 1620, **Pilgrims,** or English Protestants who rejected the Church of England, landed at what became Plymouth, Massachusetts. They wrote a **compact,** or agreement, called the Mayflower Compact. It set guidelines for governing their colony. In the 1600s and 1700s, the English created additional colonies. Many were commercial ventures or havens for religious groups. English monarchs exercised control through royal governors. Yet, English colonists enjoyed a greater degree of self-government than did French and Spanish colonists. They had their own representative assemblies that could advise the governor and decide local issues.

During the 1700s, England and France emerged as powerful rivals. In 1754, the **French and Indian War** erupted in North America and then spread to other parts of the world by 1756, where it is known as the Seven Years' War. British and colonial troops eventually captured New France's capital city, Quebec. Although the war dragged on, the British ultimately prevailed. The 1763 **Treaty of Paris** ended this worldwide conflict. France surrendered Canada and other North American possessions to Britain. Its Louisiana Territory passed to Spain.

Review Questions

1. How did Canadian winters affect French settlement?

_____

_____

2. In what way did English colonists have a greater degree of self-government than did French or Spanish colonists?

_____

_____

Note Taking Study Guide

THE ATLANTIC SLAVE TRADE

Focus Question: How did the Atlantic slave trade shape the lives and economies of Africans and Europeans?

As you read this section in your textbook, complete the following flowchart to record the sequence of events that led to millions of Africans being brought to the Americas.

Triangular trade intensifies.

CHAPTER 3 SECTION 4

Section Summary
THE ATLANTIC SLAVE TRADE

Empires grew in the 1500s, and trade increased between the Americas and other parts of the world. Spain was the first major power to import slaves into its South American colonies, but slave trade grew as other European powers established colonies. Slave labor became a way to gain greater profits, but at the expense of millions of lives.

The trade of slaves became known as **triangular trade,** a series of Atlantic sea routes joining Europe, Africa, and the Americas. On the first leg of the triangle, merchant ships brought European goods, such as guns and cloth, to Africa, where they were traded for slaves. On the second leg, known as the **Middle Passage,** slaves were brought to the Americas, where they were traded for sugar, molasses, and cotton from European-owned plantations. On the final leg, these products were traded for other colonial goods, such as furs and salt fish, then shipped to Europe, where they were traded for European goods.

The Middle Passage was a horrifying journey for Africans. **Olaudah Equiano,** who was sold into slavery as an 11-year-old in the 1750s, wrote of his experiences. During the Middle Passage, slaves were captured, bound, and forced to walk as much as a thousand miles. Many died on the way. Those who lived were restrained in holding pens in African port cities until European ships arrived. Hundreds were crammed below deck for the three-week to three-month voyages. Some committed suicide. Many died from disease, brutality, or other dangers, like storms, pirate raids, and **mutinies,** or revolts, by captives trying to return home.

The triangular trade continued, in part, because it was so profitable. It brought riches to merchants and traders, helped the colonial economies succeed, and helped European and American port cities grow. However, for Africans the outcome was devastating. African societies were torn apart, and lives were cut short or brutalized. By the mid-1800s, when the slave trade finally ended, an estimated 11 million Africans had been brought to the Americas, and another 2 million had died during the Middle Passage.

Review Questions

1. What was triangular trade, and what were the three main areas it linked?

_____

_____

2. Why did triangular trade continue, even though it devastated the lives of millions of people?

_____

_____

Focus Question: How did the voyages of European explorers lead to new economic systems in Europe and its colonies?

A. *As you read "The Columbian Exchange," complete the following flowchart to record the sequence of events that led to the Columbian Exchange, as well as the effects.*

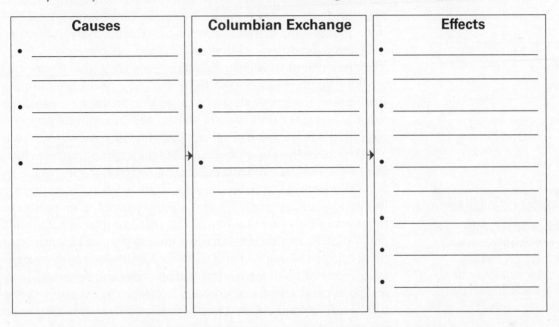

Causes	Columbian Exchange	Effects
• _____ _____	• _____ _____	• _____ _____
• _____ _____	• _____ _____	• _____ _____
• _____ _____	• _____ _____	• _____
		• _____
		• _____
		• _____

B. *As you read "A Commercial Revolution," complete the following flowchart to record the sequence of events that led to new global economic systems, as well as the effects.*

Causes	New Economic Systems	Effects
• _____ _____	• Capitalism	• _____ _____
• _____ _____	• _____	• _____ _____
• _____ _____	• _____	• _____ _____
		• _____
		• _____

CHAPTER 3 SECTION 5

Section Summary
EFFECTS OF GLOBAL CONTACT

READING CHECK

What is the name for the vast global interchange begun by Columbus' first voyage?

_____

_____

_____

VOCABULARY STRATEGY

In the underlined sentence, what does the word *dispersal* mean? Study the surrounding words, phrases, or sentences. Circle any context clues that help you decide on the meaning of *dispersal.*

READING SKILL

Recognize Sequence What happened in the 1500s that led to inflation in Europe?

_____

_____

_____

Exploration in the 1500s and 1600s led to European domination of the globe. By the 1700s, worldwide contact brought major changes to people in Europe, the Americas, Asia, and Africa.

When Columbus returned to Europe in 1493, he brought back American plants and animals. Later, he carried European plants, animals, and settlers back to the Americas. This began a vast global interchange named for Columbus, the **Columbian Exchange.** Sharing different foodstuffs and livestock helped people around the world. The dispersal of new crops from the Americas also contributed to worldwide population growth by the 1700s. Additionally, the Columbian Exchange started a migration to the Americas, the forcible transfer of millions of slaves, and brought death to millions of Native Americans from European diseases.

Another effect of global contact was great economic change. In the 1500s, the pace of **inflation** increased in Europe, fueled by silver and gold flowing in from the Americas. Inflation is a rise in prices linked to sharp increases in the money supply. This period of rapid inflation in Europe is known as the **price revolution.** Out of this change came **capitalism,** an economic system of private business ownership. The key to capitalism was **entrepreneurs,** or people who take financial risks for profits. European entrepreneurs hired workers, paid production costs, joined investors in overseas ventures, and ultimately helped convert local economies into international trading economies. Fierce competition for trade and empires led to a new economic system called **mercantilism,** which measured wealth by a nation's gold and silver. Mercantilists believed the nation must export more than it imports. They also pushed governments to impose **tariffs,** or taxes on foreign goods, giving an advantage to local goods over now costlier imports.

Economic changes, however, took centuries to affect most Europeans, who were still peasants. But by the 1700s, many social changes had taken place, too. Nobles, whose wealth was in land, were hurt by the price revolution. Merchants who invested in overseas ventures grew wealthy, and skilled workers in Europe's growing cities thrived. A thriving middle class developed.

Review Questions

1. Why did mercantilists push governments to impose tariffs?

_____

_____

2. By the 1700s, what groups were benefiting most from economic change?

_____

_____

Note Taking Study Guide

SPANISH POWER GROWS

Focus Questions: How did Philip II extend Spain's power and help establish a golden age?

As you read this section in your textbook, use the outline to identify main ideas and supporting details about Spain's power.

I. Charles V Inherits Two Crowns

   A. Ruling the Hapsburg empire

      1. Spain

      2. Holy Roman Empire and Netherlands

   B. Charles V abdicates

      1. _____

      2. _____

      3. _____

II. _____

   A. _____

      1. _____

      2. _____

   B. _____

      1. _____

      2. _____

   C. _____

      1. _____

      2. _____

   D. _____

      1. _____

      2. _____

      3. _____

      4. _____

      5. _____

(Outline continues on next page.)

CHAPTER 4 SECTION 1 — Note Taking Study Guide

SPANISH POWER GROWS

(Continued from page 63)

III. _____

    A. _____

       _____

    B. _____

       _____

    C. _____

       _____

    D. _____

       _____

    E. _____

       _____

Name_____ Class_____ Date_____

Section Summary
SPANISH POWER GROWS

In 1519, **Charles V,** the king of Spain and ruler of the Spanish colonies in the Americas, inherited the **Hapsburg empire.** This included the Holy Roman Empire and the Netherlands. Ruling two empires involved Charles in constant religious warfare. Additionally, the empire's vast territory became too cumbersome for Charles to rule effectively. His demanding responsibilities led him to abdicate the throne and divide his kingdom between his brother Ferdinand and his son Philip.

Under **Philip II,** Spanish power increased. He was successful in expanding Spanish influence, strengthening the Catholic Church, and making his own power absolute. Philip reigned as an **absolute monarch**—a ruler with complete authority over the government and the lives of the people. He also declared that he ruled by **divine right.** This meant he believed that his authority to rule came directly from God. Philip was determined to defend the Catholic Church against the Protestant Reformation in Europe. He fought many battles in the Mediterranean and the Netherlands to advance or preserve Spanish Catholic power.

To expand his empire, Philip II needed to eliminate his rivals. He saw Elizabeth I of England as his chief Protestant enemy. Philip prepared a huge **armada,** or fleet, to carry an invasion force to England. However, the English ships were faster and easier to maneuver than Spanish ships. Several disasters led to the defeat of this powerful Spanish fleet.

This defeat marked the beginning of a decline in Spanish power. Wars were costly and contributed to Spain's economic problems. However, while Spain's strength and wealth decreased, art and learning took on new importance. Philip was a supporter of the arts and founded academies of science and mathematics. The arts flourished between 1550 and 1650, a time known as Spain's *Siglo de Oro,* or "golden century." Among the outstanding artists of this period was a painter called **El Greco.** Famous for his religious paintings and portraits of Spanish nobles, his use of vibrant color influenced many other artists. This period also produced several remarkable writers. One of the most significant was **Miguel de Cervantes.** His *Don Quixote,* which mocks medieval tales of chivalry, is considered Europe's first modern novel.

Review Questions

1. What territories were included in the Hapsburg empire?

_____

_____

2. In what ways was Philip II an absolute monarch?

_____

_____

READING CHECK

Who wrote Europe's first modern novel?

_____

_____

_____

VOCABULARY STRATEGY

What does the word *cumbersome* mean in the underlined sentence? Circle context clues in the nearby words and phrases to help you figure out the meaning of *cumbersome.*

READING SKILL

Identify Main Ideas and Supporting Details What details support the main idea that the period from 1550 to 1650 was a "golden century" in Spain?

_____

_____

Note Taking Study Guide

FRANCE UNDER LOUIS XIV

Focus Question: How did France become the leading power of Europe under the absolute rule of Louis XIV?

As you read this section in your textbook, complete the concept web to identify supporting details about the rule of Louis XIV.

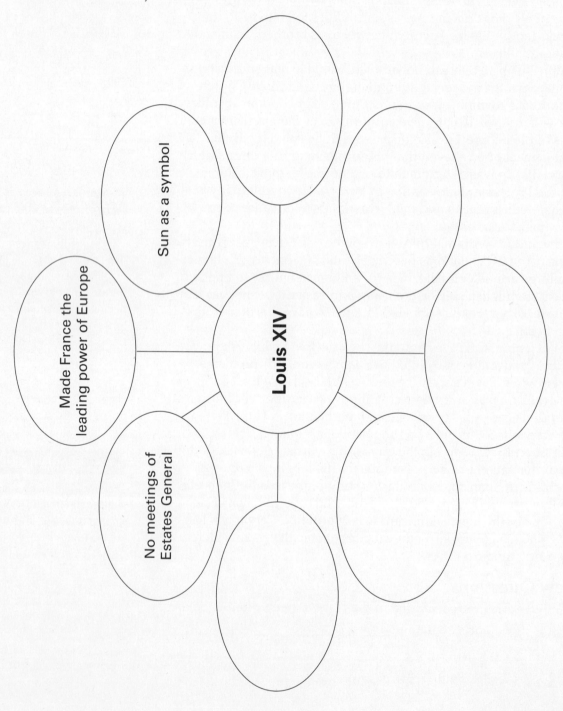

CHAPTER 4 / SECTION 2

Section Summary
FRANCE UNDER LOUIS XIV

In the late 1500s, France was torn apart by religious conflict between French Protestants, called **Huguenots,** and Catholics. In an event called the St. Bartholomew's Day Massacre, thousands of Huguenots were slaughtered. In 1598, King **Henry IV** issued the **Edict of Nantes** to protect Protestants. This granted the Huguenots religious toleration and other freedoms.

After Henry's assassination in 1610, his nine-year-old son, Louis XIII, inherited the throne. Louis appointed **Cardinal Richelieu** as his chief minister. Richelieu sought to strengthen royal power by crushing any groups that did not bow to royal authority. In 1643, five-year-old **Louis XIV** inherited the French throne. When his chief minister died, Louis XIV resolved to take complete control of the government. He believed in his divine right to rule and even called himself the Sun King to symbolize his vital role within the nation.

Louis XIV expanded the royal government and appointed **intendants**—royal officials who collected taxes, recruited soldiers, and carried out his policies in the provinces. To fuel the country's economy, Louis's finance minister, **Jean Baptiste Colbert,** expanded commerce and trade. Taxes helped finance the king's extravagant lifestyle.

Outside Paris, Louis XIV transformed a royal hunting lodge into the grand palace of **Versailles.** The palace represented the king's great power and wealth. Elaborate court ceremonies were held to emphasize the king's importance. For example, during the ritual known as the *levée*, or rising, high-ranking nobles would compete for the honor of handing the king his shoes. The purpose was to keep the nobles in Versailles to gain their support and prevent them from getting too powerful.

Under Louis XIV, France became the strongest state in Europe. However, the country's prosperity began to erode. This loss of wealth was caused by some of Louis's decisions. He fought costly wars to extend French borders, but rival rulers resisted in order to maintain the **balance of power.** Louis also revoked the Edict of Nantes, driving over 100,000 hard-working and prosperous Huguenots out of France.

Review Questions

1. How did Henry IV end religious conflict?

_____

_____

2. What was the purpose of intendants?

_____

_____

READING CHECK

What were the main reasons why France lost economic strength?

_____

_____

_____

VOCABULARY STRATEGY

What does the word *erode* mean in the underlined sentence? Do you know what *erosion* is? Use any prior knowledge you might have about the word *erosion* to help you figure out the meaning of *erode.*

READING SKILL

Identify Supporting Details How did Louis XIV strengthen the French monarchy? Identify key details that contributed to France's becoming the leading power of Europe.

_____

_____

_____

CHAPTER 4 SECTION 3
Note Taking Study Guide
PARLIAMENT TRIUMPHS IN ENGLAND

Focus Question: How did the British Parliament assert its rights against royal claims to absolute power in the 1600s?

As you read this section in your textbook, complete the flowchart to identify supporting details about the evolution of Parliament.

Tudors consult with and control Parliament.

Section Summary
PARLIAMENT TRIUMPHS IN ENGLAND

CHAPTER 4 SECTION 3

From 1485 to 1603, England was ruled by the Tudors. While believing in divine right, the Tudors also recognized the value of good relations with Parliament.

This was not the view of the first Stuart king, **James I.** He inherited the throne after Elizabeth I died childless in 1603. He claimed absolute power. Parliament, however, resisted the king's claim. James clashed often with Parliament over money. James was also at odds with **dissenters**—Protestants who disagreed with the Church of England. One such group, the **Puritans,** wanted simpler services and a more democratic church with no bishops.

In 1625, **Charles I** inherited the throne. He too behaved like an absolute monarch. Tensions between Charles and Parliament escalated into civil war. The English Civil War lasted from 1642 to 1651. Supporters of Charles were called Cavaliers. The supporters of Parliament were known as Roundheads. **Oliver Cromwell,** the leader of the Parliament forces, guided them to victory. In January 1649, Charles I was beheaded.

The House of Commons abolished the monarchy and declared England a republic under Cromwell, called the Commonwealth. Many new laws reflected Puritan beliefs. Cromwell did not tolerate open worship for Catholics; however, he did respect the beliefs of other Protestants and welcomed Jews back to England. Eventually people tired of the strict Puritan ways. Cromwell died in 1658. Two years later, Parliament invited Charles II to return to England as king.

Charles II's successor, James II, was forced from the English throne in 1688. Protestants feared that he planned to restore the Roman Catholic Church to power in England. Parliament offered the crown to James's Protestant daughter Mary and her husband William. However, William and Mary had to accept the **English Bill of Rights.** This helped establish a **limited monarchy.** This bloodless overthrow of James II was known as the Glorious Revolution.

During the next century, Britain's government became a **constitutional government,** whose power was defined and limited by law. A **cabinet,** or group of parliamentary advisors who set policies, developed. In essence, British government was now an **oligarchy**—a government that was run by a powerful few.

Review Questions

1. How did the English government change under Cromwell's leadership?

_____

_____

2. Why was James II forced from the throne?

_____

_____

READING CHECK

What was the Glorious Revolution?

_____

_____

_____

VOCABULARY STRATEGY

What does the word *tolerate* mean in the underlined sentence? Look for an alternative meaning of *tolerate* later in the same sentence. Use this context clue to figure out what *tolerate* means.

READING SKILL

Identify Supporting Details
Find two details in this Summary that support the statement, "Parliament triumphs in England."

_____

_____

_____

CHAPTER 4
SECTION 4

Note Taking Study Guide
RISE OF AUSTRIA AND PRUSSIA

Focus Question: How did the two great empires of Austria and Prussia emerge from the Thirty Years' War and subsequent events?

As you read this section in your textbook, use the table to identify supporting details about the emergence of Austria and Prussia as European powers.

Rise of Austria	Rise of Prussia
• Austrian ruler keeps title of Holy Roman Emperor.	• Hohenzollern rulers take over German states.
•	•
•	•
•	

CHAPTER 4
SECTION 4

Section Summary
RISE OF AUSTRIA AND PRUSSIA

By the seventeenth century, the Holy Roman Empire had become a mix of several hundred small, separate states. Theoretically, the Holy Roman emperor, who was chosen by seven leading German princes called **electors,** ruled these states. Yet, the emperor had little power over the numerous princes. This power vacuum led to a series of brutal wars that are together called the Thirty Years' War. It began when **Ferdinand,** the Catholic Hapsburg king of Bohemia, wanted to suppress Protestants and declare royal power over nobles. This led to several revolts and then a widespread European war.

The war devastated the German states. **Mercenaries,** or soldiers for hire, burned villages, destroyed crops, and murdered and tortured villagers. This led to famine and disease, which caused severe **depopulation,** or reduction in population.

It was not until 1648 that a series of treaties known as the **Peace of Westphalia** were established. <u>These treaties aspired to bring peace to Europe and also settle other international problems.</u>

While Austria was becoming a strong Catholic state, a region within the German states called **Prussia** emerged as a new Protestant power. The Prussian ruler **Frederick William I** came to power in 1713. He created a new bureaucracy and placed great emphasis on military values.

In Austria, **Maria Theresa** became empress after her father's death in 1740. That same year, **Frederick II** of Prussia seized the Hapsburg province of Silesia. This action sparked the eight-year **War of the Austrian Succession.** Despite tireless efforts, Maria Theresa did not succeed in forcing Frederick out of Silesia. However, she did preserve her empire and won the support of most of her people. She also strengthened Hapsburg power by reorganizing the bureaucracy and improving tax collection.

At his father's insistence, Frederick II endured harsh military training at a early age. After becoming king, he used his military education brilliantly, making Prussia a leading power. By 1750, the great European powers included Austria, Prussia, France, Britain, and Russia. These nations formed various alliances to maintain the balance of power. Often, Austria and Prussia were rivals.

Review Questions

1. What started the Thirty Years' War?

_____

_____

2. What caused the depopulation in the German states?

_____

_____

READING CHECK

What was the Peace of Westphalia supposed to accomplish?

_____

_____

_____

VOCABULARY STRATEGY

What does the word *aspired* mean in the underlined sentence? The word *strived* is a synonym for *aspired.* Apply what you already know about *strived* to help you understand the meaning of *aspired.*

READING SKILL

Identify Supporting Details List details to support the statement: The Thirty Years' War had a terrible effect on German states.

_____

_____

_____

Name_____ Class_____ Date_____

Focus Questions: How did Peter the Great and Catherine the Great strengthen Russia and expand its territory?

As you read this section in your textbook, complete the Venn diagram to identify the main ideas about the reigns of Peter the Great and Catherine the Great.

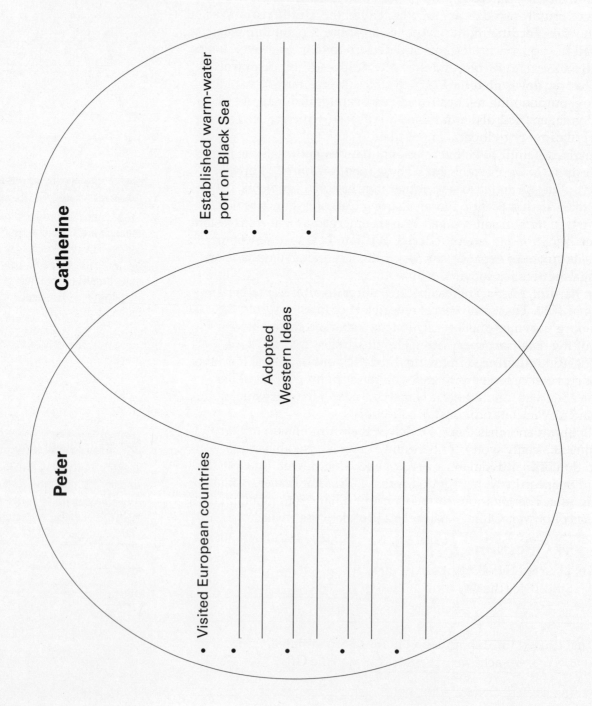

Catherine

• Established warm-water port on Black Sea

Adopted Western Ideas

Peter

• Visited European countries

Section Summary
ABSOLUTE MONARCHY IN RUSSIA

In the early 1600s, Russia was isolated from Western Europe and had remained a medieval state. It was not until the end of that century that a new tsar, **Peter the Great,** transformed Russia into a leading power.

To modernize Russia, Peter began a new policy of **westernization**—the adoption of Western ideas, technologies, and culture. Many resisted change. To enforce his new policy, Peter became an **autocratic** monarch—one who ruled with unlimited authority.

All Russian institutions were under Peter the Great's control. He executed anyone who resisted the new order. He forced the **boyars**—landowning nobles—to serve the state in civilian or military positions. Peter also stipulated that they shave their beards and wear Western-style clothes.

Peter pushed through social and economic reforms. He also increased Russia's military power and extended its borders. However, Russia still needed a **warm-water port.** This would increase Russia's trade with the West. The nearest port of this kind to Russia was on the Black Sea, but Peter could not defeat the Ottoman empire, which controlled the region.

Determined to expand Russia's territory, Peter also waged a long war against Sweden to win territory along the Baltic Sea. On this territory, he built a new capital city, **St. Petersburg.** It became the symbol of modern Russia. When Peter died in 1725, he left a mixed legacy. Although he had modernized Russia, he had used terror to enforce his absolute power.

In 1762, **Catherine the Great** ruled as an absolute monarch. She followed Peter's lead in embracing Western ideas and expanding Russia's borders. She was an efficient and energetic empress. Under her rule, laws were codified and state-supported education began for both boys and girls. After waging war, she defeated the Ottoman empire and finally won the warm-water port on the Black Sea.

In the 1770s, Russia, Prussia, and Austria each wanted Poland as part of their territory. In order to avoid war, the three kingdoms agreed to **partition,** or divide up, Poland. In 1772, Russia gained part of eastern Poland, while Prussia and Austria took over the West. Poland vanished from the map.

Review Questions

1. What did Peter the Great do to modernize Russia?

_____

_____

2. What were two achievements of Catherine the Great?

_____

_____

READING CHECK

Where was St. Petersburg built?

_____

_____

_____

VOCABULARY STRATEGY

What does *stipulated* mean in the underlined sentence? It comes from a Latin word that means "to bargain." Use this word-origins clue to help you figure out the meaning of *stipulated*.

READING SKILL

Identify Main Ideas Write a new title for this Summary that identifies its main idea.

_____

_____

_____

CHAPTER	Note Taking Study Guide
5 SECTION 1	**PHILOSOPHY IN THE AGE OF REASON**

Focus Question: What effects did Enlightenment philosophers have on government and society?

As you read this section in your textbook, complete the following table to summarize each thinker's works and ideas.

Thinkers' Works and Ideas	
Hobbes	• *Leviathan* • _____
Locke	• _____ • _____ • _____
Montesquieu	• _____ • _____ • _____
	• _____ • _____ • _____
	• _____ • _____ • _____ • _____
	• _____ • _____
	• _____ • _____ • _____

CHAPTER 5 SECTION 1	Section Summary
	PHILOSOPHY IN THE AGE OF REASON

In the 1500s and 1600s, the Scientific Revolution introduced reason and scientific method as the basis of knowledge, changing the way people looked at the world. In the 1700s, scientific successes, such as a vaccine against smallpox, convinced educated Europeans of the power of human reason. **Natural law**—rules discovered by reason—could be used to study human behavior and solve society's problems. In this way, the Scientific Revolution sparked another revolution in thinking, known as the Enlightenment.

The ideas of **Thomas Hobbes** and **John Locke,** two seventeenth-century English thinkers, were key to the Enlightenment. Hobbes argued that people are "brutish" by nature, and therefore need to be controlled by an absolute monarchy. According to Hobbes, people enter into a **social contract** with their government, giving up their freedom in exchange for an organized society. In contrast, Locke thought that people are basically reasonable and moral. He also believed that people have certain **natural rights,** including the right to life, liberty, and property. Locke rejected absolute monarchy, believing that the best kind of government had limited power. In fact, Locke felt that people could overthrow a government if it violated their natural rights.

In France, Enlightenment thinkers called *philosophes* believed that the use of reason could lead to reforms in government, law, and society. Baron de **Montesquieu** proposed the ideas of separation of powers and of checks and balances as a way to protect liberty. His ideas would deeply affect the Framers of the United States Constitution. With his biting wit, **Voltaire** exposed abuses of power and defended the principle of freedom of speech. Denis **Diderot** edited a 28-volume *Encyclopedia.* This work included articles on human knowledge, explaining new ideas on topics such as government, philosophy, and religion. **Jean-Jacques Rousseau** believed that the good of the community should be placed above individual interests. However, the Enlightenment slogan "free and equal" did not apply to women.

Other thinkers, including **Adam Smith,** focused on using natural laws for economic reform. They rejected government regulation of the economy and instead urged the policy of **laissez faire.**

Review Questions

1. How did the Scientific Revolution lead to the Enlightenment?

_____

_____

2. Identify three major ideas developed by Enlightenment thinkers.

_____

_____

READING CHECK

Who were the *philosophes* and what did they believe?

_____

_____

_____

VOCABULARY STRATEGY

What does the word *philosophy* mean in the underlined sentence? It comes from a Greek word that means "love of wisdom." Use this word-orgins clue to help you figure out what *philosophy* means.

READING SKILL

Summarize What ideas did Thomas Hobbes and John Locke have about human nature and the role of government?

_____

_____

_____

Name_____ Class_____ Date_____

Focus Question: As Enlightenment ideas spread across Europe, what cultural and political changes took place?

A. *As you read "New Ideas Challenge Society" and "Arts and Literature Reflect New Ideas," complete the following concept web to categorize how Enlightenment ideas spread.*

Salons

Spread of Enlightenment Ideas

B. *As you read "Enlightened Despots Embrace New Ideas" and "Lives of the Majority Change Slowly," complete the following concept web to summarize information about enlightened despots and their contributions.*

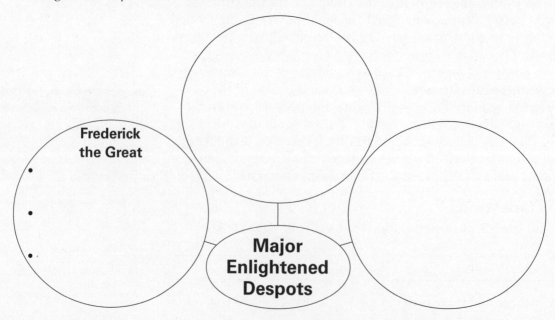

Frederick the Great

Major Enlightened Despots

Section Summary
ENLIGHTENMENT IDEAS SPREAD

Enlightenment ideas flowed from France, across Europe and beyond. Before the Enlightenment, most Europeans had accepted a society based on divine-right rule, a strict class system, and a belief in a heavenly reward for earthly suffering. The ideas of the Enlightenment, found in books such as Diderot's *Encyclopedia*, challenged those traditional beliefs and customs. In response, most government and church authorities waged a war of **censorship.** They banned and burned books, and imprisoned writers. Censorship, however, did not stop the spread of ideas. *Philosophes* and others disguised their ideas in works of fiction. Ideas continued to spread in **salons,** where people gathered to discuss new concepts in literature, the arts, science, and philosophy.

<u>In the 1600s and 1700s, the arts evolved to meet changing tastes and reflect new Enlightenment ideals.</u> In visual art and in music there was a transition from the heavier splendor of the **baroque** style to the lighter, more charming style of **rococo.** Ballets and operas—plays set to music—were performed at royal courts. Opera houses sprang up in Europe. Composers later created elegant works in a style known as classical. A growing audience of middle-class readers also led to the rise of a new type of literature—a prose form called the novel. Daniel Defoe's *Robinson Crusoe* was written at this time.

The courts of Europe were also affected by the Enlightenment as *philosophes* tried to persuade European rulers to make reforms. A few European monarchs did accept Enlightenment ideas, but retained their absolute control. These **enlightened despots** used their power to bring about some political and social changes. In Prussia, **Frederick the Great** kept tight control over his subjects yet allowed a free press and religious tolerance. **Catherine the Great** of Russia abolished torture and criticized the institution of serfdom. In Austria, **Joseph II** traveled in disguise among his subjects to learn of their problems. Despite the spread of Enlightenment ideas, however, the lives of most regular Europeans changed slowly.

Review Questions

1. How did most government and church authorities try to stop the spread of Enlightenment ideas?

_____

_____

2. What effect did Enlightenment ideas have on art, music, and literature?

_____

_____

READING CHECK

What traditional beliefs and customs did the ideas of the Enlightenment challenge?

_____

_____

_____

VOCABULARY STRATEGY

What does the word *evolved* mean in the underlined sentence? What clues can you find in the surrounding words, phrases, or sentences? Circle the context clues in the paragraph that could help you learn what *evolved* means.

READING SKILL

Summarize How did enlightened despots contribute to the Enlightenment?

_____

_____

_____

CHAPTER 5
SECTION 3

Note Taking Study Guide

BIRTH OF THE AMERICAN REPUBLIC

Focus Question: How did ideas of the Enlightenment lead to the independence and founding of the United States of America?

As you read this section in your textbook, complete the following timeline with the dates of important events that led to the formation of the United States.

French and Indian War ends.

1763

1760

CHAPTER 5 SECTION 3
Section Summary
BIRTH OF THE AMERICAN REPUBLIC

In the mid-1700s, Britain was a formidable global power. Key reasons for this status included its location, support of commerce, and huge gains in territory around the world. <u>Furthermore, the new king, **George III,** began to assert his leadership and royal power.</u>

Britain's growing empire included prosperous colonies on the east coast of North America. The colonists shared many values. These included an increasing sense of their own destiny separate from Britain. In some cases, Britain neglected to enforce laws dealing with colonial trade and manufacturing.

Tensions between the colonists and Britain grew as Parliament passed laws, such as the **Stamp Act,** that increased colonists' taxes. The colonists protested what they saw as "taxation without representation." A series of violent clashes with British soldiers intensified the colonists' anger. Finally, representatives from each colony, including **George Washington** of Virginia, met in the Continental Congress to decide what to do. Then in April 1775, colonists fought British soldiers at Lexington and Concord, and the American Revolution began.

On July 4, 1776, the Second Continental Congress adopted the Declaration of Independence. Written primarily by **Thomas Jefferson,** it reflects John Locke's ideas about the rights to "life, liberty, and property." It also details the colonists' grievances and emphasizes the Enlightenment idea of **popular sovereignty.**

At first, chances for American success looked bleak. The colonists struggled against Britain's trained soldiers, huge fleet, and greater resources. When the colonists won the Battle of Saratoga, other European nations, such as France, joined the American side. With the help of the French fleet, Washington forced the British to surrender at **Yorktown, Virginia,** in 1781. Two years later American, British, and French diplomats signed the **Treaty of Paris,** ending the war.

By 1789, leaders of the new United States, such as **James Madison** and **Benjamin Franklin,** had established a **federal republic** under the Constitution. The new government was based on the separation of powers, an idea borrowed directly from Montesquieu. The Bill of Rights, the first ten amendments to the Constitution, protected basic rights. The United States Constitution put Enlightenment ideas into practice and has become an important symbol of freedom.

Review Questions

1. What first caused tensions to rise between the colonists and Britain?

_____

_____

2. What are some Enlightenment ideas found in the Declaration of Independence?

_____

_____

READING CHECK

How did France help the Americans win the Revolution?

_____

_____

_____

VOCABULARY STRATEGY

What does the word *assert* mean in the underlined sentence? What context clues can you find in the surrounding words, phrases, or sentences that hint at its meaning? Circle the word below that is a synonym for *assert*.

1. declare

2. deny

READING SKILL

Recognize Sequence Place the events leading to the American Revolution in the correct order.

_____

_____

_____

Name_____ Class_____ Date_____

Focus Question: What led to the storming of the Bastille, and therefore, to the start of the French Revolution?

As you read this section in your textbook, complete the following chart by identifying the multiple causes of the French Revolution.

Causes of the French Revolution

Inequalities among classes

CHAPTER 6 SECTION 1

Section Summary
ON THE EVE OF REVOLUTION

Under France's **ancien régime**, there were three social classes, or **estates**. The First Estate was the clergy, who enjoyed great wealth and privilege. The Second Estate was the titled nobility. They held top jobs in government, the army, and the courts. The vast majority of the population, including the **bourgeoisie,** or middle class, formed the Third Estate. The bulk of the Third Estate consisted of rural peasants. <u>The poorest members of the Third Estate were urban workers.</u>

Members of the Third Estate resented the privileges enjoyed by their social "betters." The First and Second Estates, for example, were exempt from most taxes, while peasants paid taxes on many things, including necessities. Then Enlightenment ideas led people to question the inequalities of the old social structure. The Third Estate demanded that the privileged classes pay their share.

Economic troubles added to the social unrest. **Deficit spending** had left France deeply in debt. In the 1780s, bad harvests sent food prices soaring. **Louis XVI** chose **Jacques Necker** as an economic advisor. Later, the king was forced to dismiss Necker for proposing to tax the First and Second Estates. The crisis deepened. Powerful nobles and clergy called for a meeting of the **Estates-General** to try to control reform. Louis XVI finally set a meeting at Versailles. Beforehand, the king asked all three estates to prepare **cahiers** listing their grievances. Some lists demonstrated the high level of resentment among the classes.

The Estates-General met in May 1789. After weeks of stalemate, delegates of the Third Estate abandoned the Estates-General and formed the National Assembly. Later, when they were locked out of their meeting place, the members of the new legislature took their famous **Tennis Court Oath.** They swore never to separate until they had established a just constitution.

On July 14, 1789, the streets of Paris buzzed with rumors that royal troops were going to occupy the city. More than 800 Parisians assembled outside the **Bastille,** demanding weaponry stored there. When the commander refused, the enraged mob stormed the Bastille, sparking the French Revolution.

Review Questions

1. How was society structured under France's *ancien régime?*

_____

_____

2. What economic troubles did France face in the 1780s?

_____

_____

READING CHECK

Which group paid the most taxes?

_____

_____

_____

VOCABULARY STRATEGY

What does the word *urban* mean in the underlined sentence? Notice that the word *rural* appears in the previous sentence. *Rural* is an antonym of *urban*. Use the meaning of the antonym to help you figure out what *urban* means.

READING SKILL

Recognize Multiple Causes
Identify three causes of the French Revolution.

_____

_____

_____

CHAPTER 6 SECTION 2

Note Taking Study Guide
THE FRENCH REVOLUTION UNFOLDS

Focus Question: What political and social reforms did the National Assembly institute in the first stage of the French Revolution?

As you read this section in your textbook, complete the following outline by identifying the main ideas and supporting details in this section.

I. **Political crisis leads to revolt**
- A. The Great Fear
  - 1. Inflamed by famine and rumors
  - 2. _____
- B. _____
  - 1. _____
  - 2. _____

II. _____
- A. _____
  - 1. _____
  - 2. _____
- B. _____
  - 1. _____
  - 2. _____
- C. _____
  - 1. _____
  - 2. _____

III. _____
- A. _____
  - 1. _____
  - 2. _____
- B. _____
  - 1. _____
  - 2. _____
- C. _____
  - 1. _____
  - 2. _____

(Outline continues on the next page.)

(Continued from page 82)

IV. _____
  A. _____
   1. _____
   2. _____
  B. _____
   1. _____
   2. _____
  C. _____
   1. _____
   2. _____
  D. _____
   1. _____
   2. _____

CHAPTER 6 SECTION 2

Section Summary
THE FRENCH REVOLUTION UNFOLDS

READING CHECK

Who were the sans-culottes?

_____

_____

_____

VOCABULARY STRATEGY

What do you think the word *proclaimed* means in the underlined sentence? The words *proclamation, declaration,* and *announcement* are all synonyms for *proclaimed.* Use what you know about these synonyms to figure out the meaning of *proclaimed.*

READING SKILL

Identify Supporting Details
Identify two aspects of the Constitution of 1791 that reflect Enlightenment goals.

_____

_____

In France, the political crisis of 1789 coincided with a terrible famine. Peasants were starving and unemployed. In such desperate times, rumors ran wild. Inflamed by famine and fear, peasants unleashed their fury on the nobles. Meanwhile, a variety of **factions** in Paris competed to gain power. Moderates looked to the **Marquis de Lafayette** for leadership. However, a more radical group, the Paris Commune, replaced the city's royalist government.

The storming of the Bastille and the peasant uprisings pushed the National Assembly into action. In late August, the Assembly issued the Declaration of the Rights of Man and the Citizen. <u>It proclaimed that all male citizens were equal before the law.</u> Upset that women did not have equal rights, journalist **Olympe de Gouges** wrote a declaration that provided for this. The Assembly did not adopt it, however. Nor was King Louis XVI willing to accept reforms. Much anger was directed at the queen, **Marie Antoinette,** who lived a life of great extravagance.

The National Assembly produced the Constitution of 1791. This document reflected Enlightenment goals, set up a limited monarchy, ensured equality before the law for all male citizens, and ended Church interference in government.

Events in France stirred debate all over Europe. Some applauded the reforms of the National Assembly. Rulers of other nations, however, denounced the French Revolution. Horror stories were told by **émigrés** who had fled France. Rulers of neighboring monarchies increased border patrols to stop the spread of the "French plague" of revolution.

In October 1791, the newly elected Legislative Assembly took office, but falling currency values, rising prices, and food shortages renewed turmoil. Working-class men and women, called **sans-culottes,** pushed the revolution in a more radical direction, and demanded a **republic.** The sans-culottes found support among other radicals, especially the **Jacobins.** The radicals soon held the upper hand in the Legislative Assembly. Eager to spread the revolution, they declared war against Austria and other European monarchies.

Review Questions

1. What was the Declaration of the Rights of Man and the Citizen? Why were some people dissatisfied with it?

_____

_____

2. How did rulers of European monarchies react to the French Revolution?

_____

_____

Name_____ Class_____ Date_____

Focus Question: What events occurred during the radical phase of the French Revolution?

As you read this section in your textbook, complete the following timeline to show the sequence of events that took place during the radical phase of the French Revolution.

1795

July 1794

Sept. 1793

Jan. 1793

Sept. 1792

Aug. 1792

Mob invades royal palace

CHAPTER 6

SECTION 3

Section Summary
RADICAL DAYS OF THE REVOLUTION

Who was Robespierre?

_____

_____

_____

What do you think *radical* means in the underlined sentence? Notice that the word *more* appears before *radical.* Use the word *more* and your prior knowledge to help you figure out what *radical* means.

Recognize Sequence What occurred after the radicals took control of the Assembly in 1792?

_____

_____

_____

In 1793, the revolution entered a frightening and bloody phase. The war with Austria was not going well for France. Some felt the king was in league with France's enemies. Others wanted to restore the king's power. On August 10, 1792, a mob stormed the royal palace. Radicals then took control of the Assembly and called for the election of a new legislative body called the National Convention. **Suffrage** was to be extended to all male citizens, not just to those who owned property. <u>The Convention that met in September 1792 was a more radical body than earlier assemblies.</u> It voted to abolish the monarchy and establish the French Republic. Louis XVI and his queen were executed.

War with other European nations and internal rebellions concerned the government. The Convention created the Committee of Public Safety to deal with these issues. It had almost absolute power. Jacobin Maximilien **Robespierre** led the Committee. He was one of the chief architects of the **Reign of Terror,** which lasted from September 1793 to July 1794. During that time, courts conducted hasty trials for those suspected of resisting the revolution. Many people were the victims of false accusations. About 17,000 were executed by **guillotine.**

In reaction to the Terror, the revolution entered a third stage, dominated by the bourgeoisie. It moved away from the excesses of the Convention, and moderates created the Constitution of 1795. This set up a five-man Directory to rule, and a two-house legislature. However, discontent grew because of corrupt leaders. Also, war continued with Austria and Britain. Politicians planned to use **Napoleon** Bonaparte, a popular military hero, to advance their goals.

By 1799, the French Revolution had dramatically changed France. It had dislodged the old social order, overthrown the monarchy, and brought the Church under state control. **Nationalism** spread throughout France. From the city of **Marseilles,** troops marched to a rousing new song that would become the French national anthem. Revolutionaries also made social reforms. They set up systems to help the poor and abolished slavery in France's Caribbean colonies.

Review Questions

1. What type of government did the National Convention establish in September 1792?

_____

_____

2. Identify three changes that the French Revolution brought to France.

_____

_____

Name_____ Class_____ Date_____

Note Taking Study Guide
THE AGE OF NAPOLEON

CHAPTER **6** SECTION 4

Focus Question: Explain Napoleon's rise to power in Europe, his subsequent defeat, and how the outcome still affects Europe today.

As you read this section in your textbook, complete the flowchart to list the main ideas about Napoleon's rise to power and his defeat.

Napoleon quickly advances through military ranks.

Name_____ Class_____ Date_____

CHAPTER **6** SECTION 4	**Section Summary**
	THE AGE OF NAPOLEON

READING CHECK

What was the Napoleonic Code?

_____

_____

_____

VOCABULARY STRATEGY

What do you think the word *anticipate* means in the underlined sentence? What clues can you find in the surrounding words and phrases? Use these context clues to figure out the meaning of *anticipate*.

READING SKILL

Identify Main Ideas Write a new title for this section Summary to express the main idea in another way.

_____

_____

_____

The final phase of the revolution is known as the Age of Napoleon. When the revolution first broke out, Napoleon Bonaparte was a young lieutenant. Battle victories fueled his ambitions and his rise through army ranks. By 1804, Napoleon had acquired enough power to assume the title Emperor of the French. At each step on his rise to power, Napoleon had held a **plebiscite.** However, he still had absolute power, although he was elected.

Napoleon consolidated his power by strengthening the central government. His economic and social reforms won support across classes. Among his most lasting reforms was the **Napoleonic Code.** This new code of laws embodied Enlightenment principles of equality, religious tolerance, and the abolition of feudalism.

From 1804 to 1812, Napoleon battled the European powers and created a vast French empire. A brilliant general, before each battle Napoleon developed a new plan. <u>In this way, opposing generals could never anticipate what he would do next.</u> He rarely lost. Napoleon **annexed** the Netherlands, Belgium, and parts of Italy and Germany to build his Grand Empire. However, Britain remained outside Napoleon's grasp. His attempt to wage economic warfare against Britain through the **Continental System** failed. Many Europeans resented the scarcity of goods. Growing nationalism led to resistance against French influence. In Spain, patriots waged **guerrilla warfare** against the French.

In 1812, Napoleon invaded Russia with 600,000 soldiers. To avoid battles with Napoleon, the Russians retreated, burning crops and villages as they went. This **scorched-earth policy** left the French hungry and cold. Most of the Grand Army was destroyed. Fewer than 20,000 soldiers survived. The retreat from Moscow through the long Russian winter shattered Napoleon's reputation for success.

In 1815, British and Prussian forces crushed the French at the Battle of Waterloo. Napoleon was forced to **abdicate.** After Waterloo, diplomats met at the **Congress of Vienna** to restore stability and order in Europe after years of revolution and war. The Congress strived to create a lasting peace through the principle of **legitimacy** and by maintaining a balance of power. Leaders also met periodically in the **Concert of Europe** to discuss problems that threatened peace.

Review Questions

1. How did the French respond to Napoleon's economic and social reforms?

_____

_____

2. Why did Napoleon's invasion of Russia fail?

_____

_____

Focus Question: What events helped bring about the Industrial Revolution?

As you read this section in your textbook, complete the following flowchart to list multiple causes of the Industrial Revolution.

CHAPTER 7
SECTION 1

Section Summary
DAWN OF THE INDUSTRIAL AGE

READING CHECK

Who formed the growing labor force for the Industrial Revolution?

_____

_____

_____

The Industrial Revolution started in Britain. In 1750, most people worked the land, using handmade tools. They made their own clothing and grew their own food. With the onset of the Industrial Revolution, the rural way of life in Britain began to disappear. By the 1850s, many country villages had grown into industrial towns and cities. New inventions and scientific "firsts" appeared each year. Between 1830 and 1855, for example, an American dentist first used an **anesthetic** during surgery and a French physicist measured the speed of light.

A series of related causes helped spark the Industrial Revolution. It was made possible, in part, by another revolution—in agriculture—that greatly improved the quality and quantity of food. Farmers mixed different kinds of soils and tried out new methods of crop rotation to get higher yields. Meanwhile, rich landowners pushed ahead with **enclosure,** the process of taking over and consolidating land formerly shared by peasant farmers. As millions of acres were enclosed, farm output and profits rose. The agricultural revolution created a surplus of food, so fewer people died from starvation. <u>Statistics show that the agricultural revolution contributed to a rapid growth in population.</u>

VOCABULARY STRATEGY

What does the word *statistics* mean in the underlined sentence? What prior knowledge do you have of this word? For example, think of where you may have seen statistics before. Use your prior knowledge and context clues in the sentence to help you learn what *statistics* means.

Agricultural progress, however, had a human cost. Many farm laborers were thrown out of work. In time, jobless farm workers migrated to towns and cities. There, they formed a growing labor force that would soon operate the machines of the Industrial Revolution.

Another factor that helped trigger the Industrial Revolution was the development of new technology, aided by new sources of energy and new materials. One vital power source was coal, used to develop the steam engine. In 1764, Scottish engineer **James Watt** improved the steam engine to make it more efficient. Watt's engine became a key power source of the Industrial Revolution. Coal was also used in the production of iron, a material needed for the construction of machines and steam engines. In 1709, Adam Darby used coal to **smelt** iron, or separate iron from its ore. Darby's experiments led to the production of less-expensive and better-quality iron.

READING SKILL

Recognize Multiple Causes
Identify three events in the agricultural revolution that caused population and industry to grow.

_____

_____

_____

Review Questions

1. How did people's lifestyles change in Britain with the start of the Industrial Revolution?

_____

_____

2. Why was the steam engine important to the Industrial Revolution?

_____

_____

Note Taking Study Guide

BRITAIN LEADS THE WAY

Focus Question: What key factors allowed Britain to lead the way in the Industrial Revolution?

As you read this section in your textbook, complete the following concept webs to identify causes and effects of Britain's early lead in industrialization. Fill in the first concept web with causes. Fill in the second concept web with effects.

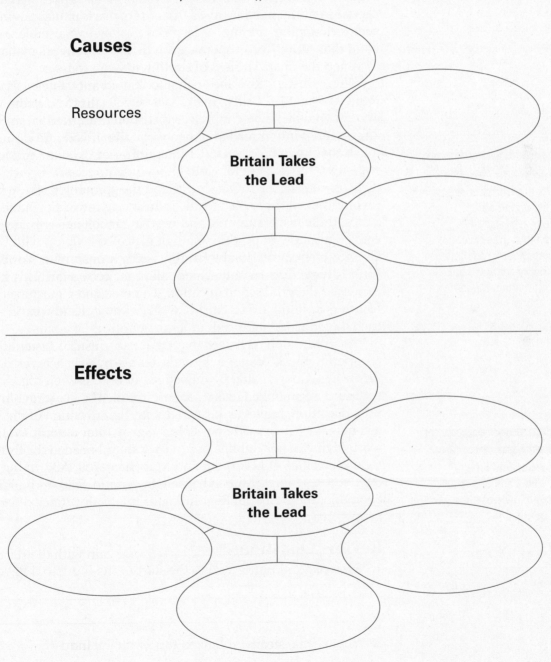

Causes

Resources

Britain Takes the Lead

Effects

Britain Takes the Lead

Name_____ Class_____ Date_____

Section Summary
BRITAIN LEADS THE WAY

READING CHECK

What machine did Eli Whitney invent?

_____

_____

_____

VOCABULARY STRATEGY

What does the word *decades* mean in the underlined sentence? The word *decades* comes from the Greek word *deka,* which means "ten." Use the meaning of the word *deka* to help you learn what *decades* means.

READING SKILL

Identify Causes and Effects Identify causes and effects of the great revolution in transportation in England.

_____

_____

_____

The start of the Industrial Revolution in Britain can be attributed to many factors, including population growth and plentiful natural resources. The growing population and ready workforce boosted demand for goods. To increase production to meet the demand, however, another key ingredient was needed—money to start businesses. Beginning with the slave trade, the business class accumulated **capital** to invest in enterprises. An **enterprise** is a business in areas such as shipping, mining, or factories. Britain had a stable government that supported economic growth. **Entrepreneurs** managed and assumed the financial risks of starting new businesses.

The Industrial Revolution first took hold in Britain's largest industry—textiles. British merchants developed the **putting-out system,** in which raw cotton was distributed to peasant families. They spun it into thread and then wove the thread into cloth, working in their own homes. Under the putting-out system, production was slow. As demand for cloth grew, inventors came up with new devices, such as the flying shuttle and the spinning jenny, which revolutionized the British textile industry. Meanwhile, in the United States, these faster spinning and weaving machines presented a challenge—how to produce enough cotton to keep up with Britain. Cleaning the raw cotton by hand was time-consuming. To solve this, **Eli Whitney** invented a machine called the cotton gin. This greatly increased the production of cotton. To house these machines, manufacturers built the first factories, where spinners and weavers came each day to work and produce large quantities of goods.

As production increased, entrepreneurs needed faster and cheaper methods of moving goods. Some capitalists invested in **turnpikes.** Goods could be moved faster on these toll roads, and turnpikes soon linked every part of Britain. The great revolution in transportation, however, occurred with the invention of the steam locomotive, which made possible the growth of railroads. The world's first major rail line began operating between the British industrial cities of **Liverpool** and **Manchester** in 1830. In the following decades, railroad travel became faster and railroad building boomed. The Industrial Revolution dramatically affected the way people lived.

Review Questions

1. What factors contributed to the start of the Industrial Revolution?

_____

_____

2. What changes revolutionized the textile industry?

_____

_____

Name_____ Class_____ Date_____

Focus Question: What were the social effects of the Industrial Revolution?

As you read this section in your textbook, complete the following table to understand the effects of industrialization.

Industrialization	
Challenges	
• Crowded cities	
•	
•	
•	
•	
Benefits	
• Created jobs	
•	
•	
•	
•	

CHAPTER
7
SECTION 3

Section Summary
SOCIAL IMPACT OF THE INDUSTRIAL REVOLUTION

READING CHECK

Who made up the new middle class that emerged during the Industrial Revolution?

_____

_____

_____

VOCABULARY STRATEGY

What does the word *contaminated* mean in the underlined sentence? What clues can you find in the surrounding words, phrases, or sentences? Circle the words in the paragraph that could help you figure out what *contaminated* means.

READING SKILL

Understand Effects How did the Industrial Revolution affect the lives of the working class?

_____

_____

_____

The Industrial Revolution brought rapid **urbanization,** or the movement of people to cities. Changes in farming, soaring population growth, and a demand for workers led masses of people to migrate from farms to cities. Almost overnight, small towns that were located around coal or iron mines grew into cities. Other cities developed around the factories in once-quiet market towns.

Those who benefited most from the Industrial Revolution were the entrepreneurs who set it in motion. The Industrial Revolution created this new middle class, whose members came from a variety of backgrounds. While the wealthy and the middle class lived in pleasant neighborhoods, vast numbers of poor struggled to survive in slums. They packed into tiny rooms in **tenements** that had no running water and no sewage or sanitation system. Sewage rotted in the streets or was dumped into rivers, which created an overwhelming stench and contaminated drinking water. This led to the spread of diseases such as cholera.

The heart of the new industrial city was the factory. Working in a factory differed greatly from working on a farm. In rural villages, people worked hard, but the work varied according to the season. Some seasons were easier than others. The factory system imposed a harsh new way of life on workers. Working hours were long, with shifts lasting from twelve to sixteen hours, six or seven days a week. Exhausted workers were injured by machines that had no safety devices. Working conditions in the mines were even worse than in the factories. Factories and mines also hired many boys and girls. These children often started working at age seven or eight; a few were as young as five.

The early industrial age brought terrible hardships. In time, however, reformers pressed for laws to improve working conditions. **Labor unions** won the right to bargain with employers for better wages, hours, and working conditions. Despite the social problems created by the Industrial Revolution—low pay, dismal living conditions—the industrial age did have some positive effects. Wages rose. Also as the cost of railroad travel fell, more people could afford to travel further and faster than ever before.

Review Questions

1. What caused rapid urbanization to occur during the Industrial Revolution?

_____

_____

2. How did the factory system change the way people worked?

_____

_____

Name_____ Class_____ Date_____

Note Taking Study Guide
NEW WAYS OF THINKING

Focus Question: What new ideas about economics and society were fostered as a result of the Industrial Revolution?

As you read this section in your textbook, complete the following outline to identify main ideas about the new economic and social theories.

I. **Laissez-faire economics**

  A. Adam Smith and free enterprise

    1. _____

    2. _____

II. **Malthus on population**

  A. _____

    1. _____

    2. _____

    3. _____

  B. _____

    1. _____

    2. _____

III. _____

  A. _____

    1. _____

    2. _____

IV. _____

  A. _____

    1. _____

    2. _____

  B. _____

    1. _____

    2. _____

(Outline continues on the next page.)

CHAPTER 7 SECTION 4
Note Taking Study Guide
NEW WAYS OF THINKING

(Continued from page 95)

V. _____
   A. _____
      1. _____
      2. _____
VI. _____
   A. _____
      1. _____
      2. _____
      3. _____
   B. _____
      1. _____
      2. _____

Section Summary
NEW WAYS OF THINKING

Many thinkers tried to understand the staggering changes taking place in the early Industrial Age. These thinkers looked for natural laws that governed the world of business and economics. Middle-class business leaders embraced the laissez-faire, or "hands-off" approach, believing that a free market would eventually help everyone, not just the rich. However, one British laissez-faire economist, **Thomas Malthus,** felt that the population would grow faster than the food supply. As long as the population kept growing, the poor would suffer. He opposed any government help including charity and vaccinations. He urged families to have fewer children.

Other thinkers sought to modify laissez-faire ideas to justify some government intervention. The British philosopher and economist **Jeremy Bentham** advocated **utilitarianism,** or the idea that the goal of society should be the "greatest happiness for the greatest number" of citizens. Bentham's ideas influenced the British philosopher and economist John Stuart Mill. Although he strongly believed in individual freedom, Mill wanted the government to step in to improve the hard lives of the working class.

To end poverty and injustice, others offered a radical solution—**socialism.** Under socialism, the people, as a whole rather than as individuals, would own and operate the **means of production—**the farms, factories, railways, and other businesses that produced and distributed goods. A number of early socialists, such as **Robert Owen,** established communities where all work was shared and all property was owned in common. These early socialists were called Utopians.

<u>**Karl Marx,** a German philosopher, formulated a new theory.</u> His theory predicted a struggle between social classes that would end in a classless society that he called communist. In a classless, communist society, the struggles of the **proletariat,** or working class, would end because wealth and power would be equally shared. In practice, **communism** later referred to a system in which a small elite controlled the economy and politics. In the 1860s, German socialists adapted Marx's beliefs to form **social democracy,** which called for a slow transition from capitalism to socialism.

Review Questions

1. Why did middle-class business leaders support laissez-faire economics?

_____

_____

2. How did utilitarians seek to modify laissez-faire ideas?

_____

_____

READING CHECK

Who were the Utopians?

_____

_____

_____

VOCABULARY STRATEGY

What does the word *formulated* mean in the underlined sentence? What clue can you find in the base word, *form*? Use the meaning of *form* to help you figure out what *formulated* means.

READING SKILL

Identify Main Ideas Explain the main ideas of Karl Marx's theory.

_____

_____

_____

<table>
<tr><td>CHAPTER
8
SECTION 1</td><td>## Note Taking Study Guide
AN AGE OF IDEOLOGIES</td></tr>
</table>

Focus Question: What events proved that Metternich was correct in his fears?

A. *As you read "Conservatives Prefer the Old Order," and "Liberals and Nationalists Seek Change," fill in the table to identify main ideas about conservatism, liberalism, and nationalism.*

Conservatism	Liberalism	Nationalism
• _____	• _____	• _____
• _____	• _____	_____
• _____	• _____	_____
• _____	• _____	
• _____	• _____	
• _____	• _____	
• _____		

B. *As you read "Central Europe Challenges the Old Order," use the table to identify supporting details about revolts in Serbia, Greece, and other countries.*

Serbia	Greece	Other Revolts
• _____	• _____	• _____
_____	_____	_____
• _____	• _____	_____
_____	_____	
• _____	• _____	• _____
_____	_____	
• _____	• _____	
_____	_____	

CHAPTER 8 SECTION 1

Section Summary

AN AGE OF IDEOLOGIES

After the Congress of Vienna, people with opposing **ideologies** plunged Europe into decades of turmoil. Conservatives, including monarchs, nobles, and church leaders, favored a return to the social order that had existed before 1789. They decided to work together in an agreement called the Concert of Europe. They wanted to restore the royal families that Napoleon had deposed. They supported a social hierarchy in which lower classes respected and obeyed their social superiors. They also backed established churches and opposed constitutional governments. Conservative leaders such as Prince Metternich of Austria sought to suppress revolutionary ideas.

Inspired by the Enlightenment and the French Revolution, liberals and nationalists challenged conservatives. Liberals included business owners, bankers, lawyers, politicians, and writers. They wanted governments based on written constitutions. They opposed established churches and divine-right monarchies. They believed that liberty, equality, and property were natural rights. They saw government's role as limited to protecting basic rights, such as freedom of thought, speech, and religion. Only later in the century did liberals come to support **universal manhood suffrage,** giving all men the right to vote. Liberals also strongly supported laissez-faire economics.

Nationalism gave people with a common heritage a sense of identity and the goal of creating their own homeland. In the 1800s, national groups within the Austrian and Ottoman empires set out to create their own states. Rebellions erupted in the Balkans, where there were people of various religions and ethnic groups. The Serbs were the first to revolt. By 1830, Russian support helped the Serbs win **autonomy,** or self-rule, within the Ottoman empire. In 1821, the Greeks revolted, and by 1830, Greece was independent from the Ottomans. Revolts spread to Spain, Portugal, and Italy. Metternich urged conservative rulers to crush the uprisings. In response, French and Austrian troops smashed rebellions in Spain and Italy.

In the next decades, sparks of rebellion would flare anew. Added to liberal and nationalist demands were the goals of the new industrial working class. <u>By the mid-1800s, social reformers and agitators were urging workers to support socialism or other ways of reorganizing property ownership.</u>

Review Questions

1. How did government views of conservatives and liberals differ?

_____

_____

2. Why did French and Austrian troops stop revolts in Spain and Italy?

_____

_____

READING CHECK

What is universal manhood suffrage?

_____

_____

_____

VOCABULARY STRATEGY

What does the word *agitators* mean in the underlined sentence? Review the surrounding words and phrases to look for clues to its meaning. Use these context clues to help you understand what an *agitator* is.

READING SKILL

Identify Main Ideas What two groups generally struggled for political control during the early nineteenth century?

_____

_____

_____

Note Taking Study Guide

REVOLUTIONS OF 1830 AND 1848

Focus Question: What were the causes and effects of the revolutions in Europe in 1830 and 1848?

As you read this section, fill in the table below with a country, date, and main idea for each revolution of 1830 and 1848.

Revolutions of 1830 and 1848	Radicals force king to abdicate.								
	1830								
	France								

CHAPTER **8** SECTION 2	**Section Summary** REVOLUTIONS OF 1830 AND 1848

When Louis XVIII died in 1824, Charles X inherited the French throne. In 1830, Charles suspended the legislature, limited the right to vote, and restricted the press. Angry citizens, led by liberals and **radicals,** rebelled and soon controlled Paris. Charles X abdicated. Radicals hoped to set up a republic, but liberals insisted on a constitutional monarchy. **Louis Philippe** was chosen king. As the "citizen king," Louis favored the bourgeoisie, or middle class, over the workers.

The Paris revolts inspired uprisings elsewhere in Europe. Most failed, but the revolutions frightened rulers and encouraged reforms. One notable success was in Belgium, which achieved its independence from Holland in 1831. Nationalists also revolted in Poland in 1830, but they failed to win widespread support. Russian forces crushed the rebels.

In the 1840s, discontent began to grow again in France. Radicals, socialists, and liberals denounced Louis Philippe's government. Discontent was heightened by a **recession.** People lost their jobs, and poor harvests caused bread prices to rise. When the government tried to silence critics, angry crowds took to the streets in February 1848. The turmoil spread, and Louis Philippe abdicated. A group of liberals, radicals, and socialists proclaimed the Second Republic. By June, the upper and middle classes had won control of the government. Workers again took to the streets of Paris. At least 1,500 people were killed before the government crushed the rebellion. By the end of 1848, the National Assembly issued a constitution for the Second Republic, giving the right to vote to all adult men. When the election for president was held, Louis Napoleon, the nephew of Napoleon Bonaparte, won. However, by 1852 he had proclaimed himself Emperor **Napoleon III.** This ended the Second Republic.

The revolts in Paris in 1848 again led to revolutions across Europe, especially in the Austrian empire. Revolts broke out in Vienna, and Metternich resigned. In Budapest, Hungarian nationalists led by **Louis Kossuth** demanded an independent government. In Prague, the Czechs made similar demands. The Italian states also revolted, and the German states demanded national unity. While the rebellions had some short-term success, most of them had failed by 1850.

Review Questions

1. What caused the rebellion in France in 1830?

_____

_____

2. In what parts of Europe did revolts take place following the Paris revolts of 1848?

_____

_____

READING CHECK

What brought the Second Republic to an end?

_____

_____

_____

VOCABULARY STRATEGY

What does the word *denounced* mean in the underlined sentence? Reread the sentences before and after the underlined sentence. Were the French people happy or unhappy with Louis Philippe's government? Note that the government "tried to silence critics." Use these context clues to help you understand the meaning of *denounce.*

READING SKILL

Identify Main Ideas What is the main idea of the last paragraph in the Summary?

_____

_____

_____

CHAPTER
8
SECTION 3

Note Taking Study Guide
REVOLTS IN LATIN AMERICA

Focus Question: Who were the key revolutionaries to lead the movements for independence in Latin America, and what were their accomplishments?

As you read this section, fill in the table below with a country, a date, and a main idea for each of the revolts in Latin America.

Revolts in Latin America										
Haiti	1791	Toussaint L'Ouverture leads an army of former slaves and ends slavery there.								

CHAPTER 8 SECTION 3
Section Summary
REVOLTS IN LATIN AMERICA

By the late 1700s, revolutionary fever had spread to Latin America, where the social system had led to discontent. Spanish-born *peninsulares,* the highest social class, dominated the government and the Church. Many **creoles**—Latin Americans of European descent who owned the haciendas, ranches, and mines—resented their second-class status. **Mestizos,** people of Native American and European descent, and **mulattoes,** people of African and European descent, were angry at being denied the status, wealth, and power that the other groups enjoyed. The Enlightenment and the French and American revolutions inspired creoles, but they were reluctant to act. However, when Napoleon invaded Spain in 1808, Latin American leaders decided to demand independence from Spain.

Revolution had already erupted in Hispaniola in 1791 when **Toussaint L'Ouverture** led a slave rebellion there. The fighting cost many lives, but the rebels achieved their goal of abolishing slavery and taking control of the island. Napoleon's army tried to reconquer the island but failed. In 1804, the island declared itself independent under the name Haiti.

In 1810, a creole priest, **Father Miguel Hidalgo,** called Mexicans to fight for independence. After some successes, he was captured and executed. **Father José Morelos** tried to carry the revolution forward, but he too was captured and killed. Success finally came in 1821 when revolutionaries led by Agustín de Iturbide overthrew the Spanish viceroy and declared independence. Central American colonies soon declared independence, too.

In the early 1800s, discontent spread across South America. **Simón Bolívar** led an uprising in Venezuela. Conservative forces toppled his new republic, but Bolívar did not give up. In a grueling campaign, he marched his army across the Andes, swooping down into Bogotá and taking the city from the surprised Spanish. Then he moved south to free Ecuador, Peru, and Bolivia. There, he joined forces with another great leader, **José de San Martín.** San Martín helped Argentina and Chile win freedom from Spain. The wars of independence ended in 1824, but power struggles among South American leaders led to destructive civil wars. In Brazil, **Dom Pedro,** the son of the Portuguese king, became emperor and proclaimed independence for Brazil in 1822.

Review Questions

1. Why were creoles ready to revolt by 1808?

_____

_____

2. How did Brazil gain its independence?

_____

_____

READING CHECK

What two leaders helped free much of South America?

_____

_____

_____

VOCABULARY STRATEGY

What does the word *proclaimed* mean in the underlined sentence? *Proclaim* comes from the Latin word *proclamare.* The prefix *pro-* means "before," and *clamare* means "to cry out" or "shout." Use these word-origin clues to help you to figure out the meaning of *proclaimed.*

READING SKILL

Identify Main Ideas In the first paragraph of the Summary, most of the sentences are supporting details. Which sentence states the main idea of that paragraph?

_____

_____

_____

Name_____ Class_____ Date_____

Focus Question: How did science, technology, and big business promote industrial growth?

As you read this section in your textbook, complete the following chart to identify main ideas about the major developments of the Industrial Revolution.

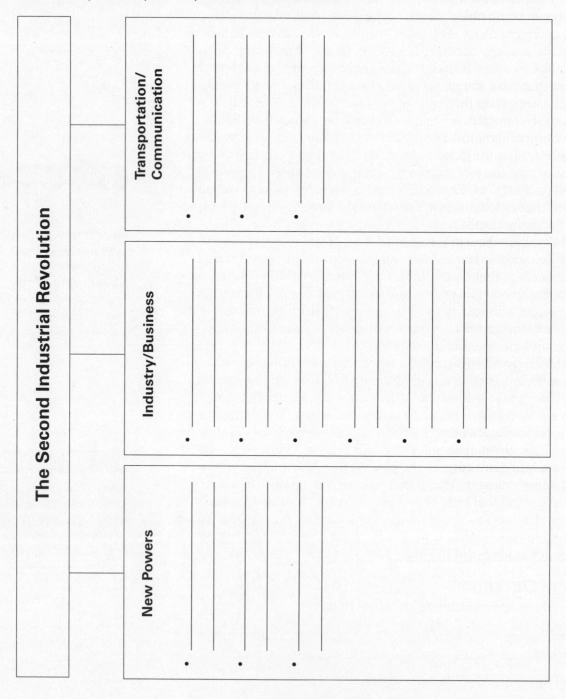

CHAPTER 9
SECTION 1

Section Summary
THE INDUSTRIAL REVOLUTION SPREADS

During the early Industrial Revolution, Britain was the world's industrial giant. Later, two new industrial powers emerged—Germany and the United States. These nations had more abundant supplies of coal, iron, and other resources than Britain. This helped them become the new industrial leaders. These nations also had the advantage of being able to follow Britain's lead, borrowing its experts and technology. The demands of an industrial society brought about many social, economic, and political changes.

Technology sparked industrial and economic growth. **Henry Bessemer** patented the process for making steel from iron. Steel became so important that industrialized countries measured their success in steel output. **Alfred Nobel** earned enough money from his invention of dynamite to fund today's Nobel prizes. Electricity replaced steam as the dominant industrial energy source. **Michael Faraday** created the first simple electric motor, as well as the first **dynamo.** In the 1870s, **Thomas Edison** made the first electric light bulb. Soon, electricity lit entire cities, the pace of city life quickened, and factories continued to operate after dark. **Interchangeable parts** and the **assembly line** made production faster and cheaper.

Technology also transformed transportation and communication. Steamships replaced sailing ships. Railroads connected cities, seaports, and industrial centers. The invention of the internal combustion engine sparked the automobile age. In the early 1900s, Henry Ford developed an assembly line to produce cars, making the United States a leader in the automobile industry. The air age began when **Orville and Wilbur Wright** flew their plane for a few seconds in 1904. Communication advances included the telegraph and telephone. **Guglielmo Marconi's** radio became the cornerstone of today's global communication network.

New technologies needed investments of large amounts of money. To get the money, owners sold **stock** to investors, growing businesses into giant **corporations.** By the late 1800s, what we call "big business" came to dominate industry. Corporations formed **cartels** to control markets.

Review Questions

1. What advantages did the new industrial powers have?

_____

_____

2. How did the development of electricity change life in cities?

_____

_____

READING CHECK

What two new industrial powers emerged in the mid-1800s?

_____

_____

_____

VOCABULARY STRATEGY

What does the word *dominate* mean in the underlined sentence? It comes from a Latin word that means "lord" or "master." Use this information about the word's origin to help you figure out what *dominate* means.

READING SKILL

Identify Main Ideas How was transportation transformed during the Industrial Revolution?

_____

_____

_____

Note Taking Study Guide

CHAPTER 9 SECTION 2

THE RISE OF THE CITIES

Focus Question: How did the Industrial Revolution change life in the cities?

As you read this section in your textbook, complete the following outline to identify main ideas and supporting details about how the Industrial Revolution changed life in the cities.

I. Medicine and the population explosion

    A. The fight against disease

        1. _____

        2. _____

    B. _____

        1. _____

        2. _____

II. _____

    A. _____

        1. _____

        2. _____

    B. _____

        1. _____

        2. _____

    C. _____

        1. _____

        2. _____

    D. _____

        1. _____

        2. _____

III. _____

    A. _____

        1. _____

        2. _____

    B. _____

        1. _____

        2. _____

Section Summary
THE RISE OF THE CITIES

Between 1800 and 1900, the population of Europe more than doubled. Advances in medicine slowed death rates and caused a population explosion. In the fight against disease, scientists speculated
about a **germ theory**. They believed that certain germs might cause
specific diseases. In 1870, French chemist **Louis Pasteur** showed that
this link is real. Ten years later, German doctor **Robert Koch** identified the bacteria that causes tuberculosis, a deadly respiratory disease. As people began to understand how germs cause diseases, they
practiced better hygiene. This helped decrease the number of deaths
from disease. Better hygiene also led to improvements in hospital
care. British nurse and reformer **Florence Nightingale** introduced
sanitary measures in hospitals. The English surgeon **Joseph Lister**
discovered how antiseptics prevent infection.

As industrialization progressed, city life underwent dramatic
changes in Europe and the United States. The most extensive **urban
renewal** took place in Paris in the 1850s. Wide boulevards, paved
streets, and splendid public buildings replaced old streets full of ten-
ement housing. Architects used steel to build soaring buildings
called skyscrapers. Electric streetlights illuminated the night,
increasing safety. Massive new sewage systems in London and Paris
provided cleaner water and better sanitation, sharply cutting death
rates from disease.

Despite these efforts, urban life remained difficult for the poor.
In the worst tenements, whole families were often crammed into a
single room. Slums remained a fact of city life. Still, millions of people were attracted to cities because of the promise of work, entertain-
ment, and educational opportunities.

However, industrialization and urban improvements did not
improve conditions for workers. Most experienced low wages, long
hours, unsafe environments, and the constant threat of unemployment. Workers protested these terrible conditions. They formed
mutual-aid societies and organized unions. Pressured by unions,
reformers, and working-class voters, governments passed laws to
regulate working conditions. Wages varied, but overall, the **standard
of living** for most workers did rise.

Review Questions
1. How did advances in medicine cause a population explosion?

_____

_____

2. What two changes in the 1800s made city life safer and healthier?

_____

_____

READING CHECK

What did Louis Pasteur do in
1870?

_____

_____

_____

VOCABULARY STRATEGY

What does the word *illuminated*
mean in the underlined sentence? The root of this word is
from *lumen*, which is Latin for
"light." How can you use the
root of *illuminated* to help you
figure out its meaning?

READING SKILL

Identify Supporting Details In
what ways were working conditions difficult for most industrial
workers?

_____

_____

_____

Note Taking Study Guide

CHANGING ATTITUDES AND VALUES

Focus Question: How did the Industrial Revolution change the old social order and long-held traditions in the Western world?

As you read this section in your textbook, complete the following table. List new issues that caused change in the first column and identify two supporting details for each in the second column.

Changes in Social Order and Values	
Issue	**Change**
• New social order	• Upper class: old nobility, new industrialists, business families • •
• Rights for women	• •
•	• •
•	• •
•	• •

Name_____ Class_____ Date_____

Section Summary
CHANGING ATTITUDES AND VALUES

In the late 1800s, the social order in the Western world slowly changed. Instead of nobles and peasants, a more complex social structure emerged, made up of three classes. The new upper class included very rich business families. Below this tiny elite were a growing middle class and a struggling lower middle class. Workers and peasants were at the bottom of the social ladder.

The middle class developed its own values and way of life, which included a strict code of rules that dictated behavior for every occasion. A **cult of domesticity** also emerged that idealized women and the home.

Demands for women's rights also challenged the traditional social order. Across Europe and the United States, many women campaigned for fairness in marriage, divorce, and property laws. Many women's groups also supported the **temperance movement.** In the United States, reformers such as **Elizabeth Cady Stanton** and **Sojourner Truth** were dedicated to achieving **women's suffrage.**

Industrialized societies recognized the need for a literate work-force. Reformers persuaded many governments to require basic education for all children and to set up public schools. More and more children attended school, and public education improved.

At the same time, new ideas in science challenged long-held beliefs. **John Dalton** developed the modern atomic theory. <u>The most controversial new idea, however, came from the British naturalist</u> <u>**Charles Darwin.**</u> His ideas upset those who debated the validity of his conclusions. Darwin argued that all forms of life had evolved over millions of years. His theory of natural selection explained the long, slow process of evolution. In natural selection, members of each species compete to survive. Unfortunately, some people applied Darwin's theory of natural selection to encourage **racism.** Others applied his ideas to economic competition.

Religion continued to be a major force in Western society. The grim realities of industrial life stirred feelings of compassion and charity. For example, the **social gospel** urged Christians to push for reforms in housing, healthcare, and education.

Review Questions

1. How did the social structure change in the late 1800s?

_____

_____

2. For what rights did women in Europe and the United States campaign?

_____

_____

READING CHECK

What new scientific theory did Charles Darwin promote to explain evolution?

_____

_____

_____

VOCABULARY STRATEGY

What does the word *controversial* mean in the under-lined sentence? Use context clues, or surrounding words and sentences, to figure out what *controversial* means.

READING SKILL

Identify Supporting Details
What changes in education were brought about by the Industrial Revolution?

_____

_____

_____

CHAPTER 9 SECTION 4

Note Taking Study Guide

ARTS IN THE INDUSTRIAL AGE

Focus Question: What artistic movements emerged in reaction to the Industrial Revolution?

As you read this section in your textbook, complete the following table. Identify supporting details about the major features of the artistic movements of the 1800s.

Major Artistic Movements of the 1800s		
Movement	**Goals/Characteristics**	**Major Figures**
Romanticism	• Rebellion against reason • • • • •	• William Wordsworth • • • • • •
Realism	• • • • •	• • • •
Impressionism	• •	• •
	•	• • •

Section Summary
ARTS IN THE INDUSTRIAL AGE

From about 1750 to 1850, a cultural movement called **romanticism** emerged in Western art and literature. The movement was a reaction against the rationality and restraint of the Enlightenment. Romanticism emphasized imagination, freedom, and emotion. In contrast to Enlightenment literature, the works of romantic writers included direct language, intense feelings, and a glorification of nature.

Poets **William Wordsworth, William Blake,** and **Lord Byron** were among the major figures of the romantic movement. Romantic novelists, such as **Victor Hugo,** were inspired by history, legend, and folklore. Romantic composers also tried to stir deep emotions. The passionate music of **Ludwig van Beethoven** combined classical forms with a stirring range of sound. Painters, too, broke free from the formal styles of the Enlightenment. They sought to capture the beauty and power of nature with bold brush strokes and colors.

By the mid-1800s, another new artistic movement, **realism,** took hold in the West. Realists sought to represent the world as it was, without romantic sentiment. Their works made people aware of the grim conditions of the Industrial Age. Many realists wanted to improve the lives of those they depicted. **Charles Dickens,** for example, vividly portrayed in his novels the lives of slum dwellers and factory workers. Some of his novels shocked middle-class readers with images of poverty, mistreatment of children, and urban crime. Painters such as **Gustave Courbet** also portrayed the realities of the time.

By the 1840s, a new art form, photography, emerged. **Louis Daguerre** produced some of the first successful photographs. Some artists questioned the effectiveness of realism when a camera could make such exact images. By the 1870s, one group had started a new art movement, **impressionism**. Impressionists, such as **Claude Monet,** sought to capture the first fleeting impression made by a scene or object on the viewer's eye. By concentrating on visual impressions, rather than realism, artists created a fresh view of familiar subjects. Later painters, called postimpressionists, developed a variety of styles. **Vincent van Gogh,** for example, experimented with sharp brush lines and bright colors.

Review Questions

1. How did the romantic movement differ from the Enlightenment?

_____

_____

2. What was the goal of the impressionist artists?

_____

_____

READING CHECK

Against what was the romantic movement a reaction?

_____

_____

_____

VOCABULARY STRATEGY

What does the word *intense* mean in the underlined sentence? What clues can you find in the surrounding words, phrases, or sentences that might have a similar meaning? Use these context clues to help you learn what *intense* means.

READING SKILL

Identify Supporting Details
Identify two supporting details for the following main idea: The artists of the realism movement made people more aware of the harsh conditions of life in the Industrial Age.

_____

_____

_____

Name_____ Class_____ Date_____

Note Taking Study Guide

BUILDING A GERMAN NATION

Focus Question: How did Otto von Bismarck, the chancellor of Prussia, lead the drive for German unity?

As you read this section in your textbook, complete the following chart to record the sequence of events that led to German unification.

Napoleon raids German lands.

CHAPTER 10 SECTION 1

Section Summary

BUILDING A GERMAN NATION

In the early 1800s, German-speaking people lived in a number of German states. Many also lived in Prussia and the Austrian empire. There was no unified German nation. However, events unfolded in the mid-nineteenth century that eventually led to the formation of one Germany. Between 1806 and 1812, Napoleon invaded these lands. He organized a number of German states into the Rhine Confederation. After Napoleon's defeat, the Congress of Vienna created the German Confederation. This was a weak alliance of German states headed by Austria. In the 1830s, Prussia created an economic union called the *Zollverein.* This union removed tariff barriers between many German states, yet they remained politically fragmented.

Otto von Bismarck, the **chancellor** of Prussia, led the drive to unite the German states—but under Prussian rule. Bismarck was a master of **Realpolitik,** or realistic politics based on the needs of the state. After creating a powerful military, he was ready to pursue an aggressive foreign policy. Over the next decade, Bismarck led Prussia into three wars. Each war increased Prussian power and paved the way for German unity.

In 1866, Bismarck created an excuse to attack Austria. The Austro-Prussian War lasted only seven weeks. Afterwards, Prussia **annexed** several north German states. In France, the Prussian victory angered Napoleon III. A growing rivalry between the two nations led to the Franco-Prussian War of 1870. Bismarck worsened the crisis by rewriting and releasing to the press a telegram that reported on a meeting between William I of Prussia and the French ambassador. Bismarck's editing of the telegram made it seem that William I had insulted the Frenchman. Furious, Napoleon III declared war on Prussia, as Bismarck had hoped. The Prussian army quickly defeated the French.

Delighted by the victory, German princes persuaded William I to take the title **kaiser** of Germany. In January 1871, German nationalists celebrated the birth of the Second **Reich.** Bismarck drafted a constitution that created a two-house legislature. Even so, the real power was in the hands of the kaiser and Bismarck.

Review Questions

1. What events occurred in the early 1800s that helped promote German unity?

_____

_____

2. How did Bismarck use war to create a united Germany under Prussian rule?

_____

_____

READING CHECK

What was Realpolitik?

_____

_____

_____

VOCABULARY STRATEGY

What does the word *editing* mean in the underlined sentence? Circle the context clues in the paragraph that could help you figure out what *editing* means.

READING SKILL

Recognize Sequence What events led Napoleon III to declare war on Prussia?

_____

_____

_____

Name_____ Class_____ Date_____

Note Taking Study Guide
GERMANY STRENGTHENS

Focus Question: How did Germany increase its power after unifying in 1871?

As you read this section in your textbook, complete the following chart to record the causes and effects of a strong German nation.

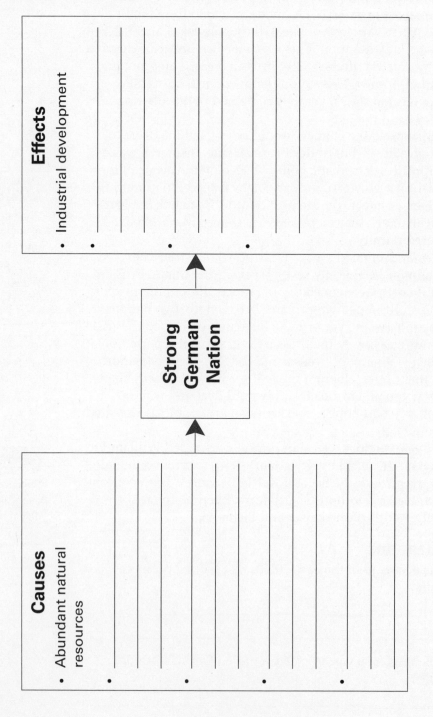

Effects
- Industrial development

Strong German Nation

Causes
- Abundant natural resources

CHAPTER 10 SECTION 2

Section Summary
GERMANY STRENGTHENS

After unification in 1871, the new German empire emerged as an industrial giant. Several factors made industrialization in Germany possible, such as ample iron and coal resources. These are the basic ingredients for industrial development. A disciplined and educated workforce also helped the economy grow. The German middle class created a productive and efficient society that prided itself on its sense of responsibility. Additionally, a growing population provided a huge home market for goods and a large supply of industrial workers.

German industrialists recognized the value of applied science in developing new products, such as synthetic chemicals and dyes. Both industrialists and the government supported scientific research and development. The government also promoted economic development. It issued a single form of currency for Germany and reorganized the banking system. The leaders of the new empire were determined to maintain economic strength as well as military power.

Bismarck pursued several foreign-policy goals. He wanted to keep France weak and build strong links with Austria and Russia. On the domestic front, Bismarck, called "the Iron Chancellor," targeted the Catholic Church and the Socialists. He believed these groups posed a threat to the new German state. He thought Catholics would be more loyal to the Church than to Germany. He also worried that Socialists would undermine the loyalty of workers and turn them toward revolution. Bismarck tried to repress both groups, but his efforts failed. For example, the *Kulturkampf* was a set of laws intended to weaken the role of the Church. Instead, the faithful rallied to support the Church. When repressing the Socialists failed to work, Bismarck changed course and pioneered social reform.

In 1888, **William II** became the kaiser. He believed that his right to rule came from God, and he shocked Europe by asking Bismarck to resign. Not surprisingly, William II resisted efforts to introduce democratic reforms. However, his government provided many **social welfare** programs to help certain groups of people. The government also provided services such as cheap transportation and electricity.

Review Questions

1. What did the German government do to promote economic development?

_____

_____

2. Why did Bismarck believe Catholics posed a threat to the new German state?

_____

_____

READING CHECK

What two ingredients are basic for industrial development?

_____

_____

_____

VOCABULARY STRATEGY

What does the word *synthetic* mean in the underlined sentence? Notice that these chemicals and dyes did not appear in nature, but were developed. Using this clue, write a definition for *synthetic*.

READING SKILL

Recognize Sequence Correctly number the following events:

_____ William II becomes Kaiser.

_____ Germany unifies in 1871.

_____ Government reorganizes the banking system.

_____ Bismarck is asked to resign.

CHAPTER 10 SECTION 3

Note Taking Study Guide

UNIFYING ITALY

Focus Question: How did influential leaders help create a unified Italy?

As you read this section in your textbook, complete the following timeline to show the sequence of events that led to Italian unification.

1870

1850

1831
Mazzini founds
Young Italy.

1830

CHAPTER 10 SECTION 3

Section Summary
UNIFYING ITALY

The peoples of the Italian peninsula had not been unified since Roman times. By the early 1800s, however, patriots were determined to build a new, united Italy. As in Germany, Napoleon's invasions had sparked dreams of nationalism.

In the 1830s, the nationalist leader Giuseppe Mazzini founded Young Italy. The goal of this secret society was "to constitute Italy, one, free, independent, republican nation." To nationalists like Mazzini, establishing a unified Italy made sense because of geography and a common language and history. It also made economic sense because it would end trade barriers among Italian states. Unification would stimulate industry, too.

Victor Emmanuel II, the constitutional monarch of Sardinia, hoped to join other states with his own and increase his power. In 1852, he made Count **Camillo Cavour** his prime minister. Cavour's long-term goal was to end Austrian power in Italy. With help from France, Sardinia defeated Austria and annexed Lombardy. Meanwhile, nationalist groups overthrew Austrian-backed leaders in other northern Italian states. In the south, **Giuseppe Garibaldi** had recruited a force of 1,000 red-shirted volunteers. He and his "Red Shirts" quickly won control of Sicily. Then they crossed to the mainland and marched triumphantly to Naples. Garibaldi turned over both regions to Victor Emmanuel. In 1861, Victor Emmanuel II was crowned king of Italy. Only Rome and Venetia remained outside the nation. However, Italy formed an alliance with Bismarck during the Austro-Prussian War and won the province of Venetia. Then, during the Franco-Prussian War, France was forced to withdraw its troops from Rome. For the first time since the fall of the Roman Empire, Italy was a united land.

However, Italy faced many problems as **anarchists** and radicals struggled against the conservative government. Tensions grew between the north and south. The north was richer and had more cities. The south was poor and rural. Still, Italy developed economically and the population grew. For many, however, **emigration** offered a chance to improve their lives. Large numbers of Italians left for the United States, Canada, and Latin America.

Review Questions

1. Why did nationalists feel that a unified Italy made sense?

_____

_____

2. Why did tensions between the north and south grow after unification?

_____

_____

READING CHECK

What was Camillo Cavour's long-term goal as prime minister?

_____

_____

_____

VOCABULARY STRATEGY

What does the word *constitute* mean in the first underlined sentence? Note that the word is a verb, which means it describes an action. Read the second underlined sentence to find out what action the nationalists wanted to take. Use this information to help you figure out what *constitute* means.

READING SKILL

Recognize Sequence What events took place between Garibaldi's recruitment of the "Red Shirts" and Victor Emmanuel II's crowning as king of Italy?

_____

_____

_____

CHAPTER 10 SECTION 4

Note Taking Study Guide

NATIONALISM THREATENS OLD EMPIRES

Focus Question: How did the desire for national independence among ethnic groups weaken and ultimately destroy the Austrian and Ottoman empires?

As you read this section in your textbook, complete the following table to record some major events in Austrian history during the 1800s.

Events in Austrian History					
	1840	1848	1859	1866	1867

Section Summary
NATIONALISM THREATENS OLD EMPIRES

In 1800, the Hapsburgs of Austria, the oldest ruling house in Europe, presided over a multinational empire. The emperor, Francis I, upheld conservative goals against growing liberal forces. He could not, however, hold back the changes that were happening throughout Europe. By the 1840s, Austria was facing the problems of industrial life, including growth of cities, worker discontent, and socialism. Nationalists were threatening the old order. The Hapsburgs ignored these demands for change and crushed revolts. Amid the turmoil, 18-year-old **Francis Joseph** inherited the Hapsburg throne. He granted some limited reforms, such as adopting a constitution. The reforms, however, satisfied only the German-speaking Austrians, but none of the other ethnic groups.

Austria's defeat in the 1866 war with Prussia brought even more pressure for change, especially from Hungarians within the empire. **Ferenc Deák** helped work out a compromise known as the **Dual Monarchy** of Austria-Hungary. Under this agreement, Austria and Hungary became separate states. Each had its own constitution, but Francis Joseph ruled both—as emperor of Austria and king of Hungary. However, other groups within the empire resented this arrangement. Restlessness increased among various Slavic groups. Some nationalist leaders called on Slavs to unite in "fraternal solidarity." By the early 1900s, nationalist unrest left the government paralyzed in the face of pressing political and social problems.

Like the Hapsburgs, the Ottomans ruled a multinational empire. It stretched from Eastern Europe and the Balkans to the Middle East and North Africa. As in Austria, nationalist demands tore at the fabric of the Ottoman empire. During the 1800s, various peoples revolted, hoping to set up their own independent states. With the empire weakened, European powers scrambled to divide up Ottoman lands. A complex web of competing interests led to a series of crises and wars in the Balkans. Russia fought several wars against the Ottomans. France and Britain sometimes joined the Russians, and sometimes the Ottomans. By the early 1900s, observers were referring to the region as the "Balkan powder keg." The "explosion" came in 1914 and helped set off World War I.

Review Questions

1. What problems threatened the Hapsburg empire in the 1840s?

_____

_____

2. What effect did nationalist unrest have on the Ottoman empire?

_____

_____

READING CHECK

What new political entity did Ferenc Deák help create?

_____

_____

_____

VOCABULARY STRATEGY

What does the word *fraternal* mean in the underlined sentence? The word derives from the Latin word *frater*, which means "brother." Use this information about the word's origin to help you figure out what *fraternal* means.

READING SKILL

Recognize Sequence What are two events that led to the decline of the Austrian empire in the late 1800s?

1. _____

_____

2. _____

_____

Name_____ Class_____ Date_____

Focus Question: Why did industrialization and reform come more slowly to Russia than to Western Europe?

As you read this section in your textbook, complete the following timeline to show the sequence of events in Russia during the late 1800s and early 1900s.

1950

1900

1850

1801
Alexander I inherits throne.

1800

Section Summary
RUSSIA: REFORM AND REACTION

By 1815, Russia was the largest, most populous nation in Europe. The Russian **colossus** had immense natural resources. Reformers hoped to free Russia from autocratic rule, economic backwardness, and social injustice. One of the obstacles to progress was the rigid social structure. Another was that, for centuries, tsars had ruled with absolute power, while the majority of Russians were poor serfs.

Alexander II became tsar in 1855 during the **Crimean War.** Events in his reign represent the pattern of reform and repression of previous tsars. The war, which ended in a Russian defeat, revealed the country's backwardness and inefficient bureaucracy. People demanded changes, so Alexander II agreed to some reforms. He ordered the **emancipation** of the serfs. He also set up a system of local, elected assemblies called **zemstvos.** Then he introduced legal reforms, such as trial by jury. These reforms, however, failed to satisfy many Russians. Radicals pressed for even greater changes and more reforms. The tsar then backed away from reform and moved toward repression. This sparked anger among radicals and, in 1881, terrorists assassinated Alexander II. In response to his father's death, Alexander III revived harsh, repressive policies. He also suppressed the cultures of non-Russian peoples, which led to their persecution. Official persecution encouraged **pogroms,** or violent mob attacks on Jewish people. Many left Russia and became **refugees.**

Russia began to industrialize under Alexander III and his son Nicholas II. However, this just increased political and social problems because nobles and peasants feared the changes industrialization brought. News of military disasters added to the unrest. On Sunday, January 22, 1905, a peaceful protest calling for reforms turned deadly when the tsar's troops killed and wounded hundreds of people. In the months that followed this "Bloody Sunday," discontent exploded across Russia. Nicholas was forced to make sweeping reforms. He agreed to summon a **Duma.** He then appointed a new prime minister, **Peter Stolypin.** Stolypin soon realized Russia needed reform, not just repression. Unfortunately, the changes he introduced were too limited. By 1914, Russia was still an autocracy, but the nation was simmering with discontent.

Review Questions

1. What effect did the Crimean War have on Russia?

_____

_____

2. What happened on January 22, 1905?

_____

_____

READING CHECK

What were zemstvos?

_____

_____

_____

VOCABULARY STRATEGY

What does the word *radicals* mean in the underlined sentence? Think about why these people were dissatisfied with Alexander II's reforms. Circle the words in the underlined sentence that help you figure out what *radical* means.

READING SKILL

Recognize Sequence What happened between Alexander II's becoming tsar and his assassination in 1881?

_____

_____

_____

CHAPTER
11
SECTION 1

Note Taking Study Guide

DEMOCRATIC REFORM IN BRITAIN

Focus Question: How did political reform gradually expand suffrage and make the British Parliament more democratic during the 1800s?

As you read this section in your textbook, complete the outline below to identify the main ideas in the section.

I. **Reforming Parliament**
    A. Reformers press for change.
        1. _____
        2. _____
    B. _____
        1. _____
        2. _____
        3. _____
    C. _____
        1. _____
        2. _____
II. _____
    A. _____
        1. _____
        2. _____
    B. _____
        1. _____
        2. _____
III. _____
    A. _____
        1. _____
        2. _____
        3. _____
    B. _____
        1. _____
        2. _____

CHAPTER 11 SECTION 1

Section Summary

DEMOCRATIC REFORM IN BRITAIN

In 1815, Britain was governed by a constitutional monarchy with a Parliament and two political parties. However, it was far from democratic. The House of Commons, although elected, was controlled by wealthy nobles and squires. The House of Lords could veto any bill passed by the House of Commons. Catholics and non-Church of England Protestants could not vote. **Rotten boroughs,** rural towns that had lost most of their voters during the Industrial Revolution, still sent members to Parliament. At the same time, new industrial cities had no seats allocated in Parliament.

The Great Reform Act of 1832 redistributed seats in the House of Commons, giving representation to new cities and eliminating rotten boroughs. It enlarged the **electorate** but kept a property requirement for voting. Protesters known as the Chartists demanded universal male suffrage, annual parliamentary elections, salaries for members of Parliament, and a **secret ballot.** In time, most of the reforms they proposed were passed by Parliament.

From 1837 to 1901, the great symbol in British life was **Queen Victoria.** She set the tone for the Victorian age that was named for her. She embodied the values of duty, thrift, honesty, hard work, and respectability. Under Victoria, the middle class felt confident. That confidence grew as the British empire expanded.

In the 1860s, a new era dawned in British politics. **Benjamin Disraeli** forged the Tories into the modern Conservative Party. The Whigs, led by **William Gladstone,** evolved into the Liberal Party. Disraeli and Gladstone alternated as prime minister and fought for important reforms. The Conservative Party pushed through the Reform Bill of 1867, which gave the vote to many working-class men. In the 1880s, the Liberals got the vote extended to farm workers and most other men.

By century's end, Britain had truly transformed from a constitutional monarchy to a **parliamentary democracy.** In this form of government, executive leaders are chosen by and responsible to the parliament, and they are members of it. In 1911, measures were passed that restricted the power of the House of Lords, and it eventually became a largely ceremonial body.

Review Questions

1. What was the result of the Great Reform Act of 1832?

_____

_____

2. How is a parliamentary democracy organized?

_____

_____

READING CHECK

What are rotten boroughs?

_____

_____

_____

VOCABULARY STRATEGY

What does the word *allocated* mean in the underlined sentence? Note that the Great Reform Act of 1832 corrected the problem described in this sentence by "redistributing" seats in the House of Commons. Use this context clue to help you understand the meaning of the word *allocated*.

READING SKILL

Identify Main Ideas What is the main idea in the first paragraph of the Summary?

_____

_____

_____

Note Taking Study Guide

SOCIAL AND ECONOMIC REFORM IN BRITAIN

Focus Question: What social and economic reforms were passed by the British Parliament during the 1800s and early 1900s?

As you read this section in your textbook, complete the chart below by listing reforms in Britain during the 1800s and early 1900s.

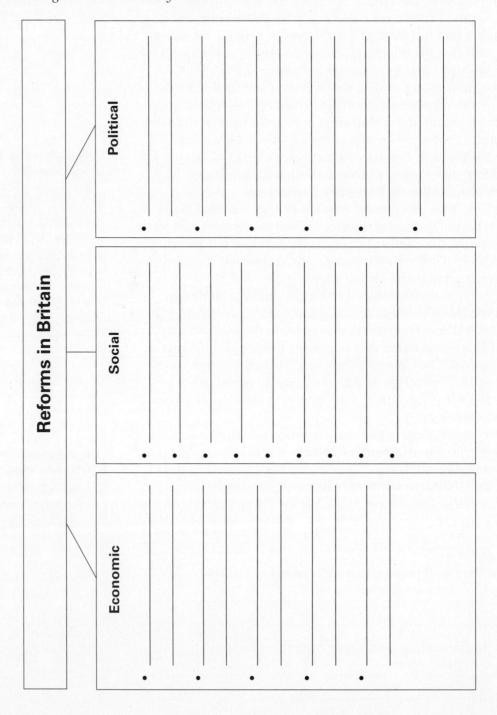

CHAPTER 11 SECTION 2	**Section Summary**
	SOCIAL AND ECONOMIC REFORM IN BRITAIN

During the 1800s, the British Parliament passed important laws. One issue was **free trade,** or trade without restrictions between countries. The Corn Laws caused fierce debate. These laws imposed high tariffs on imported grain. Farmers and landowners benefited, but the tariffs made bread more expensive. In 1846, Parliament **repealed** the Corn Laws. Another important reform, brought about by the **abolition movement,** was the end of the slave trade in 1807. By 1833, Parliament had banned slavery in all British colonies. Other reforms reduced the number of **capital offenses,** or crimes punishable by death. Instead of being put to death, many petty criminals were transported to **penal colonies** in Australia and New Zealand.

Working conditions in the industrial age were grim and often dangerous. Gradually, Parliament passed laws to regulate conditions in factories and mines. Other laws set minimum wages and maximum hours of work. Trade unions became legal in 1825 and worked to improve the lives of their members. Both the Liberal and Conservative parties enacted reforms to benefit workers, including free elementary education. The Labour Party, formed in 1900, soon became one of Britain's major parties. In the early 1900s, Parliament passed laws to protect workers with old-age pensions and accident, health, and unemployment insurance.

During this time, women struggled for the right to vote. When mass meetings and other peaceful efforts brought no results, Emmeline Pankhurst and other suffragists turned to more drastic, violent protest. They smashed windows, burned buildings, and went on hunger strikes. Not until 1918 did Parliament finally grant suffrage to women over 30.

Throughout the 1800s, Britain faced the "Irish Question." The Irish resented British rule. Many Irish peasants lived in poverty while paying high rents to **absentee landlords** living in England. Irish Catholics also had to pay tithes to the Church of England. The potato famine made problems worse. Charles Stewart Parnell and other Irish leaders argued for **home rule,** or self-government, but this was debated for decades. Under Gladstone, the government finally ended the use of Irish tithes to support the Church of England and passed laws to protect the rights of Irish tenant farmers.

Review Questions

1. Why did the Corn Laws cause fierce debate in Britain?

_____

_____

2. How did the government under Gladstone help improve conditions in Ireland?

_____

_____

READING CHECK

What are capital offenses?

_____

_____

_____

VOCABULARY STRATEGY

What does the word *drastic* mean in the underlined sentence? Note that the suffragists first tried "peaceful efforts" before turning to "more *drastic,* violent protest." The next sentence describes this. Use these context clues to help you understand what *drastic* means.

READING SKILL

Categorize Sort the laws that were passed to help workers into three categories.

_____

_____

_____

Name_____ Class_____ Date_____

Focus Question: What democratic reforms were made in France during the Third Republic?

As you read this section in your textbook, complete the timeline below by labeling the main events described in this section.

CHAPTER 11 SECTION 3

Section Summary
DIVISION AND DEMOCRACY IN FRANCE

After the revolution of 1848, **Napoleon III** established the Second Empire in France. At first, he ruled like a dictator. In the 1860s, however, he lifted some censorship and gave the legislature more power. He promoted investment in industry and ventures such as railroad building. During this period, a French entrepreneur organized the building of the **Suez Canal** in Egypt.

However, Napoleon III had major failures in foreign affairs. He tried to put the Austrian archduke Maximilian on the throne of Mexico, but Maximilian was overthrown and killed. France and Britain won the Crimean War, but France suffered terrible losses and few gains. The Franco-Prussian War was a disaster, and the Prussians captured Napoleon. He died a few years later in England.

Following Napoleon's capture, republicans established a **provisional,** or temporary, government. In 1871, an uprising broke out in Paris, and rebels set up the Paris Commune. Its goal was to save the Republic from royalists. When the rebels did not disband, the government sent troops and 20, 000 rebels were killed.

The provisional government soon became the Third Republic. Although the legislature elected a president, the **premier** had the real power. There were many political parties, and none could take control. Because of this, parties had to form **coalitions,** or alliances, to rule. Coalition governments are often unstable, and France had 50 different coalition governments in the first 10 years of the Third Republic.

A series of political scandals in the 1880s and 1890s shook public trust in the government. The most divisive scandal was the **Dreyfus affair.** Alfred Dreyfus was a Jewish army officer wrongly accused of spying for Germany. Author Émile Zola was convicted of **libel** when he charged the army and government with suppressing the truth. The affair revealed strong anti-Semitic feelings in France and led Theodor Herzl to launch modern **Zionism.**

France achieved serious reforms in the early 1900s, however. It passed labor laws regulating wages, hours, and safety conditions. Free public elementary schools were established. <u>France tried to repress Church involvement in government.</u> In 1905, it passed a law to separate church and state. Women made some gains, but they did not win the right to vote until after World War II.

Review Questions

1. What failures in foreign affairs took place under Napoleon III?

_____

_____

2. Why did French governments have to form coalitions to rule?

_____

_____

READING CHECK

What did the Dreyfus affair reveal about France?

_____

_____

_____

VOCABULARY STRATEGY

What does the word *repress* mean in the underlined sentence? Reread the sentence after the underlined sentence. What did France do to *repress* Church involvement in government? Use this context clue to help you understand the meaning of *repress.*

READING SKILL

Recognize Sequence List, in chronological order, the three French governments described in this section.

_____

_____

_____

CHAPTER 11 SECTION 4

Note Taking Study Guide

EXPANSION OF THE UNITED STATES

Focus Question: How did the United States develop during the 1800s?

As you read this section in your textbook, complete the chart below by listing key events under the appropriate headings.

Civil War	
Before	**After**

• Western expansion
 	
• _____
   _____
 	
• _____
   _____
 	
• _____
   _____
	• Fifteenth Amendment extends voting rights to all adult male citizens.
	
	• _____
	   _____
	
	• _____
	   _____
	
	• _____
	   _____
	
	• _____
	   _____
	
	• _____
	   _____
	
	• _____
	   _____
	
	• _____
	   _____

CHAPTER **11** SECTION 4	**Section Summary**
	EXPANSION OF THE UNITED STATES

In the 1800s, the United States followed a policy of **expansionism,** or extending the nation's boundaries. In 1803, the **Louisiana Purchase** nearly doubled the size of the country. More territory was soon added in the West and South. Americans believed in **Manifest Destiny,** or the idea that their nation was destined to spread across the entire continent.

Voting, slavery, and women's rights were important issues at this time. In 1800, only white men who owned property could vote. By the 1830s, most white men had the right to vote. William Lloyd Garrison, Frederick Douglass, and other abolitionists called for an end to slavery. Lucretia Mott, Elizabeth Cady Stanton, Susan B. Anthony, and others began to seek equality.

Economic differences, as well as slavery, divided the country into the North and the South. When Abraham Lincoln was elected in 1860, most Southern states **seceded,** or withdrew, from the Union. The American Civil War soon began. Southerners fought fiercely, but the North had more people, more industry, and more resources. The South finally surrendered in 1865.

During the war, Lincoln issued the Emancipation Proclamation, which declared that the slaves in the South were free. After the war, slavery was banned throughout the nation, and African Americans were granted some political rights. However, African Americans still faced restrictions, including **segregation,** or legal separation, in public places. Some state laws prevented African Americans from voting.

After the Civil War, the United States became the world leader in industrial and agricultural production. By 1900, giant monopolies controlled whole industries. <u>For example, John D. Rockefeller's Standard Oil Company dominated the world's petroleum industry.</u> Big business enjoyed huge profits, but not everyone shared in the prosperity. Reformers tried to address this problem. Unions sought better wages and working conditions for factory workers. Farmers and city workers formed the Populist Party to seek changes. Progressives sought to ban child labor, limit working hours, regulate monopolies, and give voters more power. Progressives also worked to get women the right to vote, which they did in 1920.

Review Questions

1. Why did the North win the Civil War?

_____

_____

2. How were African Americans deprived of equality after the Civil War?

_____

_____

READING CHECK

What is Manifest Destiny?

_____

_____

_____

VOCABULARY STRATEGY

What does the word *dominated* mean in the underlined sentence? Reread the sentence that precedes the underlined sentence. The Standard Oil Company was an example of the giant monopolies that "controlled" whole industries. Use this context clue to help you understand the meaning of the word *dominated.*

READING SKILL

Categorize Categorize the reforms discussed in this Summary by the group that did or would benefit from them.

_____

_____

_____

Name_____ Class_____ Date_____

Focus Question: How did Western nations come to dominate much of the world in the late 1800s?

As you read this section in your textbook, complete the chart below with the multiple causes of imperialism in the 1800s.

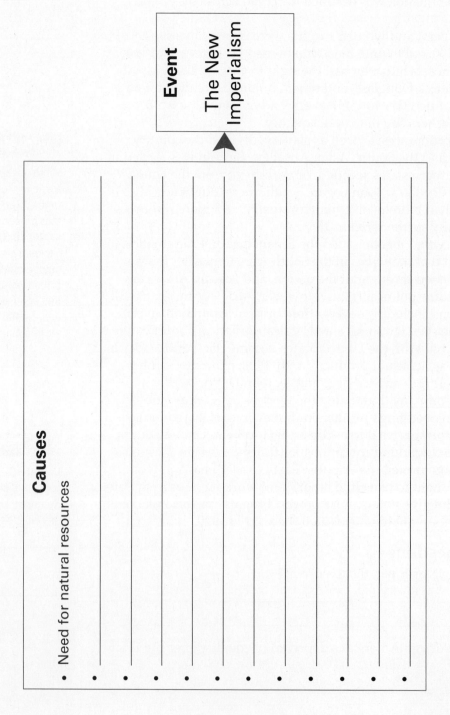

Event

The New Imperialism

Causes

Need for natural resources

• • • • • • • • • • • •

CHAPTER 12 SECTION 1

Section Summary

BUILDING OVERSEAS EMPIRES

Many western countries built overseas empires in the late 1800s. This expansion, referred to as **imperialism,** is the domination by one country of the political, economic, or cultural life of another country or region. In the 1800s, Europeans embarked on a path of aggressive expansion called the "new imperialism." There were several causes. The Industrial Revolution was one. Manufacturers wanted access to natural resources, as well as markets for their goods. Colonies also were an outlet for Europe's growing population. Leaders claimed that colonies were needed for national security. Industrial nations seized overseas islands and harbors as bases to supply their ships.

Nationalism played an important role, too. When one European country claimed an area, rival nations would move in and claim nearby areas. Europeans felt that ruling a global empire increased a nation's prestige. Missionaries, doctors, and colonial officials believed that they had a duty to spread Western civilization. Behind the idea of the West's civilizing mission was a growing sense of racial superiority. Many Westerners used Social Darwinism to justify their domination of non-Western societies. As a result, millions of non-Westerners were robbed of their cultural heritage.

Europeans had the advantages of strong economies, well-organized governments, and powerful armies and navies. Superior technology, such as riverboats, the telegraph, and the Maxim machine gun enhanced European power. Africans and Asians tried to resist Western expansion. Some people fought the invaders. Others tried to strengthen their societies by reforming their traditions. Many organized nationalist movements to expel the imperialists.

The leading imperial powers developed several systems to control colonies. The French practiced direct rule. They sent officials and soldiers from France to run the colony. Their goal was to impose French culture on the natives. The British, by contrast, often used indirect rule, governing through local rulers. In a **protectorate,** local rulers were left in place but were expected to follow the advice of European advisors on issues such as trade or missionary activity. In a **sphere of influence,** an outside power claimed exclusive investment or trading privileges, but did not rule the area.

Review Questions

1. Which aspect of the new imperialism led to non-Westerners being robbed of their cultural heritage?

_____

_____

2. What is the difference between a protectorate and a sphere of influence?

_____

_____

READING CHECK

How did Africans and Asians resist Western expansion?

_____

_____

_____

VOCABULARY STRATEGY

What does the word *prestige* mean in the underlined sentence? Notice that the word *increased* appears in the same sentence. What would ruling a global empire *increase* for a European nation? Use this context clue to help you figure out the meaning of *prestige*.

READING SKILL

Multiple Causes List the multiple causes of imperialism mentioned in this summary.

_____

_____

_____

Name_____ Class_____ Date_____

Focus Question: How did imperialist European powers claim control over most of Africa by the end of the 1800s?

As you read this section in your textbook, complete the chart below by identifying the causes and effects of the partition of Africa by European nations.

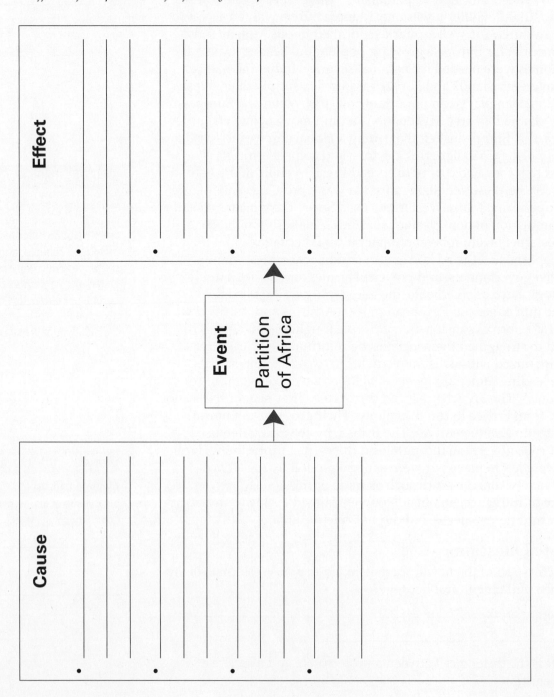

Effect

Event

Partition of Africa

Cause

CHAPTER 12 SECTION 2

Section Summary

THE PARTITION OF AFRICA

Before the scramble for colonies began in the 1800s, North Africa was under the rule of the declining Ottoman empire. West Africa experienced an Islamic revival inspired by **Usman dan Fodio.** In East Africa, port cities carried on a profitable trade. Zulus were a major force in southern Africa. A brilliant Zulu leader, **Shaka,** conquered nearby peoples. Groups driven from their homelands by the Zulus migrated north, conquering other peoples and creating powerful states.

For many years, Europeans had been trading along the African coasts. In the 1800s, contact increased as European explorers began pushing into the interior of Africa. One of the best-known was the missionary explorer **Dr. David Livingstone.** In 1869, the journalist **Henry Stanley** trekked into Africa to find Livingstone, who had not been heard from for years. Other missionaries followed explorers such as Livingstone. They built schools, churches, and medical clinics, often taking a **paternalistic** view of Africans.

About 1871, **King Leopold II** of Belgium hired Stanley to arrange trade treaties with African leaders. Leopold's action prompted Britain, France, and Germany to join in a scramble for African land. Eventually, without consulting any Africans, European leaders met in Berlin to divide the continent of Africa among themselves. In the following years, Europeans expanded further into Africa, often exploiting African people and resources. In southern Africa, the **Boer War** began when Britain wanted to claim Boer land. The Boers were descendants of Dutch farmers. The British wanted the land because gold and diamonds had been discovered there.

Africans fought back against European imperialism. In West Africa, **Samori Touré** fought French forces. **Yaa Asantewaa** was an Asante queen who led the fight against the British in West Africa. Another female leader was **Nehanda** of the Shona in Zimbabwe. In most cases resistance was not successful. However, Ethiopia was able to keep its independence. <u>Earlier, Ethiopia had been divided up among a number of rival princes who then ruled their own domains.</u> **Menelik II** modernized his country and trained an army, successfully resisting Italian invaders.

The Age of Imperialism caused a Western-educated African **elite** to emerge. Some admired Western ways. Others sought independence through nationalist movements.

Review Questions

1. Who ruled North Africa before the 1800s?

_____

_____

2. What set off a European scramble for African territories?

_____

_____

READING CHECK

Which African country was able to resist European conquest and maintain its independence?

_____

_____

_____

VOCABULARY STRATEGY

What does the word *domains* mean in the underlined sentence? Use context clues. Think about what a prince rules. What would have been divided? Use these context clues to help you figure out the meaning of *domains.*

READING SKILL

Cause and Effect What caused groups of Africans in southern Africa to migrate north? What was the effect of this?

_____

_____

_____

CHAPTER
12
SECTION 3

Note Taking Study Guide
EUROPEAN CLAIMS IN MUSLIM REGIONS

Focus Question: How did European nations extend their power into Muslim regions of the world?

As you read this section in your textbook, complete the concept web below to understand the effects of European imperialism on Muslim regions of the world.

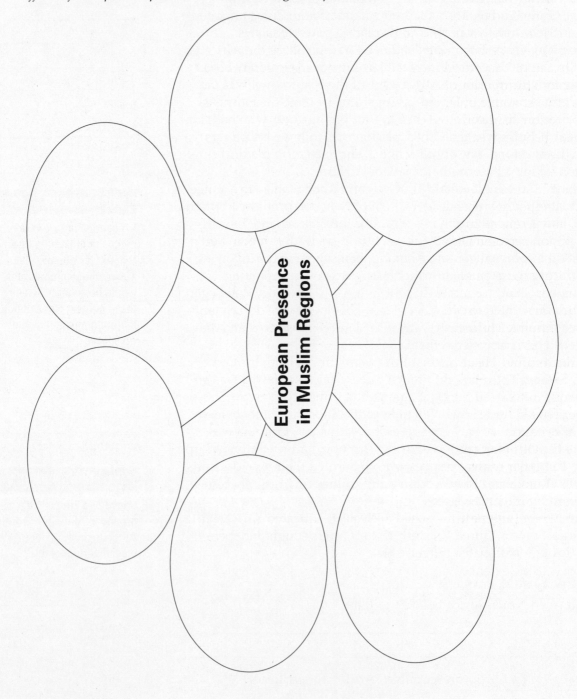

CHAPTER 12 SECTION 3

Section Summary

EUROPEAN CLAIMS IN MUSLIM REGIONS

In the 1500s, three giant Muslim empires ruled large areas of the world—the Ottomans in the Middle East, the Safavids in Persia, and the Mughals in India. By the 1700s, all three Muslim empires were in decline, in part because of corruption and discontent. Reform movements arose, stressing religious piety and strict rules of behavior. For example, in the Sudan, **Muhammad Ahmad** announced that he was the **Mahdi,** the long-awaited savior of the faith. The Mahdi and his followers fiercely resisted British expansion into the region.

At its height, the Ottoman empire extended across North Africa, Southeastern Europe, and parts of the Middle East. Ambitious **pashas** and economic problems added to the Ottoman decline. As ideas of nationalism spread from Western Europe, internal revolts by subject peoples weakened the empire. European states took advantage of this weakness to grab Ottoman territory. Some Ottoman leaders saw the need for reform. They looked to the West for ideas on reorganizing the government and its rigid rules. In the early 1700s, they reorganized the bureaucracy and system of tax collection. However, **sultans** usually rejected reform, adding to the tension. Tension between Ottoman Turkish nationalists and minority groups led to a brutal **genocide** of Christian Armenians. Turks accused Christian Armenians of supporting Russia against the Ottoman empire.

In the early 1800s, Egypt was a semi-independent province of the Ottoman empire. **Muhammad Ali** is sometimes called the "father of modern Egypt" because he introduced a number of political and economic reforms. He also conquered the neighboring lands of Arabia, Syria, and Sudan. Before he died in 1849, he had set Egypt on the road to becoming a major Middle Eastern power. His successors were less skilled, however, and in 1882 Egypt became a protectorate of Britain.

Like the Ottoman empire, Persia—now Iran—faced major challenges. The Qajar shahs exercised absolute power. Foreign nations, especially Russia and Britain, wanted to control Iran's oil fields. They were granted **concessions** and sent troops to protect their interests. These actions outraged Iranian nationalists.

Review Questions

1. What was the extent of the Ottoman empire?

_____

_____

2. Why is Muhammad Ali sometimes called the "father of modern Egypt"?

_____

_____

READING CHECK

What were the three great Muslim empires in the 1500s?

_____

_____

_____

VOCABULARY STRATEGY

What does the word *bureaucracy* mean in the underlined sentence? *Bureau* is a French word that means "office." The suffix -*cracy* means "type of government." Use these word-origin clues to help you figure out what *bureaucracy* means.

READING SKILL

Understanding Effects What was the effect of the concessions granted to Britain and Russia in Iran?

_____

_____

_____

Name_____ Class_____ Date_____

Focus Question: How did Britain gradually extend its control over most of India despite opposition?

As you read this section in your textbook, complete the flowchart below to identify the causes and effects of British colonial rule in India.

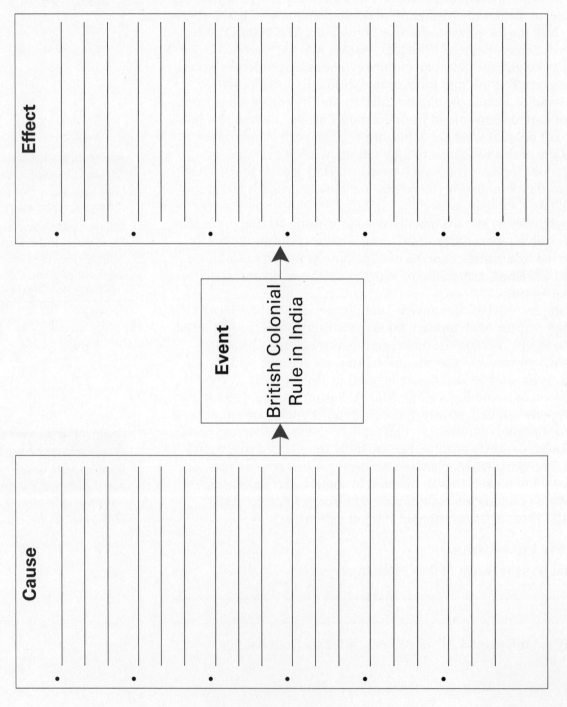

Effect

Event

British Colonial Rule in India

Cause

CHAPTER 12 SECTION 4

Section Summary

THE BRITISH TAKE OVER INDIA

Mughal rulers governed a powerful Muslim empire in India. The British East India Company had trading rights on the fringes of the Mughal empire. The main goal of the East India Company was to make money. As Mughal power declined, the East India Company extended its power. By the mid-1800s, it controlled three-fifths of India. The British were able to conquer India by exploiting its diversity, and by encouraging competition and disunity among rival princes. When necessary, the British also used force. However, British officials worked to end slavery and the caste system. They banned **sati,** a custom that called for a widow to throw herself on her husband's funeral fire. In the 1850s, the East India Company made several unpopular moves. The most serious brought about the Sepoy Rebellion. Indian soldiers, or **sepoys,** were told to bite off the tips of their rifle cartridges. This order caused a rebellion because the cartridges were greased with animal fat, violating local religious beliefs. The British crushed the revolt, killing thousands of unarmed Indians. The rebellion left a legacy of mistrust on both sides.

After the rebellion, Parliament ended the rule of the East India Company. Instead, a British **viceroy** governed India in the name of the monarch. In this way, all of Britain could benefit from trade with India as Britain incorporated India into the overall British economy. However, it remained an unequal partnership, favoring the British. Although the British built railroads and telegraph lines, they destroyed India's hand-weaving industry. Encouraging Indian farmers to grow cash crops led to massive **deforestation** and famines.

Some educated Indians urged India to follow a Western model of progress. Others felt they should keep to their own Hindu or Muslim cultures. In the early 1800s, **Ram Mohun Roy** combined both views. Roy condemned rigid caste distinctions, child marriage, sati, and **purdah,** or the isolation of women in separate quarters. He also set up educational societies to help revive pride in Indian culture. Most British disdained Indian culture and felt that Western-educated Indians would support British rule. Instead, Indians dreamed of ending British control. In 1885, Indian nationalists formed the Indian National Congress and began pressing for self-rule.

Review Questions

1. How were the British able to conquer India?

_____

_____

2. How did India benefit from Western technology?

_____

_____

READING CHECK

What was sati?

_____

_____

_____

VOCABULARY STRATEGY

What does the word *overall* mean in the underlined sentence? Notice that it is a compound word. A compound word is made from two separate words. Use the two words that make up *overall* to help you figure out what it means.

READING SKILL

Identify Causes and Effects
What caused the sepoys to rebel? What were two effects of the rebellion?

_____

_____

_____

Name_____ Class_____ Date_____

Focus Question: How did Western powers use diplomacy and war to gain power in Qing China?

As you read this section in your textbook, complete the chart below by listing the multiple causes that led to the decline of Qing China.

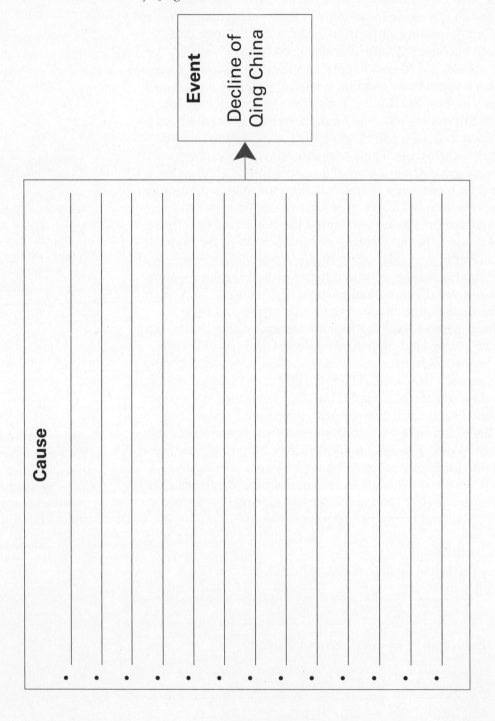

Event

Decline of
Qing China

Cause

CHAPTER 12 SECTION 5

Section Summary
CHINA AND THE NEW IMPERIALISM

For centuries, China had a favorable **balance of trade,** because of a **trade surplus.** Westerners had a **trade deficit** with China, buying more from the Chinese than they sold to them. This changed in the late 1700s when the British began trading opium grown in India in exchange for Chinese tea. The Chinese government outlawed opium and called on Britain to stop this drug trade. The British refused, leading to the **Opium War** in 1839. With outdated weapons and fighting methods, the Chinese were easily defeated. Under the Treaty of Nanjing, which ended the war, Britain received a huge **indemnity** and British citizens gained the right of **extraterritoriality.** About a decade later China lost another war. France, Russia, and the United States then each made specific demands on China. China was pressured to sign treaties stipulating the opening of more ports and allowing Christian missionaries in China.

China also faced internal problems. Peasants hated the Qing government because of corruption. The resulting **Taiping Rebellion** against this government led to an estimated 20 million to 30 million deaths. However, the Qing government survived. In addition, the Chinese were divided over the need to adopt Western ways. Some felt Western ideas and technology threatened Confucianism. Reformers who wanted to adopt Western ways in the "self-strengthening movement" did not have government support.

Meanwhile, China's defeat in the **Sino-Japanese War** of 1894 encouraged European nations to carve out spheres of influence in China. The United States feared that American merchants might be shut out. Eventually, without consulting the Chinese, the United States insisted that Chinese trade should be open to everyone on an equal basis as part of an **Open Door Policy.** Chinese reformers blamed conservatives for not modernizing China. In 1898, the emperor, **Guang Xu,** launched the Hundred Days of Reform. Conservatives opposed this reform effort and the emperor was imprisoned.

Many Chinese, including a secret society known to Westerners as the Boxers, were angry about the presence of foreigners. Antiforeign feeling exploded in the **Boxer Uprising** in 1900. Although the Boxers failed, nationalism increased. Reformers called for a republic. One of them, **Sun Yixian,** became president of the new Chinese republic when the Qing dynasty fell in 1911.

Review Questions

1. What were the results of the Opium War?

_____

_____

2. Why was the Qing government so hated?

_____

_____

READING CHECK

Who was the Chinese reformer who became president of China in 1911?

_____

_____

_____

VOCABULARY STRATEGY

What does the word *stipulating* mean in the underlined sentence? What clues can you find in the surrounding words, phrases, or sentences? Use these context clues to help you figure out what *stipulating* means.

READING SKILL

Recognize Multiple Causes
What brought about the Open Door Policy in China?

_____

_____

_____

Name_____ Class_____ Date_____

Focus Question: How did Japan become a modern industrial power, and what did it do with its new strength?

As you read this section in your textbook, complete the chart below to identify causes and effects of the Meiji Restoration.

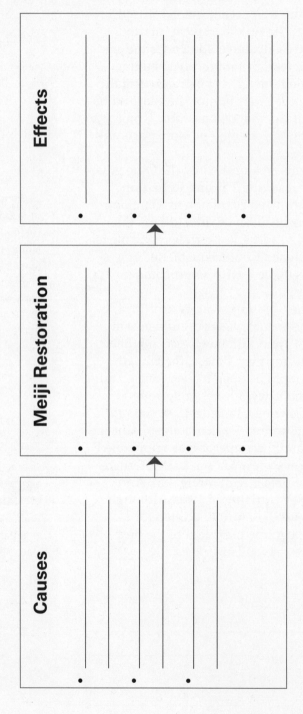

Name_____ Class_____ Date_____

Section Summary
JAPAN MODERNIZES

In 1603, the Tokugawa shoguns seized power in Japan and closed it to foreigners. For more than 200 years, Japan was isolated from other nations. Over time, unrest grew among many Japanese as they suffered financial hardship and lack of political power. The government responded by trying to revive old ways, emphasizing farming over commerce. These efforts had little success, and the shoguns' power weakened.

Then, in 1853, a fleet of well-armed U.S. ships led by Commodore **Matthew Perry** arrived. He demanded that Japan open its ports. Unable to defend itself, Japan was forced to sign treaties giving the United States trading and other rights. Humiliated by the terms of these unequal treaties, discontented daimyo and samurai led a revolt that unseated the shogun and placed the emperor Mutsuhito in power. Mutsuhito moved to the shogun's palace in the city of Edo, which was renamed **Tokyo,** and began a long reign known as the **Meiji Restoration.** This was a turning point in Japan's history.

The Meiji reformers wanted to create a new political and social system and build a modern industrial economy. The Meiji constitution gave all citizens equality before the law. A legislature, or **Diet,** was formed, but the emperor held absolute power. With government support, powerful banking and industrial families, known as **zaibatsu,** soon ruled over industrial empires. By the 1890s, industry was booming. Japan, a **homogeneous society,** modernized with amazing speed, partly due to its strong sense of identity.

As a small island nation, Japan lacked many resources essential for industry. Spurred by the need for natural resources and a strong ambition to equal the western imperial nations, Japan sought to build an empire. In 1876, Japan forced Korea to open its ports to Japanese trade. In 1894, competition between Japan and China in Korea led to the **First Sino-Japanese War,** which Japan easily won. Japan gained ports in China, won control over Taiwan, and joined the West in the race for empire. Ten years later, Japan successfully fought Russia in the **Russo-Japanese War.** By the early 1900s, Japan was the strongest power in Asia.

Review Questions

1. How did the Japanese respond to the unequal treaties signed with the United States?

_____

_____

2. How did the Meiji reformers try to modernize Japan?

_____

_____

READING CHECK

What helped to create a strong sense of identity in Japanese society?

_____

_____

_____

VOCABULARY STRATEGY

What does the word *emphasizing* mean in the underlined sentence? Look for context clues to its meaning in the surrounding words. Use the context clues to help you figure out what *emphasizing* means.

READING SKILL

Identify Causes and Effects
What were the causes and effects of the Meiji Restoration?

_____

_____

_____

Name_____ Class_____ Date_____

Focus Question: How did industrialized powers divide up Southeast Asia, and how did the colonized peoples react?

As you read this section, complete the flowchart below to identify causes, events, and effects of imperialism in Southeast Asia and the Pacific.

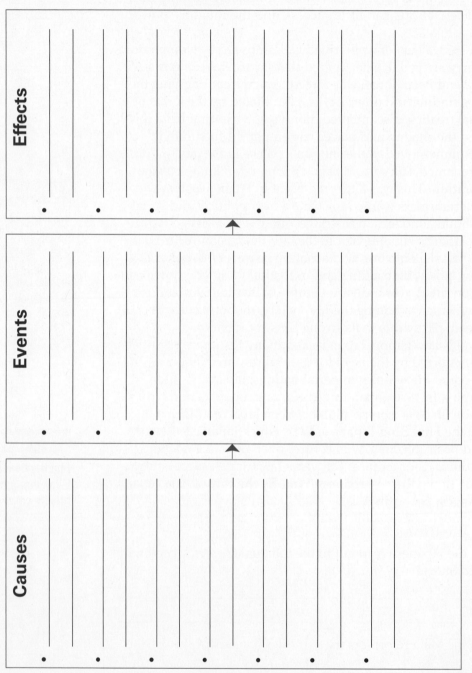

CHAPTER 13 SECTION 2

Section Summary
IMPERIALISM IN SOUTHEAST ASIA AND THE PACIFIC

By the 1700s, European merchants had gained footholds in Southeast Asia, but most of the area was still independent. In the 1800s, however, Westerners colonized much of Southeast Asia. The Dutch, for example, expanded to dominate the Dutch East Indies (now Indonesia). The British expanded from India into Burma and Malaya.

The Burmese resisted British rule and annexation but suffered disastrous defeats. The French invaded Vietnam, seeking more influence and trade markets. The Vietnamese fought fiercely but lost to superior European firepower. The French eventually took over all of Vietnam, Laos, and Cambodia and referred to these holdings as **French Indochina.** Meanwhile, the king of Siam, **Mongkut,** accepted some unequal treaties to keep Siam from becoming a European colony. By the 1890s, Europeans controlled most of Southeast Asia, where they introduced modern technology and expanded commerce and industry.

The Philippines had been under Spanish rule since the 1500s. In 1898, the **Spanish-American War** broke out. During the war, U.S. battleships destroyed the Spanish fleet stationed in the Philippines. Filipino rebel leaders declared independence and joined the Americans against Spain. In return for their help, the Filipino rebels expected the United States to recognize their independence. Instead, in the treaty that ended the war, the United States gave Spain $20 million in exchange for control of the Philippines. Bitterly disappointed, Filipinos renewed their struggle for independence, but the United States crushed the rebellion. The United States, however, did promise Filipinos a gradual transition to self-rule sometime in the future.

In the 1800s, the industrialized powers also began to take an interest in the Pacific islands. American sugar growers, for example, pressed for power in the Hawaiian Islands. When the Hawaiian queen **Liliuokalani** tried to reduce foreign influence, American planters overthrew her. In 1898, the United States annexed Hawaii. Supporters of annexation argued that if the United States did not take Hawaii, Britain or Japan might. By 1900, the United States, Britain, France, or Germany had claimed nearly every island in the Pacific.

Review Questions

1. How did the people of Burma and Vietnam respond to European attempts to colonize them?

_____

_____

2. Why did Filipino rebels renew their struggle for independence after the Spanish-American War?

_____

_____

READING CHECK

Which countries made up French Indochina?

_____

_____

_____

VOCABULARY STRATEGY

What does the word *transition* mean in the underlined sentence? Note that the word begins with the prefix *trans-*, which means "across or through." Use this knowledge to help you learn what the word *transition* means.

READING SKILL

Identify Causes and Effects
Identify the causes and effects of Liliuokalani's attempts to reduce foreign influence in Hawaii.

_____

_____

_____

Name_____ Class_____ Date_____

Focus Question: How were the British colonies of Canada, Australia, and New Zealand settled, and how did they win self-rule?

As you read this section, complete the chart below to identify the causes and effects of events in the British colonies of Canada, Australia, and New Zealand.

Cause	Event	Effect						
Loyalist Americans flee to Canada.	Up to 30,000 loyalists settle in Canada.	Ethnic tensions arise between English- and French-speaking Canadians.						

Section Summary
SELF-RULE FOR CANADA, AUSTRALIA, AND NEW ZEALAND

In Canada, Britain created two provinces: English-speaking Upper Canada and French-speaking Lower Canada. <u>When unrest grew in both colonies, the British sent Lord Durham to compile a report on the causes of the unrest.</u> In response to his report, Parliament joined the two Canadas into one colony in 1840.

As the country grew, Canadian leaders urged **confederation** of Britain's North American colonies. They felt that confederation would strengthen the new nation against the United States' ambitions and help Canada's economic development. Britain finally agreed, and Parliament passed a law that created the Dominion of Canada. As a **dominion,** Canada had its own parliament. As the growing country expanded westward, the way of life of Native Americans was destroyed. People of French and Native American descent, called **métis,** resisted in two revolts. However, government troops put down both uprisings.

In 1770, Captain James Cook claimed Australia for Britain. Like most regions claimed by imperialist powers, Australia had already long been inhabited. The **indigenous** people there are called Aborigines. When white settlers arrived in Australia, the Aborigines suffered. Britain made Australia into a **penal colony** to fill a need for prisons. Then, Britain encouraged free citizens to emigrate to Australia by offering them land and tools. As the newcomers settled in, they thrust aside or killed the Aborigines. Like Canada, Australia was made up of separate colonies scattered around the continent. To counter possible interference from other European powers and to boost development, Britain agreed to Australian demands for self-rule. In 1901, the colonies united into the independent Commonwealth of Australia.

Captain James Cook also claimed New Zealand for Britain. The indigenous people of New Zealand are the **Maori.** The Maori were determined to defend their land. In 1840, Britain annexed New Zealand. As colonists poured in, they took more and more land, leading to fierce wars with the Maori. Many Maori died in the struggle. By the 1870s, resistance crumbled. Like settlers in Australia and Canada, white New Zealanders sought self-rule. In 1907, New Zealand won independence.

Review Questions

1. Why did Britain agree to create the Dominion of Canada?

_____

_____

2. Why did Britain agree to demands for self-rule in Australia?

_____

_____

_____

READING CHECK

What happened to the Aborigines when white settlers arrived in Australia?

_____

_____

_____

VOCABULARY STRATEGY

What does the word *compile* mean in the underlined sentence? Think about research reports you have written for school. What process did you go through to create a report? Use your prior knowledge to help you learn what *compile* means.

READING SKILL

Identify Causes and Effects
Identify the causes and effects of the Maori fight against New Zealand colonists.

_____

_____

_____

Name_____ Class_____ Date_____

Focus Question: How did Latin American nations struggle for stability, and how did industrialized nations affect them?

A. *As you read this section, complete the chart below to identify multiple causes of instability in Latin America. Then, give an example of how each cause affected Mexico.*

Instability in Latin America	
Causes	**Mexican Example**

B. *As you read "The Economics of Dependence" and "The Influence of the United States," complete the chart below to identify effects of foreign influence on Latin America.*

Effects of Foreign Influence

CHAPTER 13 SECTION 4

Section Summary

ECONOMIC IMPERIALISM IN LATIN AMERICA

Many factors undermined democracy in the newly independent nations of Latin America. Constitutions in these nations guaranteed equality before the law, but inequalities remained. With no tradition of unity, **regionalism** also weakened the new nations. Local strongmen, called *caudillos,* assembled private armies to resist the central government. Power remained in the hands of a privileged few.

Mexico is an example of the challenges faced by many Latin American nations. Large landowners, army leaders, and the Catholic Church dominated Mexican politics. The ruling elite was divided between conservatives and liberals. Conservatives defended the traditional social order. <u>Liberals saw themselves as enlightened supporters of progress.</u> Bitter battles between these two groups led to revolts and the rise of dictators. When **Benito Juárez** and other liberals gained power, they began an era of reform known as **La Reforma.** Juárez offered hope to the oppressed people of Mexico. After Juárez died, however, General Porfirio Díaz ruled as a harsh dictator. Many Indians and mestizos fell into **peonage** to their employers.

Under colonial rule, Latin America was economically dependent on Spain and Portugal, which had prevented the colonies from developing their own economies. After independence, the new Latin American republics did adopt free trade, but Britain and the United States replaced Spain as Latin America's chief trading partners.

As nations like Mexico tried to build stable governments, the United States expanded across North America. To discourage any new European colonization of the Americas, the United States issued the **Monroe Doctrine.** The United States then issued a series of policies claiming "international police power" in the Western Hemisphere. Under these policies, U.S. companies continued to invest in the countries of Latin America. To protect these investments, the United States sent troops to many of these countries, which made the United States a target of increasing resentment and rebellion. When the United States built the **Panama Canal** across Central America, it was an engineering marvel that boosted trade and shipping worldwide. To people in Latin America, however, the canal was another example of "Yankee imperialism."

Review Questions

1. What limited democracy in the independent nations of Latin America?

_____

_____

2. Why did the new Latin American republics remain economically dependent after independence?

_____

_____

READING CHECK

Which Mexican leader offered hope to the oppressed people of Mexico?

_____

_____

_____

VOCABULARY STRATEGY

What does the word *enlightened* mean in the underlined sentence? Break the word into its word parts. Circle the root word, or the word part without the prefix and suffixes. Use the meaning of the root word to help you figure out what *enlightened* means.

READING SKILL

Identify Causes and Effects
Identify what caused the United States to issue the Monroe Doctrine and what its effects were on Latin America.

_____

_____

_____

CHAPTER 14 SECTION 1

Note Taking Study Guide
THE GREAT WAR BEGINS

Focus Question: Why and how did World War I begin in 1914?

As you read this section in your textbook, complete the following chart to summarize the events that led to the outbreak of World War I.

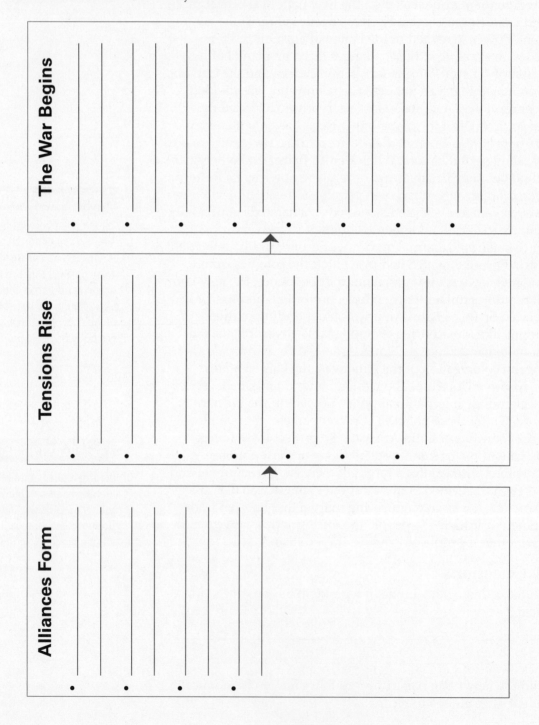

CHAPTER **14** SECTION 1	**Section Summary** THE GREAT WAR BEGINS

Although powerful forces were pushing Europe towards war, the great powers had formed alliances signing non-binding agreements, called **ententes,** to try to keep the peace. The Triple Alliance included Germany, Austria-Hungary, and Italy. Russia and France, and later Britain, formed the Triple Entente. During World War I, Germany and Austria fought together as the Central Powers. At that time, Russia, France, and Britain became known as the Allies.

In the decades before 1914, European powers competed to protect their status. <u>Overseas rivalries divided them, as they fought for new colonies in Africa and elsewhere.</u> They began to build up their armies and navies. The rise of **militarism** helped to feed this arms race. At the same time, sensational journalism stirred the public against rival nations.

Nationalism also increased tensions. Germans were proud of their military and economic might. The French yearned for the return of **Alsace and Lorraine.** Russia supported a powerful form of nationalism called Pan-Slavism. This led Russia to support nationalists in Serbia. Austria-Hungary worried that nationalism might lead to rebellions within its empire, while Ottoman Turkey felt threatened by nearby new nations in the Balkans, such as Serbia and Greece. Serbia's dreams of a South Slav state could take land away from both Austria-Hungary and Turkey. Soon, unrest made the Balkans a "powder keg." Then, in 1914, a Serbian nationalist assassinated the heir to the Austrian throne at Sarajevo, Bosnia.

Some Austrian leaders saw this as an opportunity to crush Serbian nationalism. They sent Serbia an **ultimatum,** which Serbia refused to meet completely. Austria, with the full support of Germany, declared war on Serbia in July 1914.

Soon, the network of alliances drew other great powers into the conflict. Russia, in support of Serbia, began to **mobilize** its army. Germany declared war on Russia. France claimed it would honor its treaty with Russia, so Germany declared war on France, too. When the Germans violated Belgian **neutrality** to reach France, Britain declared war on Germany. World War I had begun.

Review Questions

1. How did the network of European alliances cause World War I to develop?

_____

_____

2. What act caused Britain to declare war?

_____

_____

READING CHECK

Which countries made up the Central Powers?

_____

_____

_____

VOCABULARY STRATEGY

What does the word *overseas* mean in the underlined sentence? What clues can you find in the surrounding words, phrases, or sentences? Circle the words in the paragraph that could help you learn what *overseas* means.

READING SKILL

Summarize Describe the events that led Austria to declare war on Serbia.

_____

_____

_____

Name_____ Class_____ Date_____

Note Taking Study Guide

A NEW KIND OF WAR

Focus Question: How and where was World War I fought?

A. *As you read "Stalemate on the Western Front," "Battle on Other European Fronts," and "War Around the World," complete the following flowchart with important details about each battlefront of World War I.*

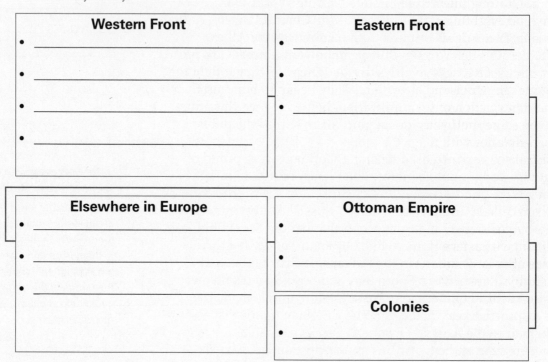

Western Front
- _____
- _____
- _____
- _____

Eastern Front
- _____
- _____
- _____

Elsewhere in Europe
- _____
- _____
- _____

Ottoman Empire
- _____
- _____

Colonies
- _____

B. *As you read "Technology of Modern Warfare," complete the following concept web to summarize information about the technology of World War I. Add ovals as needed.*

Guns

Aircraft

Technology of World War I

Poison Gas

CHAPTER **14** SECTION 2	**Section Summary**
	A NEW KIND OF WAR

The Great War was the largest conflict in history up to that time. Millions of French, British, Russian, and German soldiers mobilized for battle. German forces fought their way toward France, but Belgian resistance foiled Germany's plans for a quick victory. Both sides dug deep trenches along the battlefront to protect their armies from enemy fire. The fighting on this Western Front turned into a long, deadly **stalemate,** a deadlock that neither side could break.

Technology made World War I different from earlier wars. Modern weapons caused high casualties. In 1915, first Germany then the Allies began using poison gas. Advances in technology brought about the introduction of tanks, airplanes, and modern submarines. Germany used **zeppelins** to bomb the English coast. Both sides equipped airplanes with machine guns. <u>Pilots known as "flying aces" confronted each other in the skies, but these "dog fights" had little effect on the ground war.</u> German submarines, called **U-boats,** did tremendous damage to the Allied shipping. To defend against them, the Allies organized **convoys,** or groups of merchant ships protected by warships.

On Europe's Eastern Front, battle lines shifted back and forth, sometimes over large areas. Casualties rose higher than on the Western Front. Russia was ill-prepared and suffered a disastrous defeat when pushing into eastern Germany. In 1915, Italy declared war on Austria-Hungary and Germany. In 1917, the Austrians and Germans launched a major offensive against the Italians.

Although most of the fighting took place in Europe, World War I was a global conflict. Japan used the war to seize German outposts in China and islands in the Pacific. The Ottoman empire joined the Central Powers. Its strategic location enabled it to cut off Allied supply lines to Russia through the **Dardanelles,** a vital strait.. The Ottoman Turks were hard hit in the Middle East, however. Arab nationalists revolted against Ottoman rule. The British sent **T.E. Lawrence,** or Lawrence of Arabia, to aid the Arabs. European colonies in Africa and Asia were also drawn into the war.

Review Questions

1. Why did a stalemate develop on the Western Front?

_____

_____

2. How did technology make World War I different from earlier wars?

_____

_____

READING CHECK

What were the two battlefronts in Europe called?

_____

_____

_____

VOCABULARY STRATEGY

What does the word *confronted* mean in the underlined sentence? What clues or examples can you find in the surrounding words that hint at its meaning? Think about what the goal of these pilots was. Circle the words in the underlined sentence that could help you learn what *confronted* means.

READING SKILL

Identify Supporting Details
Identify important details that show the differences between the course of the war on the Western Front and on the Eastern Front.

_____

_____

_____

CHAPTER 14 SECTION 3
Note Taking Study Guide
WINNING THE WAR

Focus Question: How did the Allies win World War I?

As you read this section in your textbook, complete the following outline to summarize the content of this section.

I. **Waging total war**
   A. Economies committed to war production.
      1. Conscription
      2. Rationing
      3. Price controls
   B. Economic warfare
      1. _____
      2. _____
      3. _____
   C. _____
      1. _____
      2. _____
      3. _____
   D. _____
      1. _____
      2. _____
      3. _____

II. _____
   A. _____
      1. _____
      2. _____
      3. _____
   B. _____
      1. _____
      2. _____
      3. _____

(Outline continues on the next page.)

CHAPTER 14 SECTION 3

Note Taking Study Guide
WINNING THE WAR

(Continued from page 152)

III. _____

   A. _____

      1. _____

      2. _____

      3. _____

   B. _____

      1. _____

      2. _____

      3. _____

   C. _____

      1. _____

      2. _____

      3. _____

IV. _____

   A. _____

   B. _____

   C. _____

CHAPTER 14 · SECTION 3

Section Summary

WINNING THE WAR

World War I was a **total war,** in which the participants channeled all their resources into the war effort. Both sides set up systems to recruit, arm, transport, and supply their armies. Nations imposed universal military **conscription,** or "the draft," requiring all young men to be ready to fight. Women also played a critical role. As millions of men left to fight, women took over their jobs and kept national economies going.

International law allowed wartime blockades to confiscate **contraband,** but British blockades kept ships from carrying other supplies, such as food, in and out of Germany. In retaliation, German U-boats torpedoed the British passenger liner *Lusitania.* Both sides used **propaganda** to control public opinion, circulating tales of **atrocities,** some true and others completely made up.

As time passed, war fatigue set in. Long casualty lists, food shortages, and the failure to win led to calls for peace. The morale of both troops and civilians plunged. In Russia, stories of incompetent generals and corruption eroded public confidence and led to revolution.

Until 1917, the United States had been neutral, but in that year it declared war on Germany. Many factors contributed to this decision, including Germany's unrestricted submarine warfare. Also, many Americans supported the Allies because of cultural ties with Britain and sympathy for its fellow democracy, France. By 1918, about two million fresh American soldiers had joined the war-weary Allied troops on the Western Front. In that year, President Wilson also issued his **Fourteen Points,** his terms for resolving this and future wars. Among the most important was **self-determination** for peoples in Eastern Europe.

A final showdown on the Western Front began in March 1918. With American troops, the Allies drove back German forces. In September, German generals told the kaiser that the war could not be won. The kaiser stepped down and the new German government sought an **armistice** with the Allies. At 11 A.M. on November 11, 1918, the Great War at last came to an end.

Review Questions

1. What caused the morale of troops and civilians to plunge?

_____

_____

2. What are two factors that caused the United States to enter the war?

_____

_____

Name_____ Class_____ Date_____

Focus Question: What factors influenced the peace treaties that ended World War I, and how did people react to the treaties?

A. *As you read "The Costs of War," complete this concept web to summarize the costs of World War I.*

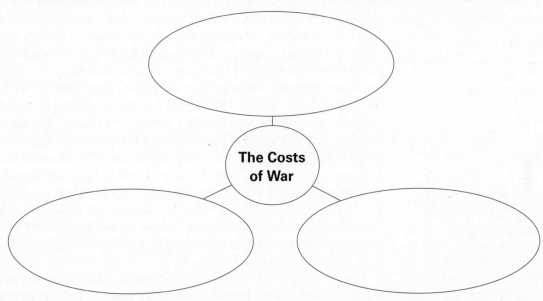

B. *As you read "The Paris Peace Conference," "The Treaty of Versailles," and "Outcome of the Peace Settlements," complete this table to categorize issues and problems that resulted from agreements made after the war.*

Issue	Treaty Settlement	Problems
War Debt		
Fear of German Strength		
Nationalism		
Colonies and Other Non-European Territories		
League of Nations		

CHAPTER 14 SECTION 4	Section Summary
	MAKING THE PEACE

Which three main Allied leaders negotiated the terms of the Treaty of Versailles?

_____

_____

_____

What does the word *widespread* mean in the underlined sentence? Look at the two words that form this compound word, and think about their meanings. Use what you know about the parts of this compound word to figure out its meaning.

Summarize How did the goals of the three main leaders at the Paris Peace Conference differ?

_____

_____

_____

The human, material, and political costs of World War I were staggering. The huge loss of life was made even worse in 1918 by a deadly **pandemic** of influenza. From France to Russia, homes, farms, factories, and roads had been bombed into rubble. Reconstruction costs and war debts would burden an already battered world. The Allies blamed the war on their defeated foes and insisted that they make **reparations.** Governments had collapsed in Russia, Germany, Austria-Hungary, and the Ottoman empire. Out of the chaos, political **radicals** dreamed of building a new social order.

The victorious Allies met at the Paris Peace Conference to discuss the fate of Europe, the former Ottoman empire, and various colonies around the world. The Central Powers and Russia were not allowed to participate. This would lead to problems regarding the issue of self-determination. The three main Allied leaders had conflicting goals. British Prime Minister David Lloyd George focused on rebuilding Britain. French leader Georges Clemenceau wanted to punish Germany severely. American President Wilson insisted on the creation of an international League of Nations, based on the idea of **collective security.** In this system, a group of nations acts as one to preserve the peace of all.

In June 1919, the Allies ordered representatives of the new German Republic to sign the Treaty of Versailles. The German delegates were horrified. The treaty forced Germany to assume full blame for the war. The treaty also imposed huge reparations that would burden an already damaged German economy and limited the size of Germany's military.

The Allies drew up treaties with the other Central Powers. Like the Treaty of Versailles, these treaties left widespread dissatisfaction, especially among many colonies that had hoped for an end to imperial rule. Many nations felt betrayed by the peacemakers. As a result of these treaties, new nations emerged where the German, Austrian, and Russian empires had once ruled. Outside Europe, the Allies added to their overseas empires. The treaties also created a system of **mandates.** The one ray of hope was the establishment of the League of Nations. The failure of the United States to support the League, however, weakened the League's power.

Review Questions

1. What were some of the human, material, and political costs of the war?

_____

_____

2. Why were German representatives at Versailles horrified?

_____

_____

Note Taking Study Guide

REVOLUTION AND CIVIL WAR IN RUSSIA

Focus Question: How did two revolutions and a civil war bring about Communist control of Russia?

As you read the section, fill in the following timeline with dates and facts about the series of events that led to Communist control of Russia. Then write two sentences summarizing the information in the timeline.

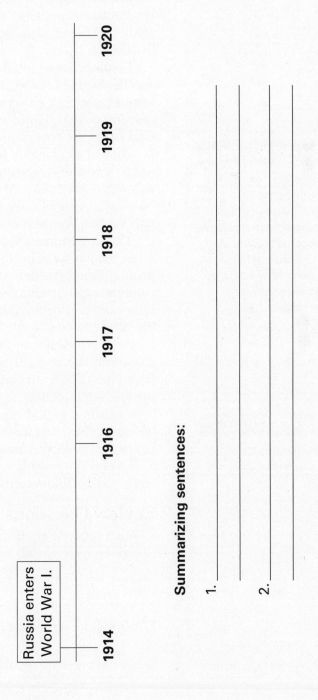

1920

1919

1918

1917

1916

Russia enters World War I.

1914

Summarizing sentences:

1. _____

2. _____

Section Summary
REVOLUTION AND CIVIL WAR IN RUSSIA

What was the name of the new Communist nation?

_____

_____

_____

What does the word *withdrawal* mean in the underlined sentence? What clues or examples can you find in the surrounding words, phrases, or sentences that hint at its meaning? Circle the words in the paragraph that could help you learn what *withdrawal* means.

Summarize Describe the events that led to Communist control of Russia.

_____

_____

_____

At the beginning of the 1900s, Russia had many political, economic, and social problems. Tsar Nicholas II resisted change. Marxists tried to ignite revolution among the **proletariat.** World War I quickly strained Russian resources. By March 1917, disasters on the battlefield and shortages at home brought the monarchy to collapse, and the tsar abdicated. While politicians set up a temporary government, revolutionary socialists set up **soviets,** or councils of workers and soldiers. These radical socialists were called Bolsheviks and were led by V. I. Lenin.

Lenin believed revolution could bring change. Leon Trotsky, another Marxist leader, helped Lenin lead the fight. To the weary Russian people, Lenin promised "Peace, Land, and Bread." In November 1917, Lenin and the Bolsheviks, renamed Communists, overthrew the government and seized power.

After the Bolshevik Revolution, events in Russia led to the nation's withdrawal from World War I. After the withdrawal, civil war raged for three years between the Communist "Reds" and the "White" armies of tsarist imperial officers. The Russians now fought only among themselves.

The Communists shot the former tsar and his family. They organized the **Cheka,** a brutal secret police force, to control their own people. Trotsky kept Red Army officers under the close watch of **commissars**—Communist Party officials. The Reds' position in the center of Russia gave them a strategic advantage, and they defeated the White armies.

After the civil war, Lenin had to rebuild a shattered state and economy. The new nation was called the Union of Soviet Socialist Republics (USSR), or Soviet Union. The Communist constitution set up an elected legislature. All political power, resources, and means of production would now belong to workers and peasants. In reality, however, the Communist Party, not the people, had all the power. Lenin did, however, allow some capitalist ventures that helped the Soviet economy recover. After Lenin's death, party leader Joseph Stalin took ruthless steps to win total control of the nation.

Review Questions

1. What brought about the tsar's abdication and the end of the monarchy in Russia?

_____

_____

2. Why did Lenin want revolution?

_____

_____

Name_____ Class_____ Date_____

Focus Question: How did Latin Americans struggle for change in the early 1900s?

A. *As you read the "The Mexican Revolution" and "Revolution Leads to Change," complete the chart by listing the causes and effects of the Mexican Revolution.*

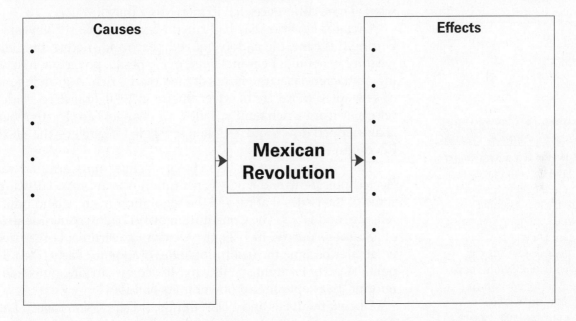

Causes	Effects
•	•
•	•
•	•
•	•
•	•

(center box: **Mexican Revolution**)

B. *As you read "Nationalism at Work in Latin America," complete the following chart as you list the effects of nationalism in Latin America.*

Effects of Nationalism in Latin America

Economic	Political	Cultural
•	•	•
•	•	•
•	•	•

Name_____ Class_____ Date_____

CHAPTER **15** SECTION 1	**Section Summary**
	STRUGGLE IN LATIN AMERICA

What was the PRI, and what was its impact on Mexico?

_____

_____

_____

What does the word *intervening* mean in the first underlined sentence? It is similar to the word *interference* in the second underlined sentence. You may have heard the word *interference* used when you watch sports. Both words begin with the prefix *inter-*, which means "between." Use the meaning of *inter-* and the context clues to help you figure out what *intervening* means.

Identify Causes and Effects
What were two effects of United States involvement in Latin America?

_____

_____

_____

In the early 1900s, exports kept Latin America's economy booming. Even though foreign investors controlled much of the natural resources, stable governments helped keep economies strong. Yet turmoil brewed because military leaders and wealthy landowners held most of the power. Workers and peasants had no say in government. These differences led to increasing unrest.

Dictator Porfirio Díaz had ruled Mexico for nearly 35 years. During this time, the nation enjoyed peace and success, but only the wealthy benefited. Peasants lived in desperate poverty while working on **haciendas,** large farms owned by the rich. A growing middle class wanted more say in government. In 1910, Francisco Madero, a reformer from a rich family, called for change. Faced with rebellion, Díaz stepped down and a violent struggle for power—the Mexican Revolution—began.

The people fought for years before Venustiano Carranza was elected president, and a new constitution was approved. It addressed some of the issues that caused the revolution, such as land reform, religion, and labor. The Constitution of 1917 allowed **nationalization** of natural resources. In 1929, the Mexican government organized what later became the Institutional Revolutionary Party (PRI). This political party brought stability to Mexico by carrying out some reforms, but kept the real power in its hands.

During the 1920s and 1930s, the Great Depression caused Latin American exports to drop and import prices to rise. As a result, **economic nationalism** became popular. Latin Americans wanted to develop their own industries. Some Latin American nations took over foreign-owned companies. The government became more powerful when people accepted authoritarian leaders, hoping that they could improve the economy. Along with economic nationalism, there was a growth in **cultural nationalism.** Artists such as Diego Rivera painted murals or large images of Mexico's history, culture, and the people's struggles. The United States also became more involved in Latin America, often intervening to protect U.S. interests or troops. This led to anti-American feelings. Under the **Good Neighbor Policy,** the United States promised less interference in Latin American affairs.

Review Questions

1. Under Porfirio Díaz, which groups had the most power?

_____

_____

2. How did the Great Depression lead to economic nationalism?

_____

_____

Note Taking Study Guide

CHAPTER 15 SECTION 2

NATIONALISM IN AFRICA AND THE MIDDLE EAST

Focus Question: How did nationalism contribute to changes in Africa and the Middle East following World War I?

As you read this section in your textbook, complete the following table to identify the causes and effects of the rise of nationalism.

Rise of Nationalism

Region	Reasons for Rise	Effects
Africa	• • • •	• • •
Turkey and Persia	• •	• • • •
Middle East	• • • •	• •

Section Summary
NATIONALISM IN AFRICA AND THE MIDDLE EAST

READING CHECK

What was the négritude movement?

_____

_____

_____

VOCABULARY STRATEGY

What does the word *advocated* mean in the underlined sentence? What clues can you find in the surrounding sentences? Think about why Britain issued the Balfour Declaration. Use this information to help you understand the meaning of *advocated*.

READING SKILL

Identify Causes and Effects
What was one effect of the Balfour Declaration?

_____

_____

_____

Europe ruled over most of Africa during the early 1900s. Improved farming methods meant more exports; however, this mostly benefited colonial rulers. Europeans kept the best lands, and African farmers were forced to grow cash crops instead of food. They also were forced to work in mines and then pay taxes to the colonial governments. Many Africans began criticizing imperial rule, but their freedoms only eroded further. An example was the system of **apartheid** in South Africa. Under this policy, black Africans were denied many of their previous rights, such as the right to vote.

During the 1920s, the **Pan-Africanism** movement called for the unity of Africans and people of African descent around the world. During the first Pan-African Congress, delegates asked world leaders at the Paris Peace Conference to approve a charter of rights for Africans. Their request was ignored. The members of the **négritude movement** in West Africa and the Caribbean protested colonial rule while expressing pride in African culture. These movements, however, brought about little real change.

In **Asia Minor,** Mustafa Kemal overthrew the Ottoman ruler and established the republic of Turkey. Also referred to as Atatürk (father of the Turks), his government promoted industrial expansion by building factories and railroads. Inspired by Atatürk's successes, Reza Khan overthrew the shah of Persia. Khan sought to turn Persia into a modern country. He, too, built factories and railroads. Khan also demanded a bigger portion of profits for Persia from British-controlled oil companies. Both leaders pushed aside Islamic traditions, replacing them with Western alternatives.

Pan-Arabism was a movement based on a shared history of Arabs living from the Arabian Peninsula to North Africa. Leaders of Arab nations and territories had hoped to gain independence after World War I, but felt betrayed when France and Britain were given control over their lands. In Palestine, Arab nationalists faced Zionists, or Jewish nationalists. To win the support of European Jews, Britain issued the **Balfour Declaration.** In it, the British advocated for a "national home for the Jewish people" in Palestine. Arabs felt the declaration favored the Jews. As a result, an ongoing conflict developed in the Middle East.

Review Questions

1. How did colonial rule hurt Africans?

_____

_____

2. How did Reza Khan change Persia?

_____

_____

CHAPTER 15 SECTION 3

Note Taking Study Guide

INDIA SEEKS SELF-RULE

Focus Question: How did Gandhi and the Congress party work for independence in India?

As you read this section in your textbook, complete the following chart by recording the causes and effects of Gandhi's leadership on India's independence movement.

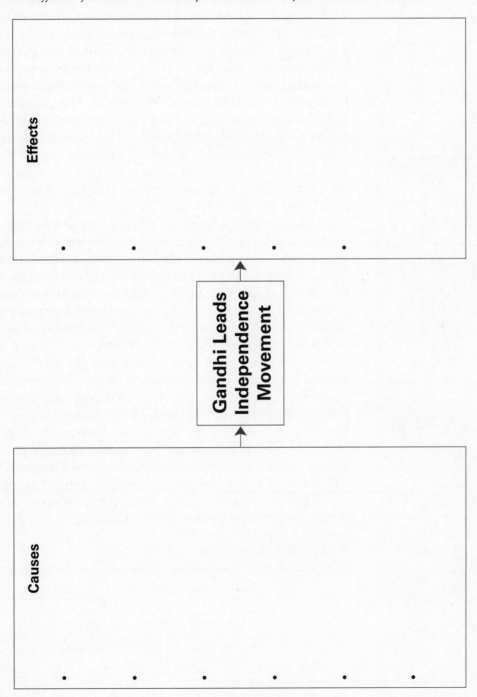

Name_____ Class_____ Date_____

What had Gandhi done before becoming a leader for Indian independence?

_____

_____

_____

What do you think the word *discriminated* means in the underlined sentence? Think about why Gandhi would have been fighting laws in South Africa. Note what the Summary says about the government of South Africa in the previous sentence.

Identify Causes and Effects
What caused the Amritsar massacre? What effect did it have on the independence movement?

Cause:_____

_____

Effect:_____

_____

In 1919, Indian protests against colonial rule led to riots and attacks on British residents. The British then banned public meetings. On April 13, 1919, a peaceful crowd of Indians gathered in an enclosed field in Amritsar. As Indian leaders spoke, British soldiers fired on the unarmed crowd. Nearly 400 people were killed and more than 1,100 were wounded. The **Amritsar massacre** convinced many Indians that independence was necessary.

During World War I, more than a million Indians served in the British armed forces. Because the British were pressured by Indian nationalists, they promised more self-government for India. After the war they failed to keep their promise. The Congress Party of India had been pressing for self-rule since 1885. After Amritsar it began to call for full independence. However, the party had little in common with the masses of Indian peasants. A new leader, Mohandas Gandhi, united Indians. Gandhi had a great deal of experience opposing unjust government. He had spent 20 years fighting laws in South Africa that discriminated against Indians.

Gandhi inspired people of all religions and backgrounds. He preached **ahimsa,** a belief in nonviolence and respect for all life. For example, he fought to end the harsh treatment of **untouchables,** the lowest group of society. Henry David Thoreau's idea of civil disobedience influenced Gandhi. This was the idea that one should refuse to obey unfair laws. Gandhi proposed **civil disobedience** and nonviolent actions against the British. For example, he called for a **boycott** of British goods, especially cotton textiles.

Gandhi's Salt March was an example of civil disobedience in action. The British had a monopoly on salt. They forced Indians to buy salt from British producers even though salt was available naturally in the sea. As Gandhi walked 240 miles to the sea to collect salt, thousands joined him. He was arrested when he reached the water and picked up a lump of salt. Newspapers worldwide criticized Britain for beating and arresting thousands of Indians during the Salt March. That protest forced Britain to meet some of the demands of the Congress Party. Slowly, Gandhi's nonviolent campaign forced Britain to hand over some power to Indians.

Review Questions

1. Why did the Congress party fail to unite all Indians?

_____

_____

2. What was the significance of the Salt March?

_____

_____

Name_____ Class_____ Date_____

Focus Question: How did China cope with internal division and foreign invasion in the early 1900s?

A. *As you read "The Chinese Republic in Trouble," complete the following chart by listing the multiple causes of upheaval in the Chinese Republic.*

Causes of Upheaval

B. *As you read "Struggle for a New China" and "Japanese Invasion," complete the chart to sequence the fighting among the Guomindang, the warlords, the Chinese Communists, and the Japanese.*

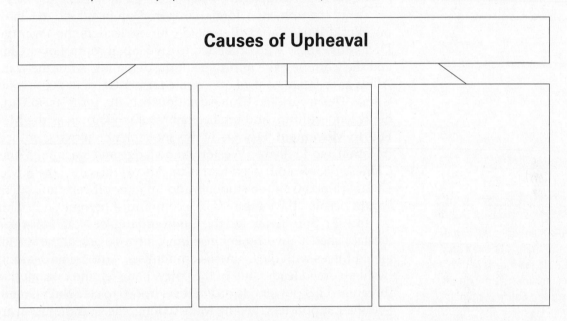

1926
• Guomindang and Communists defeat warlords.

CHAPTER
15
SECTION 4

Section Summary

UPHEAVALS IN CHINA

READING CHECK

What group of people spear-headed the May Fourth Movement?

_____

_____

_____

When the Qing dynasty collapsed in 1911, Sun Yixian became president of China's new republic. He hoped to rebuild China, but he made little progress. The country fell into chaos when local warlords seized power and the economy fell apart. Millions of peasants suffered severe hardships. Sun Yixian stepped down as president in 1912.

Amid the upheaval, foreign imperialism increased in China. During World War I, Japan presented Chinese leaders the **Twenty-One Demands.** These were intended to give Japan control over China, and the Chinese gave into some of the demands. After the war, the Allies gave Japan control over some former German possessions in China. This infuriated Chinese nationalists. As protests spread, students led a cultural and intellectual rebellion known as the **May Fourth Movement.** Leaders of this movement rejected Confucian tradition and looked to Western knowledge and learning. Other Chinese people embraced Marxism. Also at this time, the Soviet Union trained Chinese students and military officers, hoping they would become the **vanguard** of a communist revolution in China.

In 1921, Sun Yixian led the **Guomindang,** or Nationalist party, as it established a government in south China. To defeat the warlords he joined forces with the Chinese communists. After Sun's death, Jiang Jieshi assumed leadership of the party. Jiang felt the Communists threatened his power. He ordered his troops to slaughter Communists and their supporters. Led by Mao Zedong, the Communist army escaped north in what became known as the **Long March.** During the March, Mao's soldiers fought back using guerrilla tactics. Along the way, Mao's soldiers treated the peasants kindly. They paid for the goods they needed and were careful not to destroy crops. Many peasants had suffered because of the Guomindang, so they supported the Communists.

VOCABULARY STRATEGY

What does the word *intellectual* mean in the first underlined sentence? Circle the words in the second underlined sentence that could help you figure out what *intellectual* means.

While Jiang pursued the Communists across China, the Japanese invaded Manchuria, adding it to their growing empire. Then, in 1937, Japanese planes bombed Chinese cities and Japanese soldiers marched into Nanjing, killing hundreds of thousands of people. In response, Jiang and Mao formed an alliance to fight the invaders. The alliance held up until the end of the war with Japan.

Review Questions

1. How did Japan gain territory and control of areas of China during World War I?

_____

_____

READING SKILL

Recognize Multiple Causes
Why did Chinese peasants support the Communists?

_____

_____

_____

2. Why did Jiang and Mao form an alliance?

_____

_____

Name_____ Class_____ Date_____

Focus Question: How did Japan change in the 1920s and 1930s?

As you read this section in your textbook, complete the table by listing the effects of liberalism and militarism in Japan during the 1920s and 1930s.

Conflicting Forces in Japan	
Liberalism in the 1920s	**Militarism in the 1930s**
•	•
•	•
•	•
•	•

CHAPTER 15
SECTION 5

Section Summary

CONFLICTING FORCES IN JAPAN

Who became emperor of Japan in 1926?

_____

_____

_____

VOCABULARY STRATEGY

What does the word *manipulated* mean in the underlined sentence? Think about the Latin root *manus*, which means "hand" or "to handle." How did the zaibatsu "handle" politicians? Use this information about the word's root to help you understand what *manipulated* means.

READING SKILL

Understand Effects What effect did the Great Depression have on Japanese politics?

_____

_____

_____

The Japanese economy grew during World War I, based on the export of goods to the Allies and increased production. At this time, Japan also expanded its influence throughout East Asia and sought further rights in China. Additionally, Japan gained control of some former German possessions in China after the war. **Hirohito** became emperor of Japan in 1926, and during his reign, the country experienced both success and tragedy

In the 1920s, the Japanese government moved toward greater democracy. All adult men gained the right to vote, regardless of social class. Despite greater democratic freedoms, however, the zaibatsu, a group of powerful business leaders, manipulated politicians. By donating to political parties, the zaibatsu were able to push for policies that favored their interests.

Peasants and factory workers did not share in the nation's prosperity. Young Japanese rejected tradition and family authority. There was tension between the government and the military. The Great Depression fed the discontent of the military and the extreme nationalists, or **ultranationalists.** They resented Western limits on the expansion of Japan's empire. As the economic crisis worsened, the ultranationalists set their sights on **Manchuria** in northern China. In 1931, a group of Japanese army officers set explosives to blow up railroad tracks in Manchuria. They blamed it on the Chinese and used it as an excuse to invade. Without consulting government leaders, the military conquered Manchuria. Politicians objected to the army's actions, but the people sided with the military. When the League of Nations condemned the invasion, Japan withdrew from the organization.

Militarists and ultranationalists increased their power in the 1930s. Extremists killed some politicians and business leaders who opposed expansion. To please the ultranationalists, the government suppressed most democratic freedoms. Japan planned to take advantage of China's civil war and conquer the country. In 1939, however, World War II broke out in Europe. The fighting quickly spread to Asia. Earlier, Japan had formed an alliance with Germany and Italy. In September 1940, Japan's leaders signed the Tripartite Pact linking the three nations. Together, the three nations formed the Axis Powers.

Review Questions

1. Describe the economic success of Japan in the 1920s.

_____

_____

2. How did militarists and ultranationalists increase their power in the 1930s?

_____

_____

Note Taking Study Guide
POSTWAR SOCIAL CHANGES

Focus Question: What changes did Western society and culture experience after World War I?

As you read this section in your textbook, complete the concept web below to identify supporting details related to "Changes to Society" and "Cultural Changes."

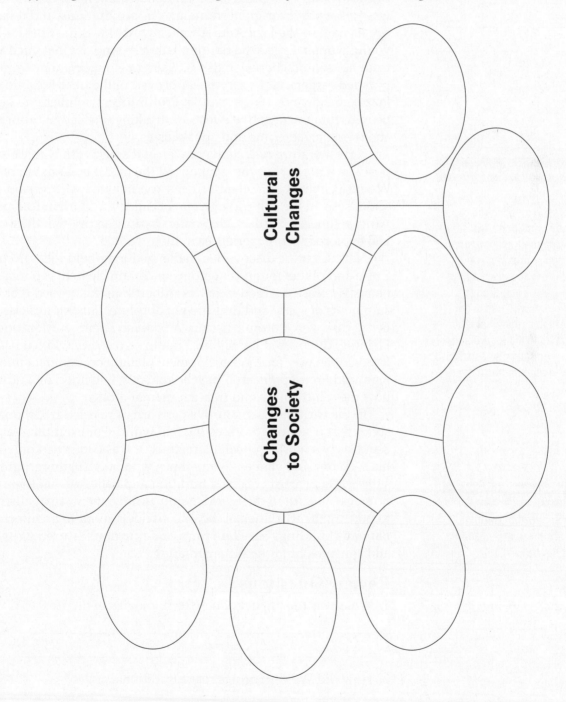

Section Summary
POSTWAR SOCIAL CHANGES

What were two symbols of American culture in the 1920s?

_____

_____

_____

What does the word *emancipation* mean in the underlined sentence? The sentence containing *emancipation* follows two sentences about women. Think about what flappers were like compared to young women who had lived before. Think about what labor-saving devices did for women. Use these context clues to figure out what *emancipation* means.

Identify Supporting Details
What were three aspects of postwar literature?

_____

_____

In reaction to World War I, society and culture in the United States and elsewhere underwent rapid changes. During the 1920s, new technologies helped create a mass culture, and to connect people around the world. American culture was characterized by a greater freedom and willingness to experiment. One symbol of this new age was jazz, with its original sound and improvisations, and it gave the age its name—the Jazz Age. Another symbol was the liberated young woman called the **flapper.** Labor-saving devices freed women from household chores. <u>In this new era of emancipation, women pursued careers</u>. Not everyone approved of the freer lifestyle of the Jazz Age, however. For example, **Prohibition** was meant to keep people from the negative effects of drinking. Instead, it brought about organized crime and **speakeasies.**

New literature reflected a powerful disgust with war. To some postwar writers, the war symbolized the moral breakdown of Western civilization. Other writers experimented with stream of consciousness. In the cultural movement called the **Harlem Renaissance,** African American artists and writers expressed pride in their culture and explored their experiences in their work.

New scientific discoveries challenged long-held ideas. Marie Curie and others found that atoms of certain elements spontaneously release charged particles. Albert Einstein argued that measurements of space and time are not absolute. Italian physicist Enrico Fermi discovered atomic fission. A Scottish scientist, Alexander Fleming, discovered penicillin, a nontoxic mold that killed bacteria. It paved the way for the development of antibiotics to treat infections. Sigmund Freud pioneered **psychoanalysis,** a method of studying how the mind works and treating mental illness.

In the early 1900s, many Western artists rejected traditional styles that tried to reproduce the real world. For example, Vasily Kandinsky's work was called **abstract.** It was composed only of lines, colors, and shapes—sometimes with no visually recognizable subject. **Dada** artists rejected tradition and believed that there was no sense or truth in the world. Another movement, **surrealism,** tried to portray the workings of the unconscious mind. In architecture, Bauhaus buildings based on form and function featured glass, steel, and concrete, but little ornamentation.

Review Questions

1. What was the impact of new technologies in the 1920s?

_____

_____

2. How did Western artists reject traditional styles?

_____

_____

Note Taking Study Guide
THE WESTERN DEMOCRACIES STUMBLE

Focus Question: What political and economic challenges did the leading democracies face in the 1920s and 1930s?

A. *As you read "Politics in the Postwar World," Postwar Foreign Policy," and "Postwar Economics," complete the chart below to identify the main ideas under each heading.*

Postwar Issues			
Country	**Politics**	**Foreign Policy**	**Economics**

B. *As you read "The Great Depression," and "The Democracies React to the Depression," complete the chart below to identify the main ideas on the causes, effects, and reactions related to the Great Depression.*

The Great Depression

Causes	Effects	Reactions
•	•	•
•	•	•
•	•	•
•		
•		

CHAPTER 16 SECTION 2

Section Summary

THE WESTERN DEMOCRACIES STUMBLE

READING CHECK

How did Britain and France pay back their war loans to the United States?

_____

_____

_____

VOCABULARY STRATEGY

What does the word *affluent* mean in the underlined sentence? *Affluent* comes from a Latin word that means "to flow." Ask yourself what people have a lot of if they are *affluent*. Use these clues to help you figure out the meaning of *affluent*.

READING SKILL

Identify Main Ideas Write a sentence that summarizes the main idea of this Summary.

_____

_____

_____

In 1919, after World War I, Britain, France, and the United States appeared powerful. However, postwar Europe faced grave problems. The most pressing issues were finding jobs for veterans and rebuilding war-ravaged lands. These problems made radical ideas more popular. Britain had to deal with growing socialism and the "Irish question." Fear of radicals set off a "Red Scare" in the United States.

The three democracies also faced international issues. Concern about a strong Germany led France to build the **Maginot Line** and insist on strict enforcement of the Versailles treaty. Many nations signed the **Kellogg-Briand Pact** promising to "renounce war as an instrument of national policy." In this optimistic spirit, the great powers pursued **disarmament.** Unfortunately, neither the Kellogg-Briand Pact nor the League of Nations had the power to stop aggression. Ambitious dictators in Europe noted this weakness.

The war affected economies all over the world. Both Britain and France owed huge war debts to the United States and relied on reparation payments from Germany to pay their loans. Britain was deeply in debt, with high unemployment and low wages. In 1926, a **general strike** lasted nine days and involved three million workers. On the other hand, the French economy recovered fairly quickly, and the United States emerged as the world's top economic power. In the affluent 1920s, middle-class Americans enjoyed the benefits of capitalism, buying cars, radios, and refrigerators.

However, better technologies allowed factories to make more products faster, leading to **overproduction** in the United States. Factories then cut back, and many workers lost their jobs. A crisis in **finance** led the **Federal Reserve** to raise interest rates. This made people even more nervous about the economy. In the autumn of 1929, financial panic set in. Stock prices crashed. The United States economy entered the **Great Depression,** which soon spread around the world.

Governments searched for solutions. In the United States, President **Franklin D. Roosevelt** introduced the programs of the **New Deal.** Although the New Deal failed to end the Depression, it did ease much suffering. However, as the Depression wore on, it created fertile ground for extremists.

Review Questions

1. After the war, what international agreement was intended to ensure peace?

_____

_____

2. What economic problems did Britain face after the war?

_____

_____

Name_____ Class_____ Date_____

Focus Question: How and why did fascism rise in Italy?

A. *As you read "Mussolini's Rise to Power" and Mussolini's Rule," complete the flowchart below as you identify the main ideas under each heading.*

Dissatisfaction and Unrest	**Mussolini Takes Power**	**Mussolini Changes Italy**
• • •	• • • •	• • •

B. *As you read "The Nature of Fascism," use the table below to identify the main ideas for each heading.*

What Is Fascism?	
Values	
Characteristics	
Differences from Communism	
Similarities to Communism	

CHAPTER 16 SECTION 3

Section Summary

FASCISM IN ITALY

After World War I, Italian nationalists were outraged when Italy received just some of the territories promised by the Allies. Chaos ensued as peasants seized land, workers went on strike, veterans faced unemployment, trade declined, and taxes rose. The government could not end the crisis. Into this turmoil stepped **Benito Mussolini,** the organizer of the Fascist party. Mussolini's supporters, the **Black Shirts,** rejected democratic methods and favored violence for solving problems. In the 1922 **March on Rome,** tens of thousands of Fascists swarmed the capital. Fearing civil war, the king asked Mussolini to form a government as prime minister.

Mussolini soon suppressed rival parties, muzzled the press, rigged elections, and replaced elected officials with Fascists. Critics were thrown into prison, forced into exile, or murdered. Secret police and propaganda bolstered the regime. In 1929, Mussolini also received support from the pope. Mussolini brought the economy under state control, but basically preserved capitalism. His system favored the upper class and industry leaders. Workers were not allowed to strike, and their wages were kept low. In Mussolini's new system, loyalty to the state replaced conflicting individual goals. "Believe! Obey! Fight!" loudspeakers blared and posters proclaimed. Fascist youth groups marched in parades chanting slogans.

Mussolini built the first modern **totalitarian state.** In this form of government, a one-party dictatorship attempts to control every aspect of the lives of its citizens. Today, we usually use the term **fascism** to describe the underlying ideology of any centralized, authoritarian governmental system that is not communist. Fascism is rooted in extreme nationalism. Fascists believe in action, violence, discipline, and blind loyalty to the state. They praise warfare. They are anti-democratic, rejecting equality and liberty. Fascists oppose communists on important issues. Communists favor international action and the creation of a classless society. Fascists are nationalists who support a society with defined classes. Both base their power on blind devotion to a leader or the state. Both flourish during economic hard times.

Fascism appealed to Italians because it restored national pride, provided stability, and ended the political feuding that had paralyzed democracy in Italy.

Review Questions

1. What was the result of the March on Rome?

_____

_____

2. How are communism and fascism similar?

_____

_____

Note Taking Study Guide
THE SOVIET UNION UNDER STALIN

Focus Question: How did Stalin transform the Soviet Union into a totalitarian state?

As you read this section in your textbook, complete the chart below by identifying the main ideas about the Soviet Union under Stalin for each heading.

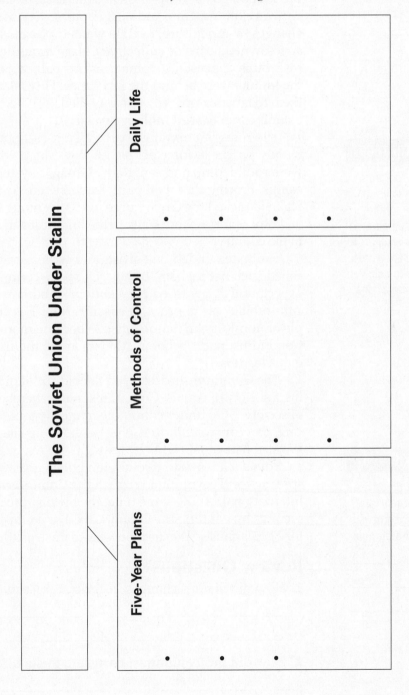

CHAPTER 16 SECTION 4

Section Summary
THE SOVIET UNION UNDER STALIN

Under Joseph Stalin, the Soviet Union grew into a totalitarian state, controlling all aspects of life, including agriculture, culture, art, and religion. The state also developed a **command economy,** in which it made all economic decisions. Stalin's five-year plans set high production goals. Despite great progress in some sectors, products such as clothing, cars, and refrigerators were scarce. Stalin forced changes in agriculture, too. He wanted peasants to farm on either state-owned farms or **collectives,** large farms owned and operated by groups of peasants. Some peasants balked. Stalin believed that the **kulaks** were behind the resistance. He took their land and sent them to labor camps, where many died. In 1932, Stalin's policies led to a famine that caused millions to starve.

The ruling Communist party used secret police, torture, and bloody purges to force people to obey. Those who opposed Stalin were rounded up and sent to the **Gulag,** a system of brutal labor camps. Fearing that rival party leaders were plotting against him, Stalin launched the Great Purge in 1934. Among the victims of this and other purges were some of the brightest and most talented people in the country.

Stalin demanded that artists and writers create works in a style called **socialist realism.** <u>If they refused to conform to government expectations, they faced persecution.</u> Another way Stalin controlled cultural life was to promote **russification.** The goal was to force people of non-Russian nationalities to become more Russian. The official Communist party belief in **atheism** led to the cruel treatment of religious leaders.

The Communists destroyed the old social order. Instead of creating a society of equals, Communist party members became the heads of society. Still, under communism most people enjoyed free medical care, day care for children, cheaper housing, and public recreation. Women had equal rights by law.

Soviet leaders had two foreign policy goals. They hoped to spread world revolution through the **Comintern,** or Communist International. At the same time, they wanted to ensure their nation's security by winning the support of other countries. These contradictory goals caused Western powers to mistrust the Soviet Union.

Review Questions

1. How did Stalin's changes in agriculture lead to a famine?

_____

_____

2. How did the Communist party and Stalin force people to obey?

_____

_____

Focus Question: How did Hitler and the Nazi Party establish and maintain a totalitarian government in Germany?

As you read this section in your textbook, complete the flowchart below to identify the main ideas about Hitler and the rise of Nazi Germany for each heading.

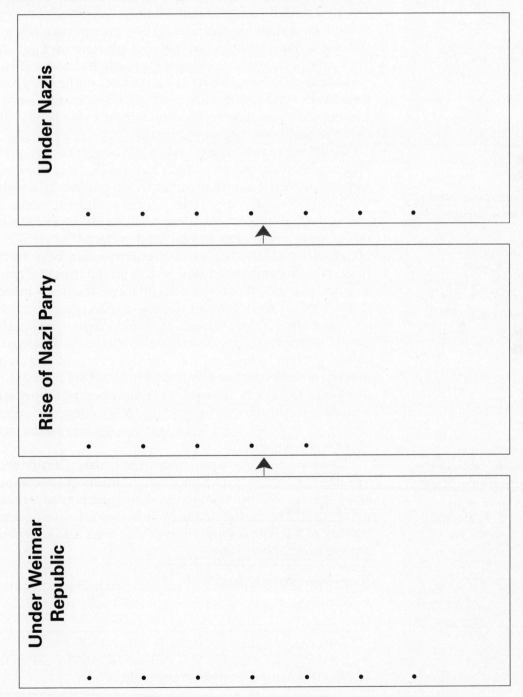

CHAPTER 16 SECTION 5

Section Summary

HITLER AND THE RISE OF NAZI GERMANY

READING CHECK

What was the purpose of the Nuremberg Laws?

_____

_____

_____

After World War I, German leaders set up a democratic government known as the Weimar Republic. The Weimar constitution established a parliamentary system led by a **chancellor.** It gave women the right to vote and included a bill of rights. However, the new republic faced severe problems. When Germany could not make its war reparations France seized the coal-rich **Ruhr Valley.** Government actions led to inflation and skyrocketing prices. The German mark was almost worthless. Many middle-class families lost their savings.

Many Germans believed that energetic leader Adolf Hitler would solve Germany's problems. As head of the Nazi party, Hitler promised to end reparations, create jobs, and rearm Germany. He was elected chancellor in 1933, and within a year he was dictator over the new fascist state in Germany.

To appeal to nationalism and recall Germany's glorious past, Hitler called his government the **Third Reich.** To combat the Depression, Hitler launched public works programs. In violation of the Versailles treaty, he rearmed Germany. Hitler relied on his secret police, the **Gestapo,** to root out opposition. He organized a brutal system of terror, repression, and totalitarian rule. A fanatical anti-Semite, Hitler set out to drive the Jews from Germany. In 1935, the Nazis passed the **Nuremberg Laws,** which deprived Jews of German citizenship and placed severe restrictions on them. The Nazis indoctrinated German youth and rewrote textbooks to reflect Nazi racial views.

VOCABULARY STRATEGY

What does the word *regime* mean in the underlined sentence? Circle the words in the sentence that refer to the phrase "the new *regime.*" What do you think is the meaning of *regime?*

Hitler also limited women's roles and encouraged "pure-blooded Aryan" women to bear many children. He sought to purge German culture of what he believed were corrupt influences. Nazis denounced modern art and jazz, but glorified German artists and myths. Hitler despised Christianity as "weak." He combined all Protestant sects into a single state church. <u>Although many clergy either supported the new regime or remained silent, some courageously spoke out against Hitler's government.</u>

Like Germany, most new nations in Eastern Europe slid from systems of democratic to authoritarian rule. Economic problems and ethnic tensions contributed to instability and helped fascist rulers to gain power. The new dictators promised to keep order, and won the backing of the military and the wealthy. They also supported the growth of anti-Semitism.

READING SKILL

Identify Main Ideas Reread the last paragraph in the Summary. Write the main idea of that paragraph on the lines below.

_____

_____

_____

Review Questions

1. What were the basic features of the Weimar constitution?

_____

_____

2. Why did many Germans support Hitler?

_____

_____

CHAPTER 17
SECTION 1

Note Taking Study Guide
FROM APPEASEMENT TO WAR

Focus Question: What events unfolded between Chamberlain's declaration of "peace in our time" and the outbreak of a world war?

A. *As you read "Aggression Goes Unchecked" and "Spain Collapses into Civil War," complete the chart below to record the sequence of events that led to the outbreak of World War II.*

Acts of Aggression	
Japan	• _____
	• _____
Italy	• _____
Germany	• _____
	• _____
Spain	• _____

B. *As you read "German Aggression Continues" and "Europe Plunges Toward War," complete the timetable below to recognize the sequence of German aggression.*

German Aggression	
March 1938	Anschluss, or union of Austria and Germany, occurs.
September 1938	
March 1939	
September 1939	

CHAPTER 17 — SECTION 1

Section Summary

FROM APPEASEMENT TO WAR

Throughout the 1930s, dictators took aggressive action. Yet, they met only verbal protests and pleas for peace from Western powers. For example, when the League of Nations condemned Japan's invasion of Manchuria in 1931, Japan simply withdrew from the League. A few years later, Japanese armies invaded China, starting the Second Sino-Japanese War. Meanwhile, Mussolini invaded Ethiopia in 1935. The League of Nations voted sanctions against Italy, but the League had no power to enforce its punishment of Mussolini. Hitler, too, defied the Western democracies by building up the German military and sending troops into the "demilitarized" Rhineland. This went against the Treaty of Versailles. The Western democracies denounced Hitler but adopted a policy of **appeasement.** Appeasement developed for a number of reasons, including widespread **pacifism.** The United States responded with a series of **Neutrality Acts.** The goal was to avoid involvement in a war, rather than to prevent one. While the Western democracies sought to avoid war, Germany, Italy, and Japan formed an alliance. It became known as the **Axis powers.**

In Spain, a new, more liberal government passed reforms that upset conservatives. General **Francisco Franco,** who was opposed to the new government, started a civil war. Hitler and Mussolini supported Franco, their fellow fascist. The Soviet Union sent troops to support the anti-Fascists, or Loyalists. The governments of Britain, France, and the United States remained neutral, although individuals from these countries fought with the Loyalists. By 1939, Franco had triumphed.

German aggression continued. In 1938, Hitler forced the **Anschluss,** or union with Austria. Next, Hitler set his sights on the **Sudentenland.** This was a part of Czechoslovakia where three million Germans lived. At the Munich Conference, which was held to discuss the situation, British and French leaders chose appeasement and allowed Hitler to annex the territory.

In March 1939, Hitler took over the rest of Czechoslovakia. Months later, Hitler and Stalin signed the **Nazi-Soviet Pact.** They agreed not to fight if the other went to war. This paved the way for Germany's invasion of Poland in September of 1939, which set off World War II.

Review Questions

1. How did the United States respond to the aggressive action of dictators in the 1930s?

_____

_____

2. What was the result of the Munich Conference?

_____

_____

Name_____ Class_____ Date_____

Focus Question: Which regions were attacked and occupied by the Axis powers, and what was life like under their occupation?

A. *As you read "The Axis Attacks," "Germany Invades the Soviet Union," and "Japan Attacks the United States," use the chart below to record the sequence of events.*

September 1939: Germany invades Poland.

B. *As you read "Life Under Nazi and Japanese Occupation," use the concept web to identify supporting details about the occupations.*

Nazi occupation

Japanese occupation

Name_____ Class_____ Date_____

READING CHECK

What was the name of the German government in southern France?

_____

_____

_____

VOCABULARY STRATEGY

Find the word *nullified* in the underlined sentence. In math class you might have learned that there is nothing, or zero, in the null set. Use this clue about related words to help you figure out the meaning of *nullified*.

READING SKILL

Sequence Events When did the United States declare neutrality?

_____

_____

In September 1939, Nazi forces launched a **blitzkrieg** against Poland. First the **Luftwaffe,** the German air force, bombed. Then, tanks and troops pushed their way in. At the same time, Stalin invaded from the east, grabbing land. Within a month, Poland ceased to exist.

Then, in early 1940, Hitler conquered Norway, Denmark, the Netherlands, and Belgium. By May, German forces had bypassed France's Maginot Line. British forces that had been sent to help the French were trapped. In a desperate scheme, the British rescued their troops from **Dunkirk.** However, in June, the French were forced to surrender. Germany occupied northern France and set up a puppet state, the **Vichy** government, in the south.

The British, led by Winston Churchill, remained defiant against Hitler. In response, Hitler launched bombing raids over British cities that lasted from September 1940 until June 1941. Despite this blitz, Hitler was not able to take Britain. Meanwhile, Hitler sent one of his best commanders, **General Erwin Rommel,** to North Africa. Rommel had a string of successes there. In the Balkans, German and Italian forces added Greece and Yugoslavia to the growing Axis territory. At the same time, the Japanese were occupying lands in Asia and the Pacific.

In June 1941, Hitler nullified the Nazi-Soviet Pact by invading the Soviet Union. Stalin was unprepared, and the Soviet army suffered great losses. The Germans advanced toward Moscow and Leningrad. During a lengthy siege of Leningrad, more than a million Russians died. The severe Russian winter finally slowed the German army.

As they marched across Europe, the Nazis sent millions to **concentration camps** to work as slave laborers. Even worse, Hitler established death camps to kill those he judged racially inferior. Among many others, some six million Jews were killed in what became known as the **Holocaust.**

The United States declared neutrality at the beginning of the war. Yet many Americans sympathized with those who fought the Axis powers. Congress passed the **Lend-Lease Act** of 1941, allowing the United States to sell or lend war goods to foes of the Axis. On December 7, 1941, the Japanese bombed the U.S. fleet at Pearl Harbor. Four days later, Congress declared war on Japan.

Review Questions

1. What countries were conquered by Germany in 1939 and 1940?

_____

_____

2. What was the purpose of the Lend-Lease Act?

_____

_____

Name_____ Class_____ Date_____

Focus Question: How did the Allies begin to push back the Axis powers?

As you read this section in your textbook, complete the chart below to record the sequence of events that turned the tide of the war in favor of the Allies.

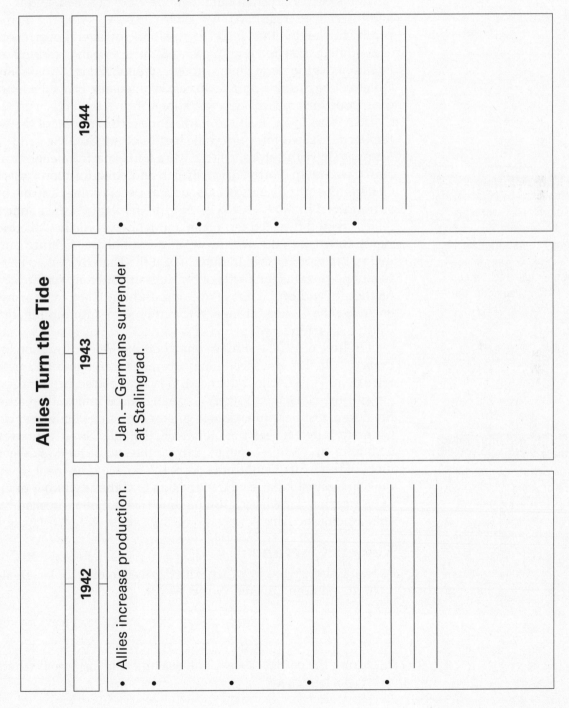

Allies Turn the Tide

1944
•   •   •   •

1943
• Jan.—Germans surrender at Stalingrad.   •   •   •

1942
• Allies increase production.   •   •   •   •

Name_____ Class_____ Date_____

READING CHECK

Who were the "Big Three"?

_____

_____

_____

VOCABULARY STRATEGY

Find the word *incessant* in the underlined sentence. Notice that the phrase "around-the-clock" follows *incessant.* They have similar meanings. Use this context clue to help you figure out the meaning of *incessant.*

READING SKILL

Recognize Sequence List the sequence of events in 1942–1943 that gave the Allies control of North Africa.

_____

_____

_____

To defeat the Axis powers in World War II, the Allies devoted all their resources to the war effort. Governments took a greater role in the economy. For example, governments ordered factories to make tanks instead of cars. Consumer goods were rationed, and wages and prices were regulated. A positive result was that the increase in production ended the Great Depression. However, governments also limited citizens' rights, censored the press, and resorted to propaganda. At the same time, women, symbolized by **"Rosie the Riveter,"** replaced men in factories. Women also played a more direct role in some military operations.

The years 1942 and 1943 marked the turning point of the war. In the Pacific, Allied forces won the battles of the Coral Sea and Midway. In both battles, attacks were launched from enormous **aircraft carriers.** In North Africa, British and American forces, led by General **Dwight Eisenhower,** soon trapped Rommel's army, and he surrendered in May 1943. With North Africa under their control, the Allies crossed the Mediterranean and landed in Sicily. Allied victories in Italy led to the overthrow of Mussolini, but fighting continued in Italy for another 18 months. On the Eastern front, a key turning point was the Battle of **Stalingrad.** After a German advance on the city and brutal house-to-house fighting, the Soviet army encircled the German troops. Without food or ammunition, the Germans surrendered.

On June 6, 1944, the Allies launched the **D-Day** invasion of France. Allied troops faced many obstacles, but the Germans finally retreated. As the Allies advanced, Germany reeled from incessant, around-the-clock bombing. A German counterattack, the Battle of the Bulge, resulted in terrible losses on both sides. However, with Germany's defeat seeming inevitable, the "Big Three"—Roosevelt, Churchill, and Stalin—met to plan for the end of the war. Key features of this **Yalta Conference** were the Soviet agreement to enter the war against Japan and the division of Germany into four zones of occupation. However, growing mistrust at Yalta foreshadowed a split among the Allies.

Review Questions

1. Name three ways in which Allied governments took a greater role in the economy during World War II.

_____

_____

2. During the battles of the Coral Sea and Midway, from where were attacks launched?

_____

_____

Focus Question: How did the Allies finally defeat the Axis powers?

As you read this section in your textbook, complete the timeline below to sequence the events that led to the defeat of the Axis powers.

Oct. 1945

June 1945

Feb. 1945

Oct. 1944

CHAPTER 17 SECTION 4 — Section Summary

VICTORY IN EUROPE AND THE PACIFIC

READING CHECK

What was the "island-hopping" campaign?

_____

_____

_____

VOCABULARY STRATEGY

What does the word *objective* mean in the underlined sentence? Say the sentence aloud and omit *objective*. Think about other words that might complete the sentence. Use this strategy to help you figure out the meaning of *objective*.

READING SKILL

Recognize Sequence Create a timeline of the events that took place in Japan from August 6 to August 10, 1945.

_____

_____

_____

In Europe, World War II officially ended on May 8, 1945, or **V-E Day.** The Allies were able to defeat the Axis powers for many reasons. Because of their location, the Axis powers had to fight on several fronts at the same time. Hitler also made some poor military decisions. For example, he underestimated the Soviet Union's ability to fight. The huge productive capacity of the United States was another factor. At the same time, Allied bombing hindered German production and caused oil to become scarce. This nearly grounded the Luftwaffe.

Although Germany was defeated, the Allies still had to defeat the Japanese in the Pacific. By May 1942, the Japanese had gained control of the Philippines, killing thousands during the **Bataan Death March.** However, after the battles of Midway and the Coral Sea, the United States took the offensive. General **Douglas MacArthur** began an **"island-hopping"** campaign to recapture islands from the Japanese. The captured islands served as stepping-stones to the next objective—Japan. The Americans gradually moved north and were able to blockade Japan. Bombers pounded Japanese cities and industries. At the same time, the British pushed Japanese forces back into the jungles of Burma and Malaya.

In early 1945, bloody battles on Iwo Jima and Okinawa showed that the Japanese would fight to the death rather than surrender. Some young Japanese became **kamikaze** pilots who flew their planes purposefully into U.S. ships. While Allied military leaders planned to invade, scientists offered another way to end the war. They had conducted research, code-named the **Manhattan Project,** that led to the building of an atomic bomb for the United States. The new U.S. president, Harry Truman, decided that dropping the bomb would save American lives. The Allies first issued a warning to the Japanese to surrender or face "utter and complete destruction," but the warning was ignored. On August 6, 1945, a U.S. plane dropped an atomic bomb on the city of **Hiroshima,** instantly killing more than 70,000 people. Many more died from radiation sickness. When the Japanese did not surrender, another bomb was dropped on **Nagasaki** on August 9. The next day, Japan finally surrendered, ending World War II.

Review Questions

1. What were two reasons why the Allies were able to defeat the Axis powers?

_____

_____

2. Why did Truman decide to drop the atomic bomb on Japan?

_____

_____

Note Taking Study Guide

THE END OF WORLD WAR II

Focus Question: What issues arose in the aftermath of World War II and how did new tensions develop?

As you read this section in your textbook, sequence the events following World War II by completing the outline below.

I. The War's Aftermath

  A. Devastation

    1. As many as 50 million are dead.

    2. _____

  B. _____

    1. _____

    2. _____

    3. _____

  C. _____

    1. _____

    2. _____

II. _____

  A. _____

    1. _____

  B. _____

    1. _____

    2. _____

  C. _____

    1. _____

    2. _____

III. _____

  A. _____

    1. _____

    2. _____

  B. _____

    1. _____

    2. _____

(Outline continues on the next page.)

CHAPTER
17
SECTION 5

Note Taking Study Guide

THE END OF WORLD WAR II

(Continued from page 187)

3. _____

IV. _____

  A. _____

    1. _____

    2. _____

    3. _____

  B. _____

    1. _____

    2. _____

    3. _____

  C. _____

    1. _____

    2. _____

    3. _____

    4. _____

  D. _____

    1. _____

    2. _____

    3. _____

  E. _____

    1. _____

    2. _____

  F. _____

    1. _____

    2. _____

CHAPTER 17
SECTION 5

Section Summary
THE END OF WORLD WAR II

While the Allies enjoyed their victory, the huge costs of World War II began to emerge. As many as 50 million people had been killed. The Allies also learned the full extent of the horrors of the Holocaust. War crimes trials, such as those at **Nuremberg** in Germany, held leaders accountable for their wartime actions. To ensure tolerance and peace, the Western Allies set up democratic governments in Japan and Germany.

In 1945, delegates from 50 nations convened to form the **United Nations.** Under the UN Charter, each member nation has one vote in the General Assembly. A smaller Security Council has greater power. It has five permanent members: the United States, the Soviet Union (today Russia), Britain, France, and China. Each has the right to veto any council decision. UN agencies have tackled many world problems, from disease to helping refugees.

However, conflicting ideologies soon led to a **Cold War.** This refers to the state of tension and hostility between the United States and the Soviet Union from 1946 to 1990. Soviet leader Stalin wanted to spread communism into Eastern Europe. He also wanted to create a buffer zone of friendly countries as a defense against Germany. By 1948, pro-Soviet communist governments were in place throughout Eastern Europe.

When Stalin began to threaten Greece and Turkey, the United States outlined a policy called the **Truman Doctrine.** This policy meant that the United States would resist the spread of communism throughout the world. To strengthen democracies in Europe, the United States offered a massive aid package, called the **Marshall Plan.** Western attempts to rebuild Germany triggered a crisis over the city of Berlin. The Soviets controlled East Germany, which surrounded Berlin. To force the Western Allies out of Berlin, the Soviets blockaded West Berlin, but a yearlong airlift forced them to end the blockade.

However, tensions continued to mount. In 1949, the United States and nine other nations formed a new military alliance called the **North Atlantic Treaty Organization (NATO).** The Soviets responded by forming the **Warsaw Pact,** which included the Soviet Union and seven Eastern European nations.

Review Questions

1. What was the purpose of the post-World War II war crimes trials?

_____

_____

2. Why did the United States offer aid under the Marshall Plan to European countries?

_____

_____

READING CHECK

What was the Cold War?

_____

_____

_____

VOCABULARY STRATEGY

What does the word *convened* mean in the underlined sentence? The word *convene* comes from the Latin *convenire.* In Latin, *con-* means "together" and *venire* means "to come." Use this word-origins clue to help you figure out the meaning of *convened.*

READING SKILL

Recognize Sequence List the sequence of events that led to the Berlin airlift.

_____

_____

_____

Name_____ Class_____ Date_____

<table>
<tr><td>CHAPTER
18
SECTION 1</td><td>## Note Taking Study Guide
THE COLD WAR UNFOLDS</td></tr>
</table>

Focus Question: What were the military and political consequences of the Cold War in the Soviet Union, Europe, and the United States?

As you read this section in your textbook, complete the following chart to summarize the consequences of the Cold War in the Soviet Union, Europe, and the United States.

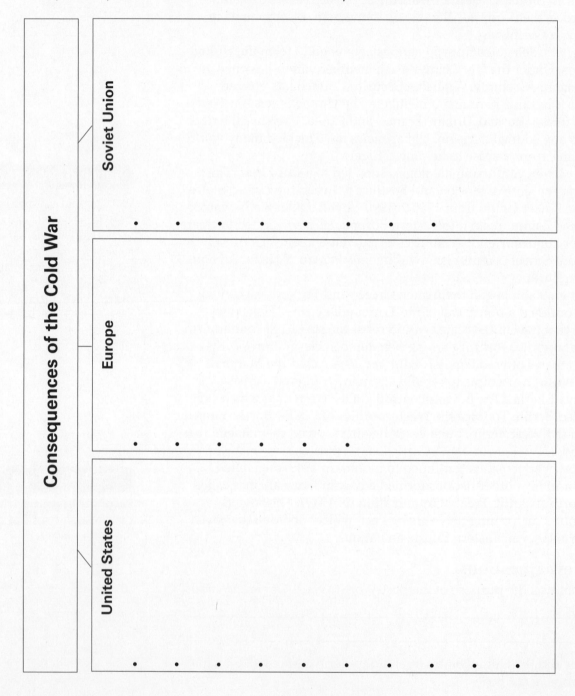

CHAPTER 18 SECTION 1	**Section Summary**
	THE COLD WAR UNFOLDS

After World War II, the United States and the Soviet Union emerged as **superpowers.** They each created military alliances made up of nations they protected or occupied. <u>The United States helped form the North Atlantic Treaty Organization (NATO), which comprised Western European allies.</u> The Soviet Union signed the Warsaw Pact with Eastern European countries. The line between the democratic West and communist East was called the Iron Curtain. Many revolts challenging Soviet domination were extinguished with military force.

The superpowers also engaged in a weapons race—both developed nuclear weapons. To reduce the threat of war, the two sides held several disarmament talks. One agreement was intended to limit the use of **anti-ballistic missiles (ABMs).** These weapons were designed to shoot down missiles launched by hostile nations. The ABMs were considered a threat because they could give one side more protection, which might encourage it to attack. Then during the 1980s, President **Ronald Reagan** proposed a missile defense program called "Star Wars." Other agreements limited the number of nuclear weapons that nations could maintain, which eased Cold War tensions. This period was called the era of **détente.** It ended, however, when the Soviet Union invaded Afghanistan in 1979.

During the 1950s, **Fidel Castro** led a revolution in Cuba and became its leader. To bring down Castro's communist regime, U.S. President **John F. Kennedy** supported an invasion of Cuba, but the attempt failed. One year later, the Soviets sent nuclear missiles to Cuba. Many feared a nuclear war. After the United States blockaded Cuba, Soviet leader **Nikita Khrushchev** agreed to remove the missiles.

The Soviets wanted to spread communist **ideology** around the globe. When Khrushchev came to power, he eased censorship and increased tolerance. However, repression returned under **Leonid Brezhnev.** American leaders followed a policy of **containment.** This was a strategy of keeping communism from spreading to other nations. In addition, a "red scare" in the United States resulted in Senator Joseph McCarthy leading an internal hunt for communists in the government and military. The House Un-American Activities Committee (HUAC) also sought out communist sympathizers.

Review Questions

1. What did the two superpowers do to reduce the threat of war during the Cold War?

_____

_____

2. What ended the period of détente between the United States and the Soviet Union?

_____

_____

READING CHECK

Who were the two superpowers during the Cold War?

_____

_____

_____

VOCABULARY STRATEGY

What does the word *comprised* mean in the underlined sentence? What clues can you find in the surrounding words, phrases, or sentences? Use these context clues to help you figure out what *comprised* means.

READING SKILL

Summarize What was the United States policy known as containment?

_____

_____

_____

CHAPTER 18 SECTION 2

Note Taking Study Guide

THE INDUSTRIALIZED DEMOCRACIES

Focus Question: How did the United States, Western Europe, and Japan achieve economic prosperity and strengthen democracy during the Cold War years?

As you read this section in your textbook, use the chart below to categorize economic and political changes in the industrialized democracies.

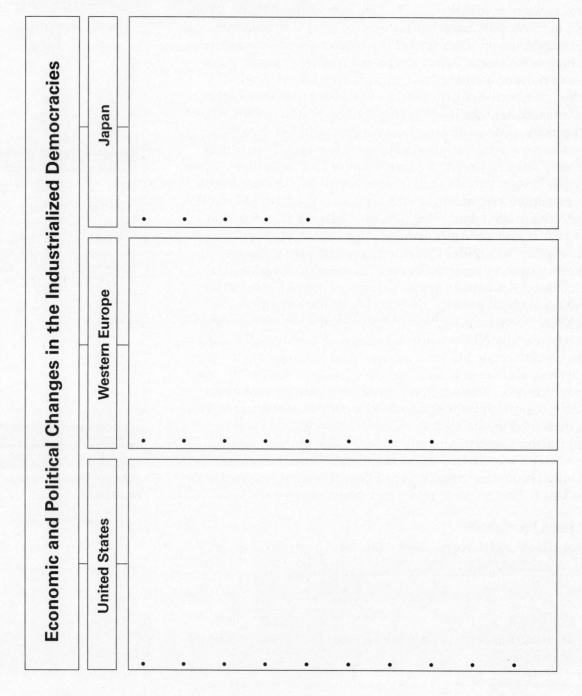

CHAPTER 18 SECTION 2

Section Summary

THE INDUSTRIALIZED DEMOCRACIES

During the postwar period, U.S. businesses expanded into the global marketplace. Other nations needed goods and services to rebuild. This led to a period of economic success that changed life in the United States. During the 1950s and 1960s, **recessions** were brief and mild. <u>As Americans prospered, they left the cities to live in the suburbs.</u> This trend is called **suburbanization.** Also, job opportunities in the Sunbelt attracted many people to that region. By the 1970s, however, a political crisis in the Middle East made Americans aware of their dependence on imported oil. The price of oil and gas rose substantially, which meant that people had less money to buy other products. The decades of prosperity ended in 1974 with a serious recession.

During the period of prosperity, African Americans and other minorities faced **segregation** in housing and education. They suffered from **discrimination** in jobs and voting. **Dr. Martin Luther King, Jr.,** emerged as the main civil rights leader in the 1960s. The U.S. Congress passed some civil rights legislation. Other minority groups were inspired by the movement's successes. For example, the women's rights movement helped to end much gender-based discrimination.

Western Europe rebuilt after World War II. The Marshall Plan helped restore European economies by providing U.S. aid. After the war, Germany was divided between the communist East and the democratic West, but reunited at the end of the Cold War in 1990. Under **Konrad Adenauer,** West Germany's chancellor from 1949 to 1963, Germany built modern cities and re-established trade. European governments also developed programs that increased government responsibility for the needs of people. These **welfare states** required high taxes to pay for their programs. During the 1980s, some leaders, such as Britain's Margaret Thatcher, reduced the role of the government in the economy. Western Europe also moved closer to economic unity with the **European Community**, an organization dedicated to establishing free trade among its members.

Japan also prospered after World War II. Its **gross domestic product (GDP)** soared. Like Germany, Japan built factories. The government protected industries by raising tariffs on imported goods. This helped create a trade surplus for Japan.

Review Questions

1. What caused a U.S. recession in 1974?

_____

_____

2. Explain how Germany rebuilt its economy after World War II.

_____

_____

READING CHECK

What is suburbanization?

_____

_____

_____

VOCABULARY STRATEGY

What does the word *prospered* mean in the underlined sentence? The word *decline* is an antonym of *prosper*. It means to "sink," "descend," or "deteriorate." Use these meanings of *decline* to figure out the meaning of *prospered*.

READING SKILL

Categorize In what ways were minorities denied equality and opportunity?

_____

_____

_____

Focus Question: What did the Communist victory mean for China and the rest of East Asia?

As you read this section in your textbook, complete the flowchart below to help you summarize the effects of the Communist Revolution on China and the impact of the Cold War on China and Korea.

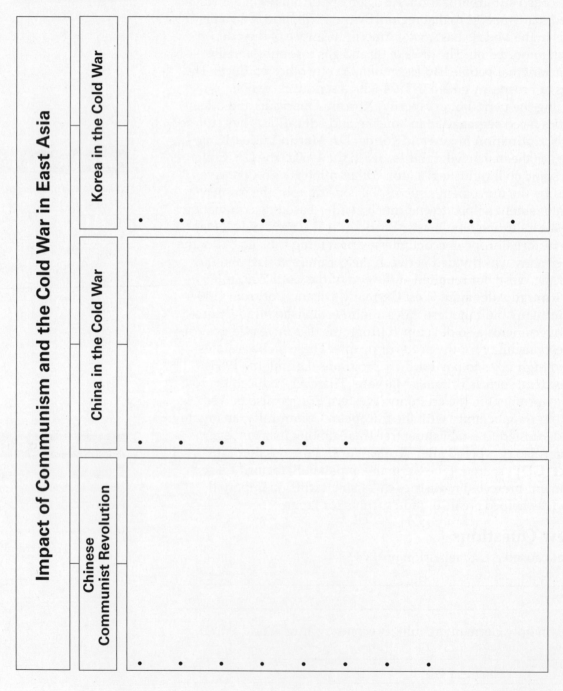

CHAPTER 18 SECTION 3

Section Summary
COMMUNISM SPREADS IN EAST ASIA

After World War II, Mao Zedong led communist forces to victory over Jiang Jieshi's Nationalists, who fled to Taiwan. Then Mao began to reshape China's economy. First, he gave land to peasants, but then called for **collectivization.** Under this system, <u>Mao moved people from their small villages and individual farms into communes of thousands of people on thousands of acres.</u> Known as the **Great Leap Forward,** the program was intended to increase farm and industrial production. Instead, it produced low quality, useless goods and less food. Bad weather also affected crops, and many people starved.

To remove "bourgeois" tendencies from China, Mao began the **Cultural Revolution.** Skilled workers and managers were removed from factories and forced to work on farms or in labor camps. This resulted in a slowed economy and a threat of civil war.

At first, the United States supported the Nationalist government in Taiwan. The West was concerned that the Soviet Union and China would become allies, but border clashes led the Soviets to withdraw aid and advisors from China. U.S. leaders thought that by "playing the China card," or improving relations with the Chinese, they would further isolate the Soviets. In 1979, the United States established diplomatic relations with China.

Korea was an independent nation until Japan invaded it in World War II. After the war, American and Soviet forces agreed to divide the Korean peninsula at the **38th parallel. Kim Il Sung**, a communist, ruled the North; and **Syngman Rhee,** allied with the United States, controlled the South. In 1950, North Korean troops attacked South Korea. The United Nations forces stopped them along a line known as the **Pusan Perimeter,** then began advancing north. Mao sent troops to help the North Koreans. UN forces were pushed back south of the 38th parallel.

In 1953, both sides signed an armistice to end the fighting, but troops remained on both sides of the **demilitarized zone (DMZ).** Over time, South Korea enjoyed an economic boom and a rise in living standards, while communist North Korea's economy declined. Kim Il Sung's emphasis on self-reliance kept North Korea isolated and poor.

Review Questions

1. What was the effect of the Cultural Revolution?

_____

_____

2. How did the North Korean economy differ from the South Korean economy?

_____

_____

READING CHECK

What is the significance of the 38th parallel?

_____

_____

_____

VOCABULARY STRATEGY

What does the word *commune* mean in the underlined sentence? The terms *group home*, *community*, and *collective farm* are all synonyms of *commune*. Use the synonyms to help you figure out the meaning of *commune*.

READING SKILL

Summarize Summarize the effects of the Great Leap Forward on the Chinese people.

_____

_____

_____

CHAPTER 18 SECTION 4
Note Taking Study Guide
WAR IN SOUTHEAST ASIA

Focus Question: What were the causes and effects of war in Southeast Asia, and what was the American role in this region?

As you read this section in your textbook, complete the flowchart below to summarize the events in Southeast Asia after World War II.

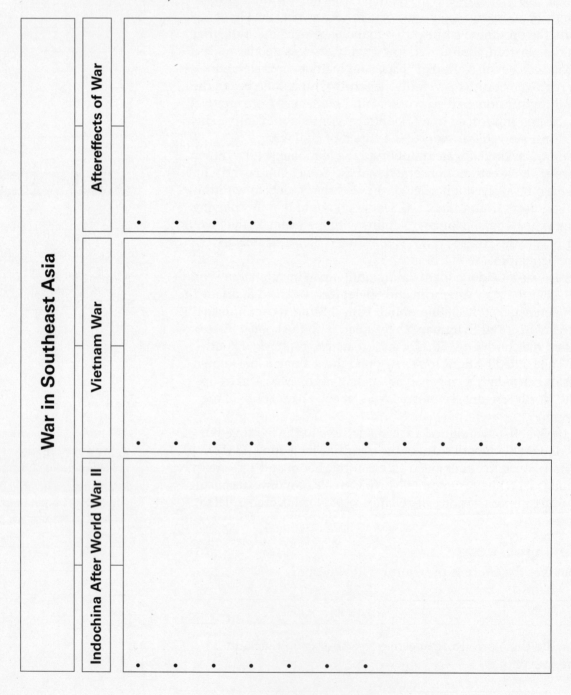

War in Southeast Asia

Aftereffects of War

• • • • • • •

Vietnam War

• • • • • • • • • • • •

Indochina After World War II

• • • • • • • •

CHAPTER 18 SECTION 4

Section Summary

WAR IN SOUTHEAST ASIA

In the 1800s, the French ruled the area in Southeast Asia called French Indochina. During World War II, Japan invaded that region, but faced resistance from **guerrillas.** After the war, the French tried to reestablish authority in Vietnam. However, forces led by communist leader **Ho Chi Minh** fought the colonialists. The French left Vietnam in 1954, after a Vietnamese victory at **Dienbienphu**. After that, Ho controlled the northern part of Vietnam while the United States supported the noncommunist government in the south.

Ho wanted to unite Vietnam. He provided aid to the National Liberation Front, or **Viet Cong,** a communist guerrilla organization in the south. American leaders saw Vietnam as an extension of the Cold War and developed the **domino theory.** This was the belief that if communists won in South Vietnam, then communism could spread to other governments in Southeast Asia. After a North Vietnamese attack on a U.S. Navy destroyer, Congress authorized the president to take military measures to prevent further communist aggression in Southeast Asia.

Despite massive American support, the South Vietnamese failed to defeat the Viet Cong and their North Vietnamese allies. During the **Tet Offensive,** the North Vietnamese attacked cities all over the south. Even though the communists were not able to hold any cities, it marked a turning point in U.S. public opinion. Upset by civilian deaths from the U.S. bombing of North Vietnam as well as growing American casualties, many Americans began to oppose the war. President Nixon came under increasing pressure to terminate the conflict. The Paris Peace Accord of 1973 established a ceasefire and American troops began to withdraw. Two years later communist North Vietnam conquered South Vietnam.

Neighboring Cambodia and Laos also ended up with communist governments. In Cambodia, guerrillas called the **Khmer Rouge** came to power. Led by the brutal dictator **Pol Pot,** their policies led to a genocide that killed about one third of the population. When Vietnam invaded Cambodia, the genocide ended. Pol Pot and the Khmer Rouge were forced to retreat. Communism did not spread any farther in Southeast Asia.

Review Questions

1. What was the domino theory?

_____

_____

2. Who were the Khmer Rouge and what role did they play in Cambodia?

_____

_____

READING CHECK

What was significant about the Tet Offensive?

_____

_____

_____

VOCABULARY STRATEGY

What does the word *terminate* mean in the underlined sentence? Note that the word is a verb. Ask yourself what action President Nixon was being pressured to take. Use this strategy to help you figure out what *terminate* means.

READING SKILL

Summarize Summarize U.S. involvement in Vietnam.

_____

_____

Name_____ Class_____ Date_____

Focus Question: What were the causes and effects of the end of the Cold War?

As you read this section in your textbook, complete this flowchart to help you categorize events connected to the end of the Cold War. Some events have been completed for you.

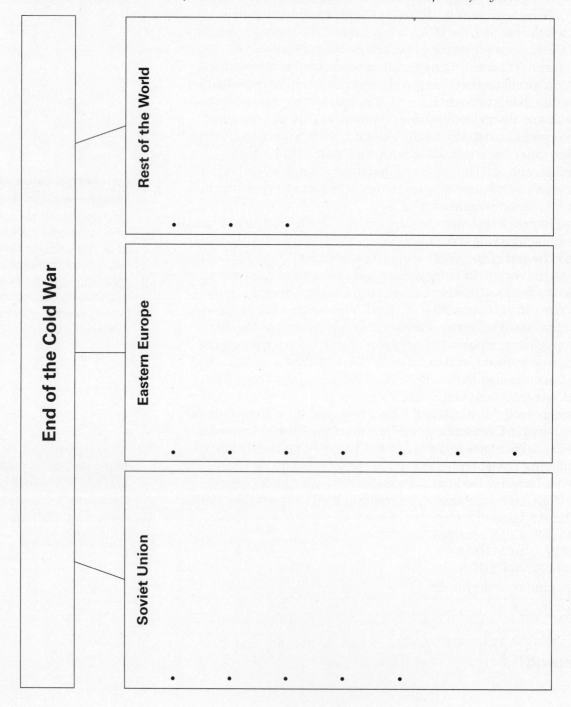

End of the Cold War

Rest of the World

• • •

Eastern Europe

• • • • • • •

Soviet Union

• • • • •

CHAPTER 18 SECTION 5

Section Summary
THE END OF THE COLD WAR

The Soviet Union emerged from World War II as a superpower, with control over many Eastern European countries. For many people, the country's superpower status brought few rewards. Consumer goods were inferior and workers were poorly paid. Because workers had lifetime job security, there was little incentive to produce high-quality goods. Still, there were some important technological successes. One example was *Sputnik I*, the first artificial satellite. Keeping up with the United States in an arms race also strained the economy. Then in 1979, Soviet forces invaded Afghanistan and became involved in a long war. The Soviets had few successes battling the **mujahedin,** or Muslim religious warriors, creating a crisis in morale in the USSR.

Then, new Soviet leader **Mikhail Gorbachev** urged reforms. He called for **glasnost.** He ended censorship and encouraged people to discuss the country's problems. Gorbachev also called for **perestroika,** or a restructuring of the government and economy. His policies, however, fed unrest across the Soviet empire.

Eastern Europeans demanded an end to Soviet rule. Previous attempts to defy the Soviets had failed. When Hungarians and Czechs challenged the communist rulers, military force subdued them. By the end of the 1980s, a powerful democracy movement was sweeping the region. In Poland, **Lech Walesa** led **Solidarity,** an independent, unlawful labor union demanding economic and political changes. When Gorbachev declared he would not interfere in Eastern European reforms, Solidarity was legalized. A year later, Walesa was elected president of Poland.

Meanwhile, East German leaders resisted reform, and thousands of East Germans fled to the West. In Czechoslovakia, **Václav Havel,** a dissident writer, was elected president. One by one, communist governments fell. Most changes happened peacefully, but Romanian dictator **Nicolae Ceausescu** refused to step down and he was executed. The Baltic States regained independence. By the end of 1991, the remaining Soviet republics had all formed independent nations. The Soviet Union ceased to exist after 69 years of communist rule.

In 1992, Czechoslovakia was divided into Slovakia and the Czech Republic. Additionally, some communist governments in Asia, such as China, instituted economic reforms.

Review Questions

1. What kinds of reforms did Gorbachev make?

_____

_____

2. What happened to the Soviet Union by the end of 1991?

_____

_____

READING CHECK

How did the arms race affect the Soviet economy?

_____

_____

_____

VOCABULARY STRATEGY

What does the word *incentive* mean in the underlined sentence? The words *motivation* and *reason* are synonyms of *incentive.* Use these synonyms to help you figure out the meaning of *incentive.*

READING SKILL

Categorize Which leaders mentioned in the summary supported reform and which leaders opposed reform?

_____

_____

_____

Focus Question: What were the consequences of independence in South Asia for the region and for the world?

As you read this section in your textbook, fill in the concept web below to identify causes and effects of events in South Asia.

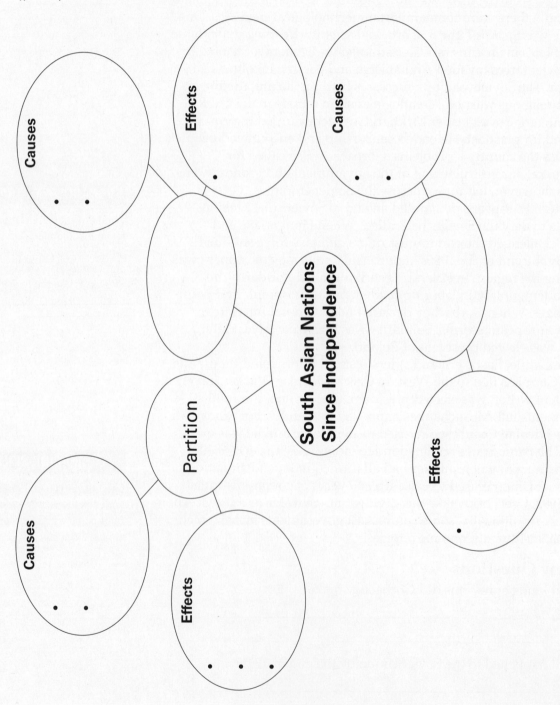

Name_____ Class_____ Date_____

<table>
<tr><td>CHAPTER
19
SECTION 1</td><td>## Section Summary
INDEPENDENT NATIONS OF SOUTH ASIA</td></tr>
</table>

In the 1940s, tensions between Hindus and Muslims in India led to violence. The ruling British decided that the only solution was a **partition,** or division, into a Muslim-majority Pakistan and a Hindu-majority India. After Pakistan and India gained their independence in 1947, Hindus in Pakistan fled to India, while Muslims in India fled to Pakistan. As they fled, Muslims, Hindus, and another religious group called **Sikhs** slaughtered one another.

Tensions have continued in the region. India and Pakistan have fought wars over **Kashmir,** a state with Muslim and Hindu populations. When India developed nuclear weapons, Pakistan began its own nuclear weapons program. In the island country of Sri Lanka, a majority are Buddhists. A Tamil-speaking Hindu minority on the island has fought for years for a separate Tamil nation.

In 1947, **Jawaharlal Nehru** became India's first prime minister. He tried to improve living conditions and end discrimination against **dalits,** or outcastes. Nehru's daughter, **Indira Gandhi,** became prime minister in 1966. While she was in office, Sikhs pressed for independence for the state of **Punjab.** In 1984, Sikh separatists occupied the **Golden Temple,** the holiest Sikh shrine. Gandhi sent troops to the temple, and thousands of Sikhs were killed. A few months later, Gandhi's Sikh bodyguards assassinated her.

In 1947, Pakistan was a divided country. A thousand miles separated West Pakistan from East Pakistan. West Pakistan dominated the nation's government. Most people in East Pakistan were Bengalis. They felt their government neglected their region. In 1971, Bengalis declared independence for East Pakistan under the name of **Bangladesh.** Pakistan tried to crush the rebels but was eventually compelled to recognize the independence of Bangladesh.

Pakistan has long lacked political stability. Islamic fundamentalists disagree with those who want a greater separation between religion and government. During the 1980s, the war in Afghanistan drove over a million Afghan refugees into Pakistan. Pakistan's Islamic fundamentalists gained power by forming ties with Afghan refugees.

Despite their differences, India and Pakistan helped organize a conference of newly independent states in 1955. This marked the birth of **nonalignment,** or political and diplomatic independence from the United States or the Soviet Union.

Review Questions

1. Why was Indira Gandhi assassinated?

_____

_____

2. Why did Bengalis want East Pakistan to be independent?

_____

_____

READING CHECK

What is nonalignment?

_____

_____

_____

VOCABULARY STRATEGY

What does the word *compelled* mean in the underlined sentence? *Compel* comes from a Latin word that means "to drive." If you substitute the word "driven" for *compelled* in the underlined sentence, it will help you figure out what *compelled* means.

READING SKILL

Identify Causes and Effects
What caused the British to partition India? What were some of the effects the partition had on Muslims and Hindus?

_____

_____

Note Taking Study Guide

CHAPTER 19 SECTION 2

NEW NATIONS OF SOUTHEAST ASIA

Focus Question: What challenges did Southeast Asian nations face after winning independence?

As you read this section in your textbook, fill in the concept web below to understand the effects of recent historical processes in Southeast Asia.

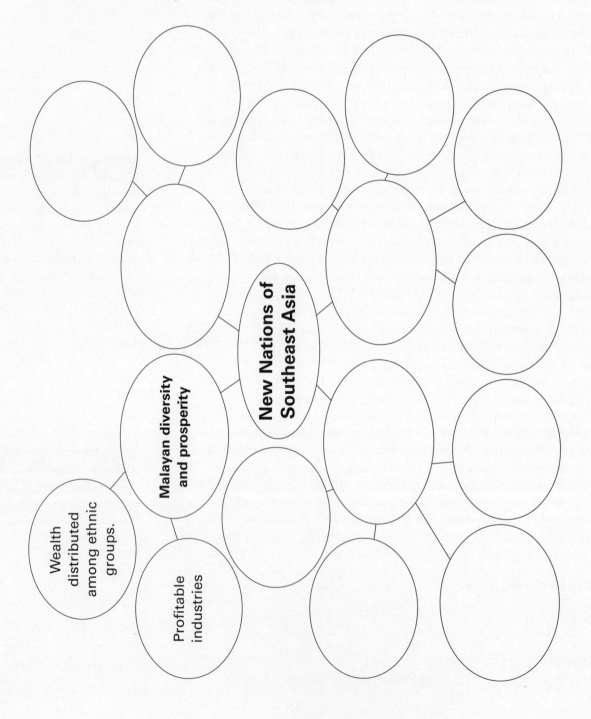

CHAPTER 19 SECTION 2

Section Summary
NEW NATIONS OF SOUTHEAST ASIA

Mainland Southeast Asia is a region of contrasts. Thailand and Malaysia have prospered as market economies. In Malaysia, people of Chinese and Indian descent have made the nation a leader in profitable industries. However, the government has also tried to include the Malay majority in the country's prosperity. By contrast, Myanmar, or Burma, has suffered under an **autocratic** government— a government that has unlimited power. The government has limited foreign trade, and living standards remain low. In 1990, elections were held in Myanmar, and a party that opposed military rule won. It was led by **Aung San Suu Kyi.** However, the military rejected the election results, and Suu Kyi was put under house arrest.

After World War II, Indonesia, formerly the Dutch East Indies, achieved its independence. Indonesia faced many obstacles to its unity. It consists of more than 13,000 islands. Javanese make up almost half of the population, but there are hundreds of ethnic groups. About 90 percent of Indonesians are Muslims, but the population includes Christians, Buddhists, and Hindus. After independence, Indonesia formed a democratic, parliamentary government under its first president, **Sukarno.** In 1966, an army general, **Suharto,** seized power and ruled as a dictator until he was forced to resign in 1998. Religious and ethnic tensions have fueled violence in parts of Indonesia. In 1975, Indonesia seized **East Timor,** a former Portuguese colony. The mostly Catholic East Timorese fought for independence, which they finally achieved in 2002.

In the Philippines, Catholics are the predominant religious group, but there is a Muslim minority in the south. In 1946, the Philippines gained freedom from United States control. Although the Filipino constitution established a democratic government, a wealthy elite controlled politics and the economy. **Ferdinand Marcos,** elected president in 1965, became a dictator and cracked down on basic freedoms. He even had **Benigno Aquino,** a popular rival, murdered. When **Corazon Aquino** was elected in 1986, Marcos tried to deny the results, but the people forced him to resign. Since then, democracy has struggled to survive in the Philippines. Communist and Muslim rebels continue to fight across the country.

Review Questions

1. What happened when Aung San Suu Kyi's party won the 1990 elections in Myanmar?

_____

_____

2. What are some obstacles to Indonesia's unity?

_____

_____

READING CHECK

What are the features of the autocratic government in Myanmar?

_____

_____

_____

VOCABULARY STRATEGY

What does *predominant* mean in the underlined sentence? Note that the second part of the sentence mentions another group that is a minority, or a smaller group. Use this context clue to help you figure out the meaning of *predominant*.

READING SKILL

Understand Effects What was the effect of Ferdinand Marcos' denial of the results of the 1986 election?

_____

_____

_____

Name_____ Class_____ Date_____

Focus Question: What challenges did new African nations face?

As you read this section in your textbook, fill in the concept web below to keep track of the causes and effects of independence in Africa.

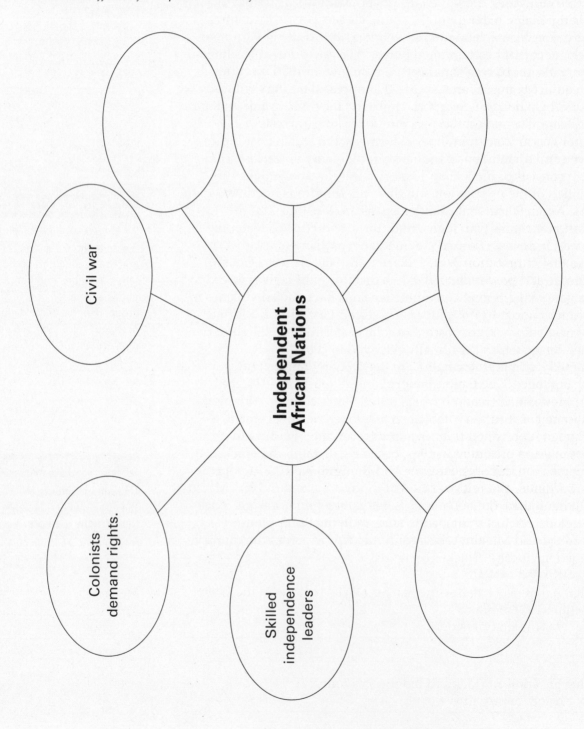

CHAPTER 19 SECTION 3	Section Summary
	AFRICAN NATIONS GAIN INDEPENDENCE

Africa is a diverse continent. Vast **savannas,** or tree-dotted grass-lands, cover much of it, but there are also rain forests and deserts. The continent also has diverse peoples, languages, and traditions.

After World War II, many Africans demanded freedom from European powers. After gaining independence, a few African nations enjoyed peace and democracy. Most faced civil wars, military rule, or corrupt dictators. European powers had drawn colonial boundaries without regard for Africa's ethnic groups. This led to ethnic conflict in many new nations once colonial powers withdrew.

In 1957, Gold Coast gained its freedom from Britain and took the name Ghana. The government of its first president, **Kwame Nkrumah,** became corrupt, and Nkrumah was overthrown in a military **coup d'etat.** Today Ghana is a democracy.

In Kenya, white settlers had passed laws to ensure their domination of the country. In the 1950s, rebels turned to guerrilla warfare, but the British crushed the rebellion. Kenya finally gained its independence in 1963. **Jomo Kenyatta,** a prominent independence leader, became the first president of the new country. In 2002, Kenya's first fair election removed the ruling party from office.

Algeria achieved independence from France in 1962. A coup in 1965 began a long period of military rule. When the government held free elections in 1992, an **Islamist** party won. The military rejected the results, and seven years of civil war followed. Although the fighting has ended, the country remains tense.

After Congo became independent from Belgium, the province of **Katanga** rebelled. The United Nations ended the rebellion in 1963. **Joseph Mobutu** ruled as a harsh military dictator from 1965 to 1997. Civil war then raged as rivals fought to control mineral resources. In 2006, Congo had its first free elections in 41 years but faced deep scars from years of conflict.

Nigeria won its independence in 1960. However, Nigeria faced ethnic, religious, and regional conflict, including a war to end a rebellion in **Biafra,** the homeland of the Ibo people in the oil-rich southeast. A series of military dictators then ruled the country, but Nigeria returned to democracy in 1999. However, ethnic conflict continued, including attacks by rebels seeking a share of oil wealth in the southeast.

Review Questions

1. Why was the first president of Ghana overthrown?

_____

_____

2. What resource provides wealth in southeastern Nigeria?

_____

_____

READING CHECK

What is a coup d'etat?

_____

_____

_____

VOCABULARY STRATEGY

What does the word *ensure* mean in the underlined sentence? The prefix *en-* means to "make" or "cause to be." Think about what the root word, *sure*, means. Use these clues about word parts to help you understand the meaning of *ensure*.

READING SKILL

Identify Causes and Effects
How did past decisions made by European powers cause ethnic conflict in many new African nations?

_____

_____

Focus Question: What are the main similarities and differences among Middle Eastern nations?

As you read this section in your textbook, fill in the concept web below to identify causes and effects of events in the Middle East since 1945.

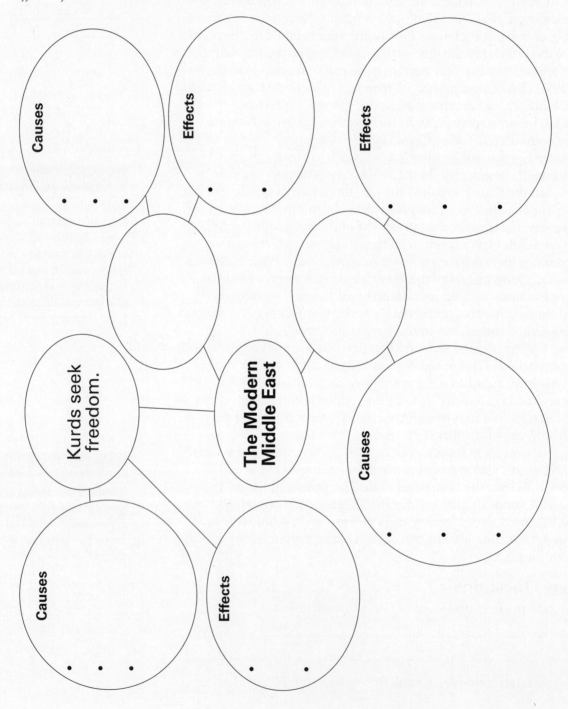

CHAPTER **19** SECTION 4	**Section Summary** THE MODERN MIDDLE EAST

Most of the people in the Middle East are Muslims, but there are also Christian communities and the predominantly Jewish nation of Israel. Most countries also have large ethnic or religious minorities. The Kurds are an example of an ethnic minority. They live in Iran, Iraq, Syria, and Turkey and have faced discrimination in each country.

The Holocaust created support for a Jewish homeland after World War II. In 1947, the UN drew up a plan to divide Palestine into an Arab and a Jewish state. In 1948, Jews proclaimed the independent state of Israel. This led to Arab-Israeli conflicts that forced 700,000 Palestinians from their homes. Despite the conflicts, Israel has developed rapidly due to a skilled workforce. Kibbutzim work on what is called a **kibbutz,** or collective farm.

Resources and religion have led to conflicts in the Middle East. The region has the world's largest oil and gas reserves. As a result, it has strategic importance. Some Middle Eastern countries have adopted **secular,** or non-religious, government and laws. However, many Muslim leaders argue that a renewed commitment to Islamic doctrine is needed. In Iran and Saudi Arabia, women are required to wear **hejab,** the traditional Muslim garments.

Egypt, the most populous Arab country, is important because it controls the **Suez Canal.** Under **Gamal Abdel Nasser,** Egypt fought two unsuccessful wars against Israel. His successor, **Anwar Sadat,** made peace with Israel. Islamists were angry about government corruption and the failure to end poverty. In 1981, Sadat was assassinated by Muslim fundamentalists.

In Iran, Shah Mohammad Reza Pahlavi ruled with the support of the United States, which helped oust one of his opponents, **Mohammad Mosaddeq.** The shah's secret police terrorized critics. In the 1970s, the shah's enemies rallied behind Ayatollah **Ruhollah Khomeini.** Protests forced the shah into exile, and Khomeini established an Islamic **theocracy,** or government ruled by religious leaders.

Saudi Arabia has the world's largest oil reserves and is the location of Islam's holy land. Kings from the Sa'ud family have ruled Saudi Arabia since the 1920s. Fundamentalists have criticized the kingdom's close ties to Western nations, and some opponents have adopted violent tactics that threaten to disrupt the Saudi oil industry.

Review Questions

1. What makes the Middle East of strategic importance?

_____

_____

2. Why have some Islamic fundamentalists criticized the Saudis?

_____

_____

READING CHECK

What is a theocracy?

_____

_____

_____

VOCABULARY STRATEGY

What does the word *doctrine* mean in the underlined sentence? The words *policy*, *dogma*, and *tenet* are all synonyms of doctrine. Use what you may know about these synonyms to help you figure out the meaning of the word *doctrine*.

READING SKILL

Identify Causes and Effects What effect did the proclamation of an independent state of Israel have on Palestinians?

_____

_____

_____

Focus Question: Why have ethnic and religious conflicts divided some nations?

As you read this section in your textbook, fill in the flowchart below to help you recognize the sequence of events that took place in Northern Ireland, Chechnya, and Yugoslavia.

CHAPTER	Section Summary
20 **SECTION 1**	**CONFLICTS DIVIDE NATIONS**

In recent decades, many wars and conflicts have arisen over ethnic differences. For example, in Sri Lanka, the Sinhalese Buddhists are the majority. Sinhalese nationalists discriminated against the Tamil Hindy minority. This and other policies led to a civil war between the Buddhists and Tamils. A ceasefire slowed the fighting. By early 2009, government forces had nearly defeated the Tamil rebels.

In some countries, however, conflicts have been peacefully resolved. In Canada the democratic government worked to discourage French-speaking Quebec from seeking independence.

Northern Ireland was the scene of another long-term conflict. When Britain granted independence to Ireland in 1922, it kept control of six northern counties with Protestant majorities. Many Catholics in those counties wanted to join with Ireland, which has a Catholic majority. Beginning in the 1960s, extremists on both sides turned to violence. Peace talks dragged on for years. Finally, in 1998, Protestants and Catholics signed the **Good Friday Agreement,** a peace accord.

Ethnic and religious minorities in several former Soviet republics also fought for independence. The fiercest struggle occurred in **Chechnya,** where Chechens fought to free Chechnya from Russian control. Russia crushed a Chechen revolt in the mid-1990s, and many civilians were killed. When a 1997 peace treaty failed, some Chechens turned to terrorism. In Nagorno-Karabakh, ethnic Armenians fought against Azerbaijanis.

Ethnic tensions also tore Yugoslavia apart during the 1990s. Before 1991, Yugoslavia was a **multiethnic,** communist country. <u>The Serbs dominated Yugoslavia, which was controlled by the Communist Party.</u> The fall of communism led to nationalist unrest and fighting between ethnic Serbs and Croats in Croatia. Soon the fighting spread to neighboring Bosnia. During the war, all sides committed atrocities. In Bosnia, the Serbs conducted a vicious campaign of **ethnic cleansing.** In 1995, the war in Bosnia ended.

Then, however, another crisis broke out in the Serbian province of **Kosovo.** In 1989 Serbian president **Slobodan Milosevic** began oppressing Kosovar Albanians. NATO launched air strikes against Serbia and Serbian forces withdrew. In 2008 Kosovo declared its independence.

Review Questions

1. What two groups are in conflict in Sri Lanka?

_____

_____

2. Why did Chechnya become an area of conflict in Russia?

_____

_____

READING CHECK

In which country did ethnic tensions not lead to war?

_____

_____

_____

VOCABULARY STRATEGY

What does *dominated* mean in the underlined sentence? What clues can you find in the surrounding words, phrases, or sentences? Use these context clues to help you figure out what *dominated* means.

READING SKILL

Recognize Sequence What happened in Ireland after independence to cause conflict?

_____

_____

_____

CHAPTER
20
SECTION 2

Note Taking Study Guide
STRUGGLES IN AFRICA

Focus Question: Why have conflicts plagued some African countries?

A. *As you read "South Africa Struggles for Freedom," "South Africa's Neighbors Face Long Conflicts," and "Ethnic Conflicts Kill Millions," record the sequence of events in the conflicts in South Africa and its neighbors.*

1910: White minority controls government of independent South Africa.
1948:

B. *As you read "Ethnic Conflicts Kill Millions," identify the causes and effects of the conflicts in Rwanda, Sudan, Burundi, and Darfur.*

CHAPTER 20 SECTION 2

Section Summary
STRUGGLES IN AFRICA

In the 1950s and 1960s, many new nations won independence in Africa. Several other African nations suffered internal conflicts and civil wars. In 1910, South Africa achieved self-rule from Britain. Most civil rights, however, were limited to white settlers. The black majority had few rights under a legal system of racial segregation called **apartheid.** Under apartheid, nonwhites faced many restrictions. <u>For example, laws banned marriages between races and stipulated segregated restaurants, beaches, and schools.</u>

The **African National Congress (ANC)** opposed apartheid and led the struggle for majority rule. In 1960, police gunned down 69 people during a protest in **Sharpeville,** a black township. The government then outlawed the ANC. **Nelson Mandela,** an ANC leader, was sentenced to life imprisonment.

In the 1980s, international demands for an end to apartheid and for Mandela's release increased. In 1984, Bishop **Desmond Tutu** won the Nobel Peace Prize for his nonviolent opposition to apartheid. In 1990, South African president **F.W. de Klerk** ended apartheid and freed Mandela, who was elected president in 1994.

South Africa's neighbors also experienced long conflicts to attain independence. Angola and Mozambique fought for 15 years until Portugal granted them independence in 1975. However, the United States and South Africa supported rebel groups in these countries. Fighting continued in Mozambique until 1992 and in Angola until 2002.

After independence, ethnic conflicts plagued many nations. In Rwanda, one of Africa's deadliest wars occurred. There, the **Hutus** were the majority, but the minority **Tutsis** dominated the country. In 1994, extremist Hutus slaughtered about 800,000 Tutsis and moderate Hutus. Millions of Rwandans lost their homes.

In Sudan, non-Muslim peoples in the south fought Arab Muslims from the north. This, along with drought and famine, killed millions. By 2005 there was peace in the south. However, a new ethnic conflict had emerged. In Darfur, in western Sudan, government-backed Arabs attacked non-Arab Muslim villagers and drove them off their land. Deprived of the land that fed them, the villagers faced possible starvation in refugee camps. Signs of war crimes and genocide brought calls for UN peacekeepers.

Review Questions

1. Describe conditions under apartheid in South Africa.

_____

_____

2. What led to deadly war in Rwanda?

_____

_____

READING CHECK

Which two African countries gained independence from Portugal?

_____

_____

_____

VOCABULARY STRATEGY

What does the word *stipulated* mean in the underlined sentence? Note that *stipulated* refers to laws. The previous sentence has a reference to restrictions that non-whites faced. Use these context clues to help you understand the meaning of the word *stipulated.*

READING SKILL

Recognize Sequence Did the South African government outlaw the ANC before or after the protest in Sharpeville?

_____

_____

_____

CHAPTER
20
SECTION 3

Note Taking Study Guide
CONFLICTS IN THE MIDDLE EAST

Focus Question: What are the causes of conflict in the Middle East?

As you read the section in your textbook, use the flowchart to record the sequence of events relating to the conflicts in the Middle East.

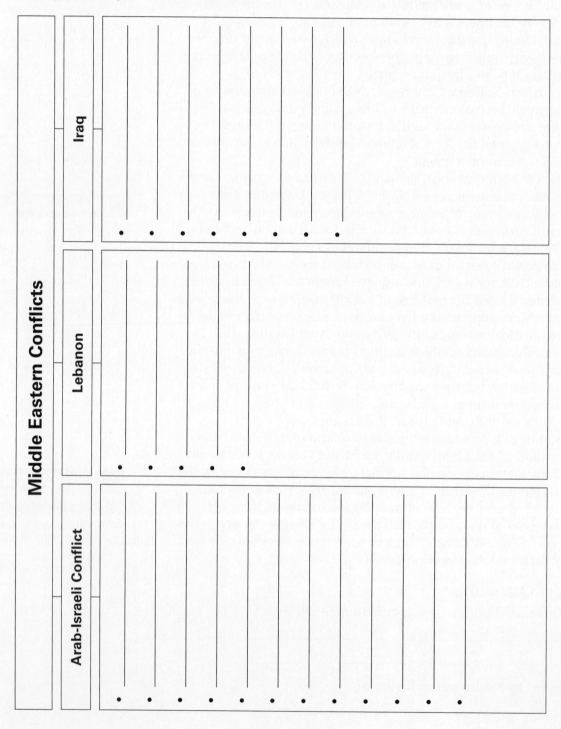

Middle Eastern Conflicts

Iraq

Lebanon

Arab-Israeli Conflict

Name_____ Class_____ Date_____

The Middle East has seen many conflicts. Modern Israel was created in 1948. Palestinian Arabs claimed the same land. After Arab countries attacked Israel in 1967, Israel took control of lands that came to be called the **occupied territories.**

The Palestine Liberation Organization, led by **Yasir Arafat,** fought against the Israelis. In the occupied territories, some Palestinians took part in uprisings called **intifadas,** and suicide bombers spread terror inside Israel. The Israelis responded with armed force, and Palestinian bitterness increased. Israeli Prime Minister **Yitzhak Rabin** signed a peace accord. There were many stumbling blocks, however, such as disagreements over **Jerusalem,** a city sacred to Jews, Christians, and Muslims. In recent years, new conflicts flared between Israel and the Palestinians that set back hopes for peace.

Lebanon is home to diverse ethnic and religious groups. There is a delicate balance among Arab Christians, Sunni Muslims, Shiite Muslims, and Druze. In 1975, civil war broke out. Later, Israel and Syria were drawn into the fighting. Peace came only after 16 years of fighting. Hezbollah fought a brief but destructive war with Israel.

Conflicts also plagued Iraq. Iraq's Sunni Arab minority had long dominated the country. Iraq's Kurdish minority and Shiite Arab majority were excluded from power. In 1979, **Saddam Hussein** took power as a dictator. He fought a prolonged war against neighboring Iran in the 1980s. In 1990, Iraq invaded Kuwait. In response, the United States led a coalition that liberated Kuwait and crushed Iraqi forces in 1991. This conflict was known as the Gulf War. Saddam Hussein remained in power and used terror to impose his will. The U.N. set up **no-fly zones** to protect the Kurds and Shiites. It worked to keep Saddam Hussein from building biological, nuclear, or chemical weapons, called **weapons of mass destruction (WMDs).**

In 2003, the United States led a coalition that invaded Iraq and overthrew Saddam Hussein. In 2005, national elections were held for the first time. However, **insurgents** and ethnic division were still obstacles. Nevertheless, leaders remained hopeful for peace.

Review Questions

1. How did Israel come to control the occupied territories?

_____

_____

2. What were the results of the Gulf War in 1991?

_____

_____

READING CHECK

Which groups in Iraq were excluded from power?

_____

_____

_____

VOCABULARY STRATEGY

What does the word *diverse* mean in the underlined sentence? Notice how in the next sentence four ethnic groups are mentioned. Use this context clue to help you understand the meaning of *diverse.*

READING SKILL

Recognize Sequence Circle the phrase in the sentence below that signals sequence.

In 1990, Iraq invaded Kuwait. In response, the United States led a coalition against the invasion.

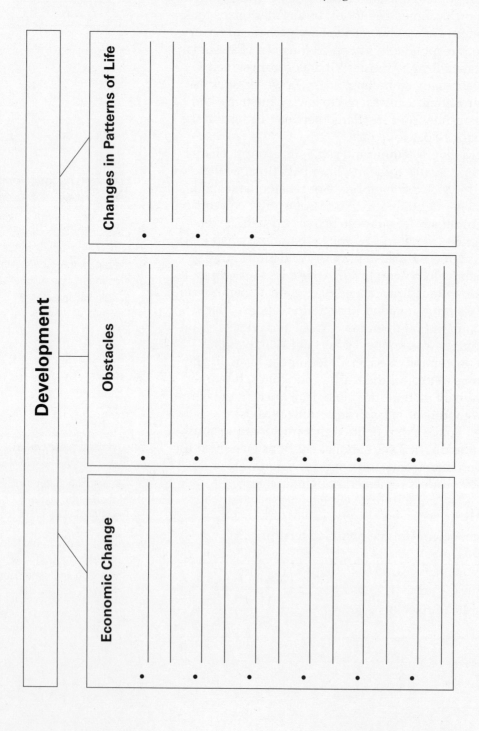

CHAPTER
21
SECTION 1

Note Taking Study Guide
THE CHALLENGES OF DEVELOPMENT

Focus Question: How have the nations of the developing world tried to build better lives for their people?

As you read this section in your textbook, complete the chart below with supporting details from the text about economic development and developing countries.

Section Summary
THE CHALLENGES OF DEVELOPMENT

After World War II, a central goal in Africa, Asia, and Latin America was **development,** or creating a more advanced economy and higher living standards. Nations that are working toward this are referred to as the **developing world.** They are also called the global South, because most of these nations are south of the Tropic of Cancer. Most industrialized nations are north of the Tropic of Cancer, so they are sometimes called the global North. Nations of the global South have tried to develop economically by improving their agriculture and industry. They have also built schools to increase **literacy.**

To pay for development, many countries in the global South procured large loans from industrialized nations. For centuries, most people in the global South had lived and worked in **traditional economies.** After gaining independence from European colonists, some of these countries experimented with government-led command economies. However, when these countries had trouble paying off their loans, lenders from the global North required many of them to change to market economies. Now many developing nations depend on the global North for investment and exports.

Beginning in the 1950s, improved seeds, pesticides, and mechanical equipment led to a **Green Revolution** in many parts of the developing world. This increased agricultural production, feeding many more people. It also benefited large landowners at the expense of small farmers. These farmers sold their land and moved to cities.

The global South still faces many challenges. Some developing nations produce only one export product. If prices for that product drop, their economies suffer. Also, the population in many of these countries has grown rapidly. Many people are caught in a cycle of poverty. When families are forced to move to cities, they often find only low-paying jobs. As a result, many children must work to help support their families. With so many moving to cities, many people are forced to live in crowded and dangerous **shantytowns.**

Economic development has brought great changes to the developing world. In many countries, women have greater equality. However, some religious **fundamentalists** oppose these changes and have called for a return to the basic values of their faiths.

Review Questions

1. What happened when nations in the global South had trouble repaying their loans?

_____

_____

2. What problems do people in the developing world often face when they move to cities?

_____

_____

READING CHECK

What is development?

_____

_____

_____

VOCABULARY STRATEGY

What does the word *procured* mean in the underlined sentence? Notice that *procured* refers to loans. Use this clue to help you figure out the meaning of the word *procured*.

READING SKILL

Identify Supporting Details
Record details that support this statement: "The global South faces many challenges."

_____

_____

_____

Focus Question: What challenges have African nations faced in their effort to develop their economies?

As you read this section in your textbook, complete the concept web below to record the main ideas about challenges faced by African nations, and details that support those main ideas.

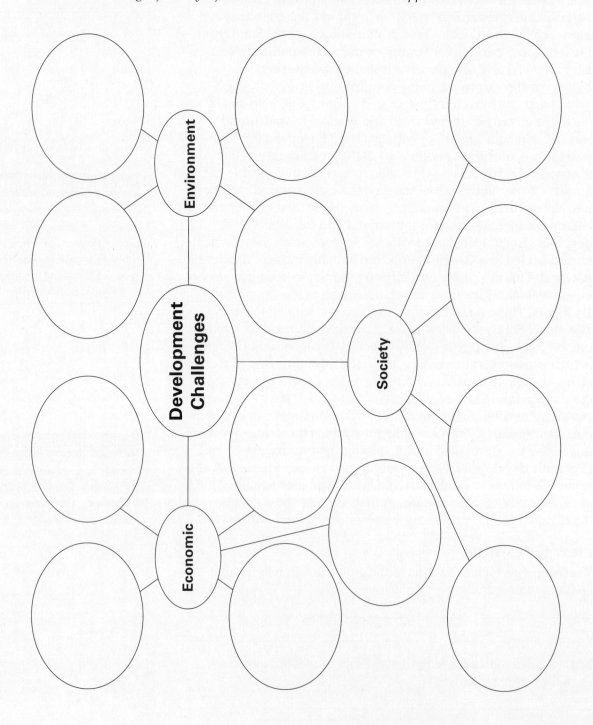

CHAPTER 21 SECTION 2

Section Summary
AFRICA SEEKS A BETTER FUTURE

After World War II, African nations had little capital to invest, so they had to make difficult economic choices. Some nations chose **socialism,** a system in which the government controls parts of the economy. The leaders of these governments hoped to end foreign influence in their countries and to close the gap between the rich and the poor. However, socialism sometimes led to large, inefficient bureaucracies. Other nations relied on capitalism, or market economies. These economies were often more efficient, but foreign owners of businesses took profits out of the country. Some governments tried to fund development by growing crops for export, rather than food crops. However, this forced them to import food to replace the food crops. <u>Governments then had to subsidize part of the cost of importing food from overseas.</u>

African nations faced many obstacles to development. Droughts led to famine in parts of Africa. This was especially true in the Sahel, where overgrazing and farming led to **desertification.** People in African nations also faced the devastating disease AIDS. Since the 1980s, millions of children in Africa have been orphaned by AIDS. **Urbanization** has also created problems in Africa. This shift from rural areas to cities has meant hardship for many and has weakened traditional cultures and ethnic ties. However, in West Africa, the growth of urban markets has increased opportunities for women.

Another concern in Africa is environmental threats. Many of Africa's animal habitats have been destroyed, causing many animals to become **endangered species.** Other animal species are being killed for their tusks or fur. One environmental activist, **Wangari Maathai,** has fought back by starting the Green Belt Movement. This organization promotes reforestation. It also helps local women with projects of **sustainable development** that aim to provide lasting benefits for future generations.

A close look at Tanzania reveals the problems that many African counties have faced. In the 1960s, the government embraced "African socialism." However, attempts to build on African traditions of cooperation failed to increase agricultural production. In 1985, new leaders introduced economic reforms. However, Tanzania remains poor and has had to rely on foreign loans to avoid economic crisis.

Review Questions

1. Why did some African nations choose socialism?

_____

_____

2. Why are many animal species in Africa endangered?

_____

_____

READING CHECK

What is urbanization?

_____

_____

_____

VOCABULARY STRATEGY

What does the word *subsidize* mean in the underlined sentence? *Subsidize* comes from a Latin word that means "aid" or "support." Use this clue to help you figure out the meaning of the word *subsidize*.

READING SKILL

Identify Main Ideas What is the main idea of this Summary?

_____

_____

_____

CHAPTER 21 SECTION 3 — Note Taking Study Guide

CHINA AND INDIA: TWO GIANTS OF ASIA

Focus Question: How do China and India compare in building strong economies and democratic governments?

As you read this section in your textbook, complete the table below to record the main ideas about reform and change in China and India.

Reform and Change in China and India

Type	China	India
Economic	• Free market • • • • • •	• • • • •
Political	• • •	• • •

CHAPTER 21 SECTION 3 — Section Summary
CHINA AND INDIA: TWO GIANTS OF ASIA

After Mao Zedong died, moderate leaders took control of China. **Deng Xiaoping** began a program called the Four Modernizations, which allowed some features of a free-market economy. Some private ownership of property was permitted, and entrepreneurs could set up businesses. Farmers were allowed to sell surplus produce and keep the profits. Foreign investment was also welcomed. These reforms brought a surge of economic growth, although a gap developed between poor farmers and wealthy city dwellers. After 30 years of reforms, China's economic output quadrupled.

Despite these economic reforms, however, Communist leaders refused to allow more political freedom. Demonstrators seeking democratic reforms occupied **Tiananmen Square** in Beijing in May 1989. When the demonstrators refused to disperse, the government sent in troops and tanks. Thousands were killed or wounded.

China continues to face many challenges. Its population is the largest in the world. The government started the **one-child policy** to prevent population growth from hurting economic development. Population growth slowed. Many rural workers have moved to cities, but they often live in poverty there. Pollution and HIV/AIDS are also problems. Critics of the government are jailed, and human rights abuses continue.

By contrast, India has a democratic government. After gaining independence, India's government adopted a socialist model, but development was uneven. The Green Revolution in the 1960s improved crop output, but most farmers continued to use traditional methods. Since the 1980s, India has shifted to a free-market system. Despite setbacks, it has developed more industry and technology.

Despite these improvements, India's population growth has hurt efforts to improve living conditions. The Indian government backed family planning, but it had limited success. More than one-third of Indians live below the poverty line. Many rural families moved to overcrowded cities like **Kolkata** and **Mumbai.** To help the urban poor, **Mother Teresa** founded the Missionaries of Charity.

Changes in India have brought improvements for India's lowest social castes and women. India's constitution bans discrimination against **dalits**, people in the lowest caste, but prejudice persists. The constitution also grants equal rights to women.

Review Questions

1. What impact have economic reforms had in China?

_____

_____

2. Name two groups that have benefited from changes in India.

_____

_____

READING CHECK

Which country, India or China, has had more success in limiting population growth?

_____

_____

_____

VOCABULARY STRATEGY

What does the word *disperse* mean in the underlined sentence? Notice that demonstrators occupied, or gathered in, Tiananmen Square and then refused to *disperse.* Use this clue to help you figure out the meaning of the word *disperse.*

READING SKILL

Identify Main Ideas In your own words, write the main idea of the first paragraph of this Summary.

_____

_____

_____

CHAPTER 21 SECTION 4

Note Taking Study Guide

LATIN AMERICA BUILDS DEMOCRACY

Focus Question: What challenges have Latin American nations faced in recent decades in their struggle for democracy and prosperity?

As you read this section in your textbook, complete this outline to identify the main ideas and supporting details about challenges faced by Latin American nations.

I. Economic and Social Forces

    A. Society

        1. _____

        2. _____

        3. _____

        4. _____

    B. _____

        1. _____

        2. _____

        3. _____

        4. _____

II. _____

    A. _____

        1. _____

        2. _____

        3. _____

    B. _____

        1. _____

        2. _____

    C. _____

        1. _____

        2. _____

        3. _____

        4. _____

        5. _____

        6. _____

        7. _____

(Outline continues on the next page.)

(Continued from page 220)

D. _____
    1. _____
    2. _____
E. _____
    1. _____
    2. _____
III. _____
    A. _____
        1. _____
        2. _____
    B. _____
        1. _____
        2. _____
        3. _____
        4. _____
        5. _____

CHAPTER 21 SECTION 4

Section Summary

LATIN AMERICA BUILDS DEMOCRACY

In the 1950s and 1960s, many governments in Latin America encouraged industries to manufacture goods that had previously been imported. This is called **import substitution.** More recently, government policies have focused on producing goods for export. Governments have also tried to open more land to farming, but much of the best land belongs to large **agribusinesses.** In many countries, a few people control the land and businesses, and wealth is distributed unevenly. Another problem is population growth, which has contributed to poverty. Many religious leaders have worked for justice and an end to poverty in a movement known as **liberation theology.**

Because of poverty and inequality, democracy has been difficult to achieve in Latin America. Between the 1950s and 1970s, military leaders seized power in Argentina, Brazil, Chile, and other countries. From the 1960s to the 1990s, civil wars shook parts of Central America. In Guatemala, the military targeted the **indigenous** population and slaughtered thousands of Native Americans.

The United States has had a powerful influence in Latin America. It has dominated the **Organization of American States (OAS).** During the Cold War, the United States backed dictators who were anti-communist. When socialist rebels called **Sandinistas** came to power in Nicaragua, the United States supported the **contras,** guerrillas who fought the Sandinistas. The United States has also pressed Latin American governments to help stop the drug trade. Many Latin Americans alleged that the problem was not in Latin America but was based on the demand for drugs in the United States.

By the 1990s, democratic reforms led to free elections in many countries. In Mexico, the Institutional Revolutionary Party (PRI) had dominated the government since the 1920s. However, in 2000, an opposition candidate was elected president. Argentina experienced years of political upheavals beginning in the 1930s. **Juan Perón,** Argentina's president from 1946 to 1955, enjoyed great support from workers but was ousted in a military coup. The military seized control again in 1976 and murdered or kidnapped thousands. Mothers whose sons and daughters were missing protested and became known as the **Mothers of the Plaza de Mayo.** By 1983, the military was forced to allow elections.

Review Questions

1. Why was democracy difficult to achieve in Latin America?

_____

_____

2. Why did the United States support dictators in Latin America during the Cold War?

_____

_____

Name_____ Class_____ Date_____

Focus Question: How did the end of the Cold War affect industrialized nations and regions around the world?

As you read this section in your textbook, complete the chart below to compare and contrast developments in industrialized nations after the Cold War.

Asia	
•	• • • •

Russia/United States

Russia
• • • •

United States
• • • •

Europe

1991 — Germany is reunified.
• • • • • •

CHAPTER 22 SECTION 1 — Section Summary
INDUSTRIALIZED NATIONS AFTER THE COLD WAR

READING CHECK

Which four Pacific Rim countries are called the "Asian tigers"?

_____

_____

_____

VOCABULARY STRATEGY

What does the word *inflation* mean in the underlined sentence? Think about what happens when you *inflate* a tire. In this sentence, *inflation* refers to prices. If prices are *inflated*, would you expect them to be higher or lower? Use these clues to help you understand the meaning of *inflation*.

READING SKILL

Compare and Contrast Compare and contrast the U.S. economy in the early 1990s with the economy in the early 2000s.

_____

_____

_____

The beginning of a new global economy began with the end of the Cold War. The division between communist Eastern and democratic Western Europe crumbled. Business and travel became easier. At the same time, new challenges emerged, including a rise in unemployment and in immigration from the developing world. One exciting change was the reunification of Germany. However, East Germany's economy was weak and had to be modernized.

In the 1990s, the European Economic Community became the **European Union** (EU). The **euro** soon became the common currency for most of Western Europe. More than a dozen countries have joined the EU, including some Eastern European nations. The expanded EU allowed Europe to compete economically with the United States and Japan. However, older members of the EU worried that the weak economies of Eastern European nations might harm the EU.

After the breakup of the Soviet Union, Russia struggled to forge a market economy. Prices soared, and criminals flourished. In 1998, Russia **defaulted** on much of its foreign debt. High inflation and the collapse of the Russian currency forced banks and businesses to close. When **Vladimir Putin** became president in 2000, he promised to end corruption and strengthen Russia's economy. However, he also increased government power at the expense of civil liberties.

After the Cold War, the United States became the world's only superpower. It waged wars in Afghanistan and Iraq. An economic boom in the 1990s produced a budget **surplus** in the United States. Within a decade, however, slow economic growth and soaring military expenses led to huge budget **deficits.**

The **Pacific Rim** nations have become a rising force in the global economy. Following World War II, Japan became an economic powerhouse and dominated this region. However, by the 1990s, Japan's economy began to suffer, while China's economy boomed. Other powerhouses include the "Asian tigers"—Taiwan, Hong Kong, Singapore, and South Korea—which are known for their electronics exports. All of these economies suffered during the global recession that began in 2008.

Review Questions

1. When did the global economy begin to develop?

_____

_____

2. What economic challenges did Russia face after the breakup of the Soviet Union?

_____

_____

Focus Question: How is globalization affecting economies and societies around the world?

As you read this section in your textbook, use the Venn diagram to compare the effects of globalization on developed and developing nations.

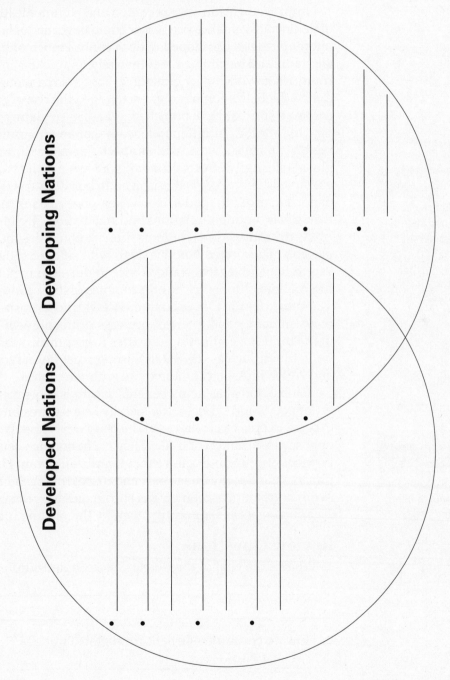

Name_____ Class_____ Date_____

READING CHECK

What is globalization?

_____

_____

_____

VOCABULARY STRATEGY

What does the word *assets* mean in the underlined sentence? Think about what it means if someone says that you are an *asset* to the team. Use this clue to help you figure out the meaning of *assets*.

READING SKILL

Compare and Contrast Compare and contrast the effect of borrowing capital on rich and poor nations.

_____

_____

_____

Globalization defines the post-Cold War world. It is the process by which national economies, politics, and cultures become integrated with those of other nations. One effect of globalization is economic **interdependence.** This means that countries depend on one another for goods, resources, knowledge, and labor.

Improvements in transportation and communication, the spread of democracy, and the rise of free trade have made the world more interdependent. Developed nations control much of the world's capital, trade, and technology. Yet they rely on workers in developing countries, to which they **outsource** jobs to save money or increase efficiency. Globalization has also encouraged the rise of **multinational corporations** that have branches and assets in many countries.

One effect of interdependence is that an economic crisis in one region can have a worldwide impact. For example, any change to the global oil supply affects economies all around the world. Another example is debt. Poor nations need to borrow capital from rich nations in order to modernize. When poor nations cannot repay their debts, both poor nations and rich nations are hurt.

Many international organizations and treaties make global trade possible. The United Nations deals with a broad range of issues. The World Bank gives loans and advice to developing nations. The International Monetary Fund promotes global economic growth. The **World Trade Organization (WTO)** tries to ensure that trade flows smoothly and freely. It opposes **protectionism**—the use of tariffs to protect a country's industries from competition. Regional trade **blocs,** such as the EU in Europe, NAFTA in North America, and APEC in Asia, promote trade within regions.

Global trade has many benefits. It brings consumers a greater variety of goods and services. It generally keeps prices lower. It also exposes people to new ideas and technology. However, some people oppose globalization of trade. They claim that rich countries exploit poor countries. Some believe that globalization hurts indigenous peoples by taking away their lands and disrupting their cultures. Others say that the emphasis on profits encourages too-rapid development. This endangers **sustainability,** thereby threatening future generations.

Review Questions

1. What is the goal of the World Trade Organization?

_____

_____

2. How do consumers benefit from global trade?

_____

_____

Focus Question: How do poverty, disease, and environmental challenges affect people around the world today?

As you read this section in your textbook, complete the chart below to compare aspects of globalization.

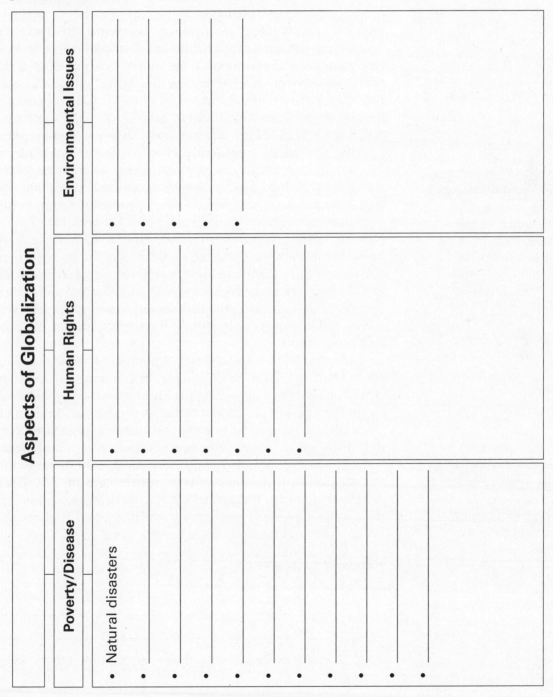

CHAPTER	Section Summary
22 SECTION 3	SOCIAL AND ENVIRONMENTAL CHALLENGES

READING CHECK

What is an epidemic?

_____

_____

_____

Poverty, disasters, and disease are still challenges today. The gap between rich and poor nations is growing. Half the world's population earns less than $2 a day. Poverty is a complex issue with many causes. Many poor nations owe billions in debt and have little money to spend to improve living conditions. Political upheavals, civil war, corruption and poor planning inhibit efforts to reduce poverty. Rapid population growth and urbanization also contribute to poverty.

Natural disasters cause death and destruction around the world. One example is the **tsunami** in the Indian Ocean in 2004. Other natural disasters include earthquakes, floods, avalanches, droughts, fires, hurricanes, and volcanic eruptions. Natural disasters can cause unsanitary conditions that lead to disease. Global travel makes it possible for diseases to spread quickly. When a disease spreads rapidly, it is called an **epidemic.** HIV/AIDS is an epidemic that has killed millions. Natural disasters can also cause **famine.** Wars and problems with food distribution also contribute to famine. Poverty, disasters, and wars have forced many people to become **refugees.**

VOCABULARY STRATEGY

What does the word *inhibit* mean in the underlined sentence? The words *help* and *aid* are antonyms of *inhibit.* Use what you know about these antonyms to help you understand the meaning of the word *inhibit.*

International agreements, such as the Universal Declaration of Human Rights and the Helsinki Accords, have tried to guarantee basic human rights around the world. However, human rights abuses continue. Women in both the developed and developing world often lack equal rights. Worldwide, children suffer terrible abuses. In some nations, they are forced to serve as soldiers or slaves. Indigenous people around the world also face discrimination and exploitation.

Industrialization and the world population explosion have caused damage to the environment. Strip mining, chemical pesticides and fertilizers, and oil spills are all environmental threats. Gases from power plants and factories produce **acid rain.** Pollution from nuclear power plants is another threat. Desertification and **deforestation** are major problems in certain parts of the world. Deforestation can lead to **erosion** and is a special threat to the rain forests. One hotly debated issue is **global warming.** Many scientists believe that Earth's temperature has risen because of gases released during the burning of fossil fuels. Others argue that global warming is due to natural fluctuations in Earth's climate.

READING SKILL

Compare Compare the two theories about global warming mentioned in the Summary.

_____

_____

_____

Review Questions

1. What are some causes of poverty?

_____

_____

2. What environmental problem is a special threat to the rain forests?

_____

_____

Note Taking Study Guide

SECURITY IN A DANGEROUS WORLD

Focus Question: What kinds of threats to national and global security do nations face today?

As you read this section in your textbook, complete the chart below to compare threats to global security.

Threats to Security	Nuclear weapons are unsecured in Soviet Union.					
	Nuclear Weapons					

CHAPTER 22 SECTION 4

Section Summary

SECURITY IN A DANGEROUS WORLD

READING CHECK

What is terrorism?

_____

_____

_____

VOCABULARY STRATEGY

What does the word *priority* mean in the underlined sentence? Notice the sentences that follow it. What did the United States do because security was a *priority?* Use this context clue to help you understand the meaning of the word *priority.*

READING SKILL

Compare and Contrast Compare and contrast information about nuclear weapons before and after the Nuclear Nonproliferation Treaty.

_____

_____

_____

During the Cold War, the United States and the Soviet Union built up arsenals of nuclear weapons. To ensure that nuclear weapons did not **proliferate,** or spread rapidly, many nations signed the Nuclear Nonproliferation Treaty (NPT) in 1968. However, the treaty does not guarantee that nuclear weapons will not be used. Some nations have not signed the treaty. Others are suspected of violating it. Stockpiles of nuclear weapons in the former Soviet Union are a special concern. This is because the Russian government has not had money to secure the weapons properly.

Recently, terrorist groups and "rogue states" have begun to use WMDs for their own purposes. **Terrorism** is the use of violence, especially against civilians, to achieve political goals. Terrorist groups use headline-grabbing tactics to draw attention to their demands. Regional terrorist groups, such as the Irish Republican Army (IRA), operated for decades. Increasingly, the Middle East has become a training ground and source for terrorism. Islamic fundamentalism motivates many of these groups. One important Islamic fundamentalist group is **al Qaeda,** whose leader is Osama bin Laden. Al Qaeda terrorists were responsible for the attacks on the United States on September 11, 2001.

In response to these attacks, the United States and other nations made fighting terrorism a priority. In 2001, Osama bin Laden and other al Qaeda leaders were living in **Afghanistan.** Afghanistan's government was controlled by the **Taliban,** an Islamic fundamentalist group. When the Taliban would not surrender the terrorists, the United States and its allies overthrew the Taliban and supported the creation of a new government. Because President Bush claimed that Iraq had WMDs, the United States later declared war on Iraq.

During the early 2000s, concerns grew that North Korea was developing nuclear weapons. In 2006, North Korea actually tested such a weapon. Meanwhile, Iran announced plans to develop nuclear power plants. The United States and other nations, however, believed that Iran aimed to build nuclear weapons, too. The United States and other countries worked to stop this nuclear proliferation.

Review Questions

1. Why are nuclear weapons in the former Soviet Union a special concern?

_____

_____

2. Why did the United States declare war on Afghanistan?

_____

_____

CHAPTER 22 SECTION 5

Note Taking Study Guide

ADVANCES IN SCIENCE AND TECHNOLOGY

Focus Question: How have advances in science and technology shaped the modern world?

As you read this section in your textbook, complete the chart below to compare the impacts of modern science and technology.

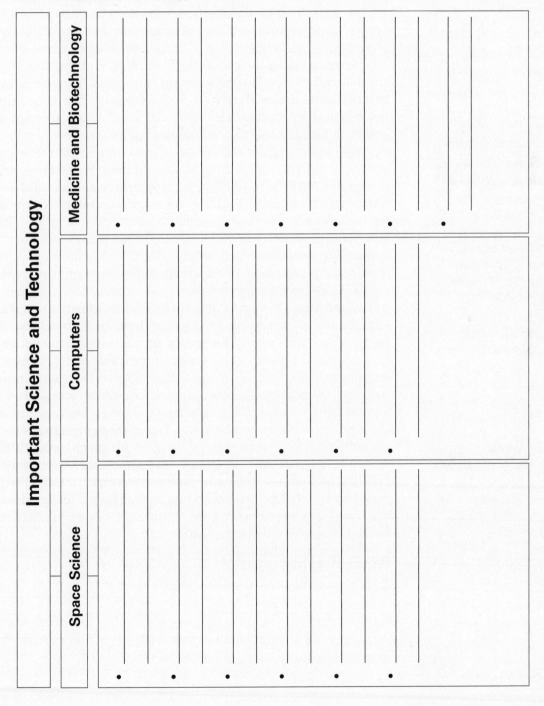

Name_____ Class_____ Date_____

READING CHECK

What is biotechnology?

_____

_____

_____

Since 1945, scientific research and technological developments have transformed human existence. One example is the exploration of space. During the Cold War, the United States and the Soviet Union competed in a "space race." This began in 1957 when the Soviet Union launched *Sputnik,* the first **artificial satellite.** By 1969, the United States had landed the first human on the moon. Both superpowers explored military uses of space and sent spy satellites to orbit Earth.

However, since the end of the Cold War, nations have worked in space together. For example, several countries are involved in the **International Space Station (ISS).** Thousands of artificial satellites belonging to many countries now orbit Earth. They are used for communication, observation, and navigation.

Another important technological development is the invention of the computer. It has led to the "Information Age." **Personal computers**, or **PCs**, have replaced typewriters and account books in homes and businesses. Factories now use computerized robots, and computers remotely control satellites and probes in space. The **Internet** links computer systems worldwide and allows people to communicate instantly around the globe. It also allows people to access vast storehouses of information that were unavailable before.

VOCABULARY STRATEGY

What does the word *manipulation* mean in the underlined sentence? It comes from the Latin word *manus,* meaning "hand." Use this word-origins clue to help you figure out the meaning of the word *manipulation.*

Other important developments have occurred in medicine and **biotechnology**—the application of biological research to industry, engineering, and technology. Vaccines have been developed that help prevent the spread of diseases. In the 1970s, surgeons learned to transplant human organs. **Lasers** have made many types of surgery safer and more precise. Computers and other technologies have helped doctors diagnose and treat diseases. The fields of genetics and genetic engineering have made dramatic advances. **Genetics** is the study of genes and heredity. <u>Genetic engineering is the manipulation of genetic material to produce specific results.</u> Genetic research has produced new drug therapies to fight human diseases and has created new strains of disease-resistant fruits and vegetables. Genetic cloning has many practical applications in raising livestock and in research. However, cloning raises ethical questions about the role of science in creating and changing life.

READING SKILL

Compare How have people benefited from advances in science and technology since the space race began?

_____

_____

_____

Review Questions

1. What are the three uses of artificial satellites?

_____

_____

2. Why is cloning controversial?

_____

_____

Concept Connector Journal

Belief Systems

 Essential Question: How do religions and belief systems help shape society?

I. WARM-UP

Throughout history, religions and belief systems have influenced how people act and what they value. A national survey conducted among 2,003 adults had the following findings about how Americans felt about the influence of religion in the United States.

Influence of Religion

	On American Life (%)	On American Government (%)
Increasing	34	42
Good thing	21	15
Bad thing	11	24
Decreasing	59	45
Good thing	6	8
Bad thing	50	36
No change	2	2
Don't know	5	7
NET: Want more*	71	51
NET: Want less**	17	32

* Increasing is good or decreasing is bad
** Increasing is bad or decreasing is good
Source: Pew Research Center for the People & the Press and the Pew Forum on Religion & Public Life, 2006

1. What generalization can you make about people's feelings about the influence of religion in the United States?

_____

_____

Concept Connector Journal

2. According to the U.S. Constitution, Congress cannot make laws establishing a religion or prohibiting the exercise of religion. List three ways this law affects you.

a. _____

_____

b. _____

_____

c. _____

_____

3. Indicate on the scale below whether you think religion or belief systems have had a major impact on American life and government.

Strongly ⟵————————————⟶ **Strongly**
Agree   **Disagree**

II. EXPLORATION

Whether or not you have been aware of it, religion and belief systems have influenced traditions and laws in the United States. As you complete the following journal entries, you will see that religion and belief systems have shaped societies throughout history.

1. Animism: How did ancient people's belief that gods inhabited nature affect rituals and the structure of ancient society?

Early drawings made in caves may have been part of religious ritual. People appealed

to many gods, such as river gods and sun gods. They built temples to gods. Ceremonies

required the full-time attention of priests, who had special training and knowledge.

_____

2. Early religions: Match the civilization in Column A with an impact of religion in Column B.

Column A		Column B
____D____	1. Sumer	A. Belief in teachings of Zoroaster helped unite the empire.
____A____	2. Persians	B. Prophets taught a strong code of ethics.
____C____	3. Egypt	C. Belief in afterlife led to elaborate burial procedures.
____B____	4. Israelites	D. Ziggurats were dedicated to the chief god or goddess.

Concept Connector Journal

3. WebQuest: Religion and Belief Systems How has what you have learned about religion in current societies affected your ideas about the impact of belief systems?

> **Transfer Your Knowledge**
> **For:** WebQuest **Web Code:** nbh-0308

_____

_____

_____

4. Egyptian and Indian Religions: Ancient Egyptians believed that the god Osiris would judge them after death. The evil would be condemned and the good would live forever in bliss. How did Hinduism and Buddhism shape expectations of right behavior?

Both religions stressed nonviolence and believed in karma (the actions of a person's

life that affect his or her fate in the next life), dharma (the religious and moral duties

of an individual), and a cycle of rebirth. Buddhists rejected the caste system and

offered the hope of nirvana (or union with the universe) regardless of birth.

5. Christianity: How did Christianity become influential in Western Civilization?

* In the first century A.D., Jesus begins teaching.
* After the death of Jesus, followers spread message to Jews of Judea.
* Paul spreads message to Greece and Asia Minor.
* Unity of Roman empire provides protection for missionaries.
* Edict of Milan in A.D. 313 ends persecution of Christians.
* In the 400s, Rome falls and Christianity becomes a central institution of Western civilization for 1000 years.

6. Byzantine Empire: How did religion influence the Byzantine Empire?

a. Great Schism: Eastern Orthodox Church separated from the Roman Catholic Church.

b. Crusades: Venetians gained control of Byzantine trade, draining the wealth from the empire.

c. Heritage: Byzantines blended Christian religious beliefs with Greek science, philosophy, arts, and literature.

Concept Connector Journal

7. Islam: How did the teachings of Islam appeal to conquered peoples?

<u>Early Umayyad caliphates did not attempt to convert Jews, Christians, and Zoroastrians.</u>
<u>Some people were attracted because Islam emphasized equality of all believers, regardless</u>
<u>or race, gender, class, or wealth.</u>

8. China: Confucianism is a belief system that supports the following values.

* Harmony results when people accept their place in society.
* Respect for one's parents is above all other duties.
* A ruler should rule by example, not by harsh laws.
* The superior man understands righteousness; the inferior man understands profit.

How did Confucianism affect China's response to the West and Western influence? How did China's choices affect its history? *(Chapter 12, Section 5)*

_____
_____
_____
_____
_____

III. ESSAY

Bring together what you have read in your textbook with the information you have gathered online about this concept. **On a separate sheet of paper, answer the essential question: How do religions and belief systems affect society?**

Concept Connector Journal

Conflict

 Essential Question: When, if ever, should people go to war?

I. WARM-UP

Conflict is a part of everyone's life. Usually, conflicts are resolved in a way acceptable to all parties; sometimes conflicts escalate into serious problems.

1. Think of a conflict that you have recently had with someone—a friend, sibling, parent, or even an organization. Write what the conflict was about on the line below, and then fill in the speech balloons to show the opposing points of view.

_____

_____

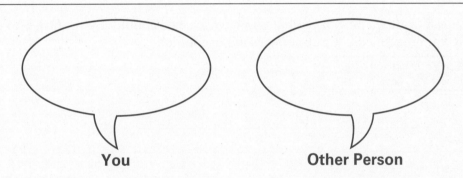

You   **Other Person**

2. What does it take to resolve a conflict?

_____

_____

_____

II. EXPLORATION

Too often throughout history, conflict has led to violence or war. As you complete the following journal entries, you will see how conflict has resulted in turning points for people and nations.

1. The Persian War: Why did Alexander want to conquer Persia?

He was ambitious and he wanted to extend his empire. He dreamed of conquering all of

Asia.

_____

Concept Connector Journal

2. Roman Imperialism: How did imperialism lead to conflict in the Roman Republic?

a. Incredible riches from trade routes poured into Rome and created <u>a new class of people</u> who bought up <u>huge farming estates</u>.

b. As Romans captured more and more land, they forced <u>war prisoners to work as slaves on the latifunda</u>.

c. Landless farmers flocked to Rome where they joined unemployed workers and began to <u>riot</u>.

d. Two tribunes who favored reform angered the senate and were <u>killed in street violence instigated by senators</u>.

e. Popular political leaders and senators disagreed over reform measure for the poor because the senators saw the reforms as a threat to their <u>political power</u>.

3. WebQuest: Conflict How has what you have learned about why countries do or do not go to war broadened your understanding of conflict?

> **Transfer Your Knowledge**
> **For:** WebQuest **Web Code:** nbh-0808

_____

_____

_____

_____

_____

4. Crusades: In the late 1000s, the Byzantine emperor asked Pope Urban II for Christian knights to help him fight the Seljuk Turks, who were Muslims. The pope called for a crusade to free the Holy Land from the Seljuk Turks.

a. Pilgrims were prevented from going to the Holy Land. _____

b. The Seljuk Turks had overrun Byzantium, threatening the Byzantine Empire. _____

c. Urban hoped to increase his power in Europe and to heal the schism between the

Roman and Byzantine churches. _____

Concept Connector Journal

5. European Exploration: Complete the web to identify factors that would lead to conflict between two European nations in the 1600s and 1700s. *(Chapter 2, Section 3)*

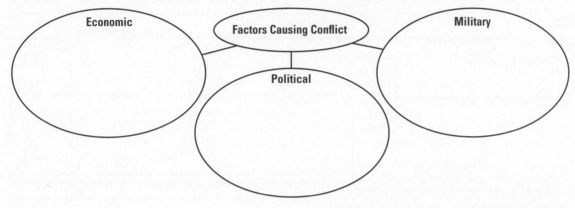

6. Enlightenment Ideas: Read the Enlightenment ideas below. Then explain why these ideas might cause conflict between colonists and their rulers. *(Chapter 5, Section 1)*

- Government's power comes from the people.
- People have natural rights to life, liberty, and property.

_____

_____

_____

_____

_____

7. Opposing Ideologies: Fill in the chart to show what Europeans with different ideologies wanted in the early 1800s. *(Chapter 8, Section 1)*

Conservatives	Liberals	Metternich
•	•	•
•	•	•
•	•	•

Concept Connector Journal

8. European Revolutionaries: Complete the cause-and-effect charts to show the immediate results of the revolutions of 1830 and 1848 in France. *(Chapter 8, Section 2)*

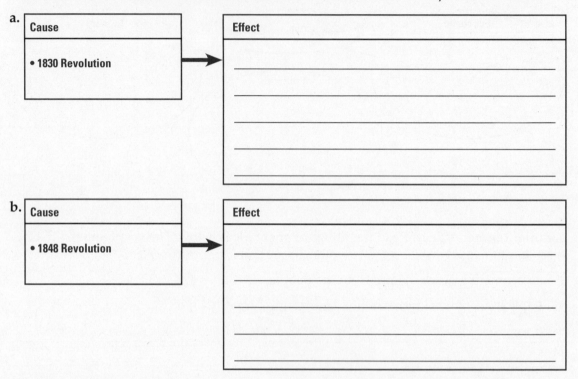

9. Nationalism: Why was nationalism a factor in Austria's declaration of war on Serbia in 1914? *(Chapter 14, Section 1)*

_____

_____

_____

10. World War II: The end of World War II was followed by the establishment of the United Nations as a peacekeeping organization. However, new conflicts soon arose among the former allies of the war. Why were the United States and the Soviet Union on opposing sides during the Cold War? *(Chapter 17, Section 5)*

_____

_____

_____

Concept Connector Journal

11. Religious Conflict: Complete the chart below to show examples of places in the world where religious differences have caused conflict. *(Chapter 20, Sections 1, 2, and 3)*

Country or Region	Religions Involved

III. ESSAY

Bring together what you have read in your textbook with the information you have gathered online about this concept. **On a separate sheet of paper, answer the essential question: When, if ever, should people go to war?**

Concept Connector Journal

Cooperation

Essential Question: With whom should we cooperate and why?

I. WARM-UP

Cooperation is working together for a common benefit. You have the opportunity to cooperate with others in many aspects of your life. Consider how you do or don't do this and the outcome.

1. Complete the table below.

Place	Action	Cost/Benefits
Home		
School		
Team/community		

2. Suppose that you are a highly skilled ball player who knows that a college scout is in the stands. Should you make every effort to be the star of the game, scoring as many points as you can, or should you make every effort to be a "team player" and set up shots for others to execute? Which approach would you take, and why?

_____

_____

_____

_____

II. EXPLORATION

Cooperation can yield great benefits or, at times, exact great costs. As you complete the following journal entries you will see how cooperation has played a role in the outcome of world events.

1. Iroquois League: Why did competing Iroquois groups create the Iroquois League?

In order to keep peace among themselves, five Iroquois nations met together in

councils to deal with common issues.

_____

Name _____ Class _____ Date _____

Concept Connector Journal

2. Defeat of the Aztecs: What were the short-term and long-term effects of the cooperation of Aztec enemies with the Spanish conquistador, Cortes? Complete the cause and effect chart below. *(Chapter 3, Section 1)*

Causes	Events	Effects
•	• Cortes joins with Aztec enemies	•
•		
•	• Cortes overthrows Moctezuma	•

3. American Revolution, 1776: How did cooperation influence the outcome of the American Revolution? *(Chapter 5, Section 3)*

_____

_____

_____

4. Coalition Against Napoleon: Sometimes a state becomes powerful and tries to impose its way on others. At some point, other states join together in opposition. Fill in the blanks to show how Napoleon lost power. *(Chapter 6, Section 4)*

In ancient times, the Athenians sought to dominate their world: Athens creates Delian League ⟶ Establishes Athenian Empire by force ⟶ Sparta creates Peloponnesian League ⟶ Athenians defeated in Peloponnesian War ⟶ Athens declines.

In the early 1800s, Napoleon tried to dominate the world: Napoleon gains

control of France ⟶ _____

_____ ⟶ _____

_____ ⟶ Napoleon is exiled.

5. The Opening of Japan: Was the Japanese decision to open its ports to the United States in 1854 a wise decision? Why or why not? *(Chapter 13, Section 1)*

_____

_____

_____

Name _____ Class _____ Date _____

Concept Connector Journal

Cooperation (continued)

6. Political Alliances: Sometimes groups of people, or factions, form coalitions to achieve their goals. Describe what each of the following did and the outcome. *(Chapter 11)*

a. Whigs and Tories in Great Britain, 1830 (reforming Parliament)

_____

_____

b. Liberals and republicans in France, 1890s (Dreyfus Affair)

_____

_____

c. Confederate states, United States, 1861 (slavery)

_____

_____

d. Farmers and city workers, United States, 1890s (reform)

_____

_____

7. Competing Alliances: Complete the web of alliances to show how Europe was enmeshed in entangling alliances. *(Chapter 13, Section 1)*

Concept Connector Journal

8. Munich Pact: How would you judge Neville Chamberlain's decision to cooperate with Adolph Hitler at the Munich Conference? Why? *(Chapter 17, Section 1)*

_____

_____

_____

9. United Nations: With the failure of the League of Nations to prevent war, nations looked for a better way to work together. Fill in the chart below. *(Chapter 17, Section 5)*

Organization/Membership	Terms of Agreement
League of Nations—40 nations, but not including the United States	• Negotiate disputes • Take common action against aggressors • No power over nonmembers
United Nations, including the United States	• •

10. European Community: In 1993, the European Union was established. In 2002, twelve European Union nations replaced their individual currencies with the euro. How did the European Community set the stage for this increased economic cooperation? *(Chapter 18, Section 2)*

_____

_____

_____

11. WebQuest: Cooperation How did the WebQuest affect your ideas about when and when not to cooperate? *(Chapter 18, Section 1)*

> **Transfer Your Knowledge**
> **For:** WebQuest **Web Code:** nbh-3008

_____

_____

_____

Concept Connector Journal

12. NGOs: Why is assistance from nongovernment agencies important for providing help around the world? *(Chapter 22, Section 2)*

_____

_____

_____

III. ESSAY

Bring together what you have read in your textbook with the information you have gathered online about this concept. **On a separate sheet of paper, answer the essential question: With whom should we cooperate and why?**

Concept Connector Journal

Cultural Diffusion

 Essential Question: How does cultural diffusion occur?

I. WARM-UP

Today, thanks to immigrants from all over the world, Americans enjoy foods from many cultures. This is just one example of cultural diffusion in the United States.

1. What are some other ways that cultural diffusion affects Americans? Write an example for each category on the web below.

2. How has cultural diffusion enriched your life?

_____

_____

II. EXPLORATION

Cultural diffusion began in ancient times when people first began trading and migrating. As you complete the following journal entries, you will see how various aspects of cultures have spread.

1. Alphabet: What role did trade play in the Greek alphabet?

Traders from Greece returned to their homeland from Phoenicia with new ideas such as

the Phoenician alphabet. As the Greeks expanded overseas, Greek settlers and traders

carried their ideas and their culture.

2. Spread of Roman Culture: The graphic organizer below shows the traditions that produced the Greco-Roman civilization.

Concept Connector Journal

3. Byzantine Empire: See the chart below to compare how the Byzantines spread their culture with how the Romans spread theirs.

	Roman Culture	Byzantine Culture
a. Language and Learning	Used Latin in literature	Preserved Roman learning, developed own, used Greek language
b. Religion	Diverse religions, then rise of Christianity with pope as head	Byzantine Church with emperor as patriarch or head
c. Art and Architecture	Sculpture, frescoes, mosaics, columns, arches, domed roof, aqueducts	Mosaics, icons, improved Roman arches
d. Political Ideas	Civil law, law of the nations	Justinian's Code based on Roman law
e. Where Culture Spread	Throughout Mediterranean, Northern Africa, Europe, Asia Minor	Mediterranean and Black Seas, Balkans, Middle East, and Northern Africa
f. How Culture Spread	Conquest, trade	Trade routes, migration

4. Spread of Islam: List at least four reasons that help explain how Islam spread.

a. A shared faith that united many formerly competing Arab tribes

b. Conquests of weakened empires like the Persians and Byzantines

c. Conversions of people drawn to the message of Islam and its emphasis, in principle, on equality

d. Tolerance of other beliefs, such as those of Jews, Christians, and Zoroastrians

5. WebQuest: Cultural Diffusion How has what you have learned about the movement of goods and ideas expanded your understanding of cultural diffusion?

> **Transfer Your Knowledge**
> For: WebQuest **Web Code:** nbh-1108

_____

_____

Concept Connector Journal

6. Mongols: In what ways did Kublai Khan try to maintain Mongol identity after he defeated China?

In addition to keeping the Chinese from serving in the military, Kublai Khan reserved the highest government positions for Mongols and had Arab architects design his palace.

7. a. What ideas of the Abbasid dynasty (750–850) and the Renaissance helped make these periods golden ages? *(Chapter 1, Section 1)*

_____

_____

_____

b. How were these ideas spread?

_____

_____

_____

8. Roots of Democracy: Complete the graphic organizer to show four ideas of the Enlightenment that were the roots of the United States Constitution. *(Chapter 5, Sections 1 and 3)*

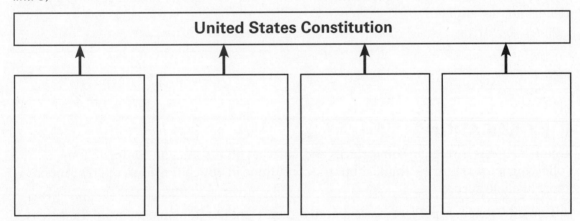

United States Constitution

III. ESSAY

Bring together what you have read in your textbook with the information you have gathered online about this concept. **On a separate sheet of paper, answer the essential question: How does cultural diffusion occur?**

Concept Connector Journal

Democracy

 Essential Question: Under what conditions is democracy most likely to succeed?

I. WARM-UP

As you know, nations have different forms of government. The government of the United States is a democracy. The government gets its power from the people.

1. What does living in a democracy mean to you? Write your ideas on the web below.

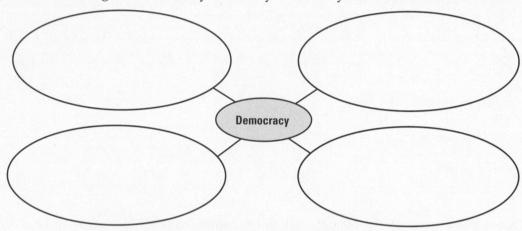

Democracy

2. Why do you think the U.S. government has served as a model for nations seeking a democratic government?

_____

_____

_____

II. EXPLORATION

Democracy has thrived in some places and failed in others. As you complete the following journal entries, think about the conditions in which this form of government is most likely to succeed.

1. Roman Citizenship: Plebeians expanded their rights as Roman citizens in the early days of the Roman Republic.

a. They gained the right to elect their own officials. _____

b. They forced the senate to choose plebeians as consuls. _____

c. They got Roman laws written down, making it possible for plebeians to appeal

judgments of patrician judges. _____

Concept Connector Journal

2. Edward I: How did King Edward I give the common people of England a voice in government, and how did that affect the monarchy?

In 1295, King Edward called for inclusion of representatives of the common people in Parliament. Since Parliament had to approve his spending, this step limited the power of the monarchy. Later, this Parliament became known as the Model Parliament because it set up the framework of England's legislature.

3. English Bill of Rights: List two ways that the English Bill of Rights, laws passed by Parliament in 1629, increased the rights of English subjects. List two ways that this document lessened the power of the monarch. *(Chapter 4, Section 3)*

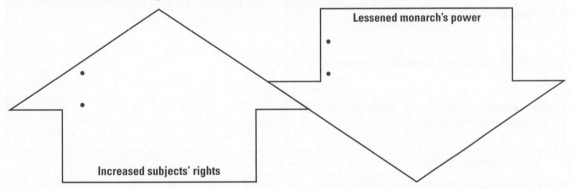

Lessened monarch's power
•
•

Increased subjects' rights

4. American Declaration of Independence: During the 1600s, government changed in England through inheritance, civil war, and the Glorious Revolution. By the end of the century, Britain had a constitutional government, but it was still an oligarchy, ruled by the few. The government established by the Americans went beyond its British roots. On what principles expressed in the Declaration of Independence was American constitutional government based? *(Chapter 5, Section 3)*

_____

_____

_____

_____

5. Napoleon: At the end of the French Revolution, Napoleon Bonaparte moved from victorious general to powerful political leader. *(Chapter 6, Section 4)*

a. How did he weaken democratic gains in France?

_____

_____

_____

Concept Connector Journal

b. How did he strengthen democracy in France?

_____

_____

_____

6. Simón Bolivar: Complete the chart to compare the outcome of the American Revolution with those in Latin America. Use these points of comparison: social classes, constitutions, and cooperation between colonies. *(Chapter 8, Section 3)*

American Revolution	Latin American Revolutions
• Embraced the ideas of liberty and equality	•
• Constitution called for a democratic government.	•
• Worked together to form federal government made up of states with own governments	•

7. Democratic Reforms: Identify some of the democratic reforms that Britain, France, and the United States achieved during the 1800s. *(Chapter 11, Sections 1–4)*

Britain	France	United States
•	•	•
•	•	•
•	•	•

Concept Connector Journal

8. Democracy in India: Complete the sentences in the flowchart to show how Gandhi's protests led to a democratic movement in India. *(Chapter 15, Section 3)*

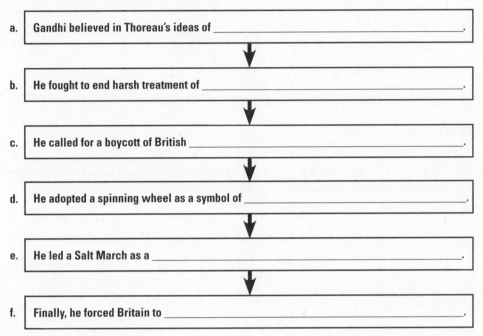

a. Gandhi believed in Thoreau's ideas of _____.

b. He fought to end harsh treatment of _____.

c. He called for a boycott of British _____.

d. He adopted a spinning wheel as a symbol of _____.

e. He led a Salt March as a _____.

f. Finally, he forced Britain to _____.

9. Internment of Japanese Americans: Are actions by a democratic government that limit the individual rights of citizens ever justified? Show where you stand on this issue by checking a box on the continuum. Then explain your reasons. *(Chapter 17, Section 3)*

Always Justified ☐ ☐ ☐ ☐ ☐ Never Justified

_____

_____

_____

10. WebQuest: Democracy How has what you have learned about democratic countries expanded your understanding of why democracy succeeds or fails?

> **Transfer Your Knowledge**
> **For:** WebQuest **Web Code:** nbh-3308

_____

_____

_____

Concept Connector Journal

11. Communications and Democracy: Make a prediction about how advances in communication might increase democracy throughout the world. *(Chapter 24)*

_____

_____

_____

_____

III. ESSAY

Bring together what you have read in your textbook with the information you have gathered online about this concept. **On a separate sheet of paper, answer the essential question: Under what conditions are democracies most likely to succeed?**

Concept Connector Journal

Dictatorship

 Essential Question: Why do people sometimes support dictators?

I. WARM-UP

How do governments remain in power? President Ronald Reagan offered his view.

> *Someone once said that every form of government has one characteristic peculiar to it and if that characteristic is lost, the government will fall. In a monarchy, it is affection and respect for the royal family. If that is lost the monarch is lost. In a dictatorship, it is fear. If the people stop fearing the dictator he'll lose power. In a representative government such as ours, it is virtue. If virtue goes, the government fails.* —Ronald Reagan

How would you define *dictatorship*? Why might fear be a key part of the success of a dictatorship?

_____

_____

_____

II. EXPLORATION

During times of turmoil and great change, people often turn to powerful leaders to solve problems. As you complete the following journal entries, you will see how dictators have risen and why people sometimes support dictatorships.

1. Reasons for Dictatorships: What circumstances gave rise to dictators in Europe after World War I? Complete the web below. (*Chapter 16, Section 2*)

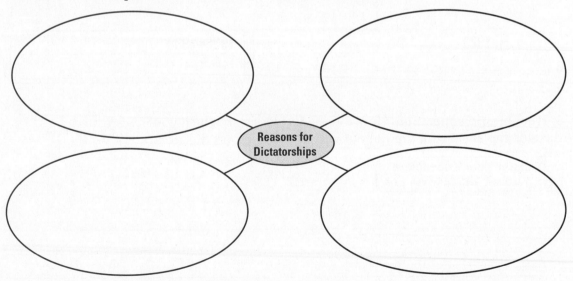

Concept Connector Journal

2. Italy and Russia: A totalitarian state is a form of government in which a one-party dictatorship tries to regulate all aspects of the lives of its citizens.

a. Complete this timeline to show the steps in the rise to power of Benito Mussolini.

Rise of Mussolini

b. Complete this timeline to show the steps in the rise to power of Joseph Stalin.

Rise of Stalin

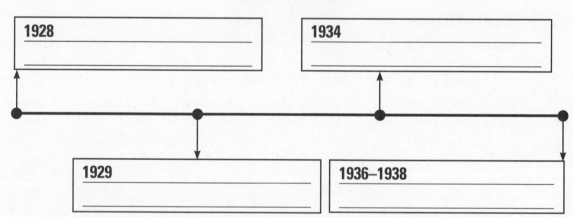

3. WebQuest: Cooperation How did the WebQuest in which you investigated dictatorship affect your view about why people support dictators?

> **Transfer Your Knowledge**
> **For:** WebQuest **Web Code:** nbh-2808

_____

_____

_____

Concept Connector Journal

4. Cultural Revolution: Complete the chart below to show the impact of aspects of Mao Zedong's Cultural Revolution on Chinese society. *(Chapter 18, Section 3)*

Impact of Cultural Revolution on Chinese Society	
Red Guards	
Propaganda	
Forced labor camps	
Civil war	

Did Mao's Cultural Revolution strengthen or weaken his control over China? Explain.

_____

_____

_____

5. Africa: a. Make generalizations about how one-party rule affected each of the following elements after African nations gained independence. *(Chapter 19, Section 3)*

- Political systems _____

_____

- Economies _____

_____

- Civil wars _____

_____

- Regional conflict _____

_____

b. Despite conflicts and divisions, why do you think people in the new African nations often supported dictators?

_____

_____

Concept Connector Journal

6. Iraq: a. Describe the outcome of these events in Iraq during the rule of Saddam Hussein. *(Chapter 20, Section 3)*

• Saddam Hussein begins war with Iran. _____

_____

• Iraq invades neighboring Kuwait. _____

_____

• Saddam Hussein crushes revolts by minorities. _____

_____

• UN imposes economic sanctions on Iraq. _____

_____

• UN coalition forces invade Iraq. _____

_____

b. Given the outcome of events under Saddam Hussein's rule, why did he keep power so long?

_____

_____

7. Latin America: Why would the following issues lead the United States to support dictatorships or repressive governments in Latin America? Fill in the chart. *(Chapter 21, Section 4)*

Issues	Reasons for U.S. Support
Cold war	
Containment policy	
Economy	

III. ESSAY

Bring together what you have read in your textbook with the information you have gathered online about this concept. **On a separate sheet of paper, answer the essential question: Why do people sometimes support dictatorships?**

Concept Connector Journal

Economic Systems

? **Essential Question:** How should resources and wealth be distributed?

I. WARM-UP

An economic system is the method used by a society to produce and distribute goods and services. As trade and industrialization become more complex, societies develop economic systems to meet their needs.

1. Suppose you and your classmates are holding a bake sale in the school lobby to raise money for a class trip. In a market economy, you need to consider certain elements when you price the goods you have made. On the chart below, write a question you might ask to help you decide on a price.

Economic Element	My Question
Supply and Demand	a.
Competition	b.
Self-Interest	c.

2. Suppose you have unsold items at the end of the sale. Would you lower the price or give away the leftover goods? Why?

_____

_____

_____

II. EXPLORATION

An economic system reflects how a society chooses to use its resources to meet the needs and wants of its people. As you complete the following journal entries, you will see how economic systems are linked to history.

1. Mercantilism and Manorialism: In the Middle Ages, under the feudal system, wealth was based on how much land a noble owned and how many peasants provided labor to work the land. Who gained in wealth after the rise of mercantilism? What was the source of this wealth? (*Chapter 3, Section 5*)

_____

_____

Concept Connector Journal

2. Middle Ages and Industrial Revolution: Complete the web to show how labor unions that arose during the Industrial Revolution played a similar role to the guilds that arose during the Middle Ages trade revival. *(Chapter 9, Section 2)*

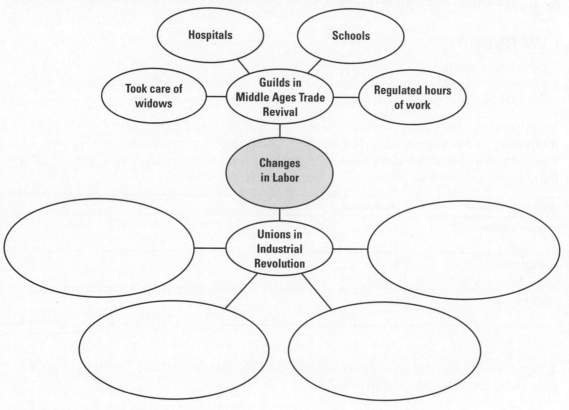

3. WebQuest: Economic Systems How has what you have learned as you completed your WebQuest affected your view about how economic systems differ?

> **Transfer Your Knowledge**
> **For:** WebQuest **Web Code:** nbh-1908

_____

_____

_____

_____

4. Market Economy: List three key elements of a market economy. *(Chapter 7, Section 4)*

a. _____

b. _____

c. _____

Concept Connector Journal

5. Centrally Planned Economy: Who makes the key economic decisions in a centrally planned economy? What are some drawbacks to this kind of economy? *(Chapter 7, Section 4)*

_____

_____

_____

_____

6. Mixed Economy: What is the goal of a mixed economy? *(Chapter 7, Section 4)*

_____

_____

7. Capitalism and Socialism: Write a statement in the chart to compare how wealth is attained and distributed in capitalism and socialism. *(Chapter 7, Section 4)*

Capitalism	Socialism

8. Globalization: Give an example of how globalization links the rich and poor nations of the world. *(Chapter 22, Section 2)*

_____

_____

_____

III. ESSAY

Bring together what you have read in your textbook with the information you have gathered online about this concept. **On a separate sheet of paper, answer the essential question: How should resources and wealth be distributed?**

Concept Connector Journal

Empire

 Essential Question: How does a state gain or lose power over others?

I. WARM-UP

1. Power can be defined as the possession of control, authority, or influence over others. In the first web below, indicate whom you have power over. In the second web, indicate who has power over you.

2. How did you get power over others? How have others gained power over you?

_____

_____

II. EXPLORATION

Throughout history, empires have played a critical role. As you complete the following journal entries, you will see how these empires have gained and lost power.

1. Darius I: How did the Persian emperor Darius I unite his vast empire through his policies in the following areas?

a. established a bureaucracy that followed set rules, divided empire into provinces ruled by a governor, set up a single code of laws

_____

b. respected customs of diverse people in the empire, new empire-wide religious belief

_____

c. built hundreds of roads for transportation and communication

_____

d. common weights and measures, use of single Persian coinage

_____

e. Greeks rebelled against Persian rule and united to throw off Persian control. Persians defeated in several naval battles with the Greeks.

_____

Concept Connector Journal

2. Roman Empire: How did the expansion of the Roman Empire contribute to its ultimate decline?

Through conquest and trade, wealthy Romans lived lives of luxury, which fostered greed and corruption, while ordinary Romans remained poor. Heavy taxes were needed to support the military and the bureaucracy. The upper classes devoted themselves to luxury. "Bread and circuses" were costly and may have undermined the self-reliance of the masses.

3. Aztecs and Incas: Compare the time span, location, and reason for decline of the Aztec and Incan empires.

Empire	Time Span	Place	Reason for Decline
Aztec	1300–1400s	Mexico	Defeated by the Spanish conquistador, Hernan Cortes
Inca	1438–1525	Coastal area of South America west of the Andes	Defeated by the Spanish conquistador, Francisco Pizarro

4. In 768, Charlemagne became king of the Franks. He briefly united Western Europe—France, Germany and part of Italy. How did the following policies of Charlemagne enable him to keep control of his vast empire?

• Close relations with the Church spread Christianity and created a unified empire.

• Use of *missi dominici* made sure that provincial rulers were governing justly. They also checked on roads and listened to grievances.

• Promotion of scholarship spread learning across the empire, encouraged schools.

5. Byzantine Empire: (a) Complete the following chart about the Byzantine Empire.

Empire	Time Span	Geographic Limits	Reason for Decline
Byzantine	300s–1400s	At its height, the Balkans, Middle East, North Africa	Struggles over succession, court intrigues, constant wars, plunder by Crusaders, loss of trade routes to Venice, defeat by Ottoman Turks

(b) How did the influence of the Byzantine Empire continue after its political decline?

Byzantine accomplishments in religious art and architecture influence Western styles to the present time. The Byzantines preserved and spread ancient Greek literature and produced works on history. Their knowledge of Greek and Byzantine culture contributed to the European Renaissance.

Concept Connector Journal

6. Abbasid, Mughal, and Ottoman Empires: Compare the time span, location, and reason for decline of the Abbasid, Mughal, and Ottoman empires.

Empire	Time Span	Place	Reason for Decline
Abbasid	750–1258	Northern Africa, Arabian peninsula, Persian Empire	Control fragmented, independent dynasties arose, Shiite rulers came to power, a series of invasions led to chaos
Mughal	1526–1857	Northern India	Persecution of Hindus, economic hardships and discontent sparked rebellions, Europeans got a foothold because of discontent
Ottoman	1400s–early 1900s	At its height, Eastern Europe and Balkans to Middle East	Corrupt government, weak commerce and military technology, local rulers broke away; later, provinces revolt and establish independent nations and autonomous regions, territory divided up by European powers

7. Tang Empire: Describe how the following contributed to the economy and strength of the Tang Empire.

- tributary states <u>forced to pay tribute and taxes on land to central government</u>

- land reform <u>redistribution of land to peasants strengthened the economy through more tax revenues and weakened power of large land owners</u>

- central government <u>bureaucracy rebuilt, new flexible law code developed</u>

8. Qing Empire: Explain how these Qing dynasty policies contributed to the expansion of its empire. *(Chapter 2, Section 4)*

- adopted Confucian system of government _____

_____

- able military leaders _____

_____

- imported new crops _____

_____

- encouraged silk, cotton, porcelain industries _____

_____

Concept Connector Journal

9. Spanish and British Empires: Complete the chart to compare the establishment of the Spanish and British empires in the Americas as you study Chapter 3 and Chapter 5. *(Chapter 3, Sections 1, 2, 3, 5; Chapter 5, Section 3)*

	Spanish Empire	British Empire
Political systems		
Economic systems		
Religion		

10. Second Reich: (a) Fill in the timeline below to show actions Chancellor Otto von Bismarck took that resulted in the formation of the Second Reich. *(Chapter 10, Section 1)*

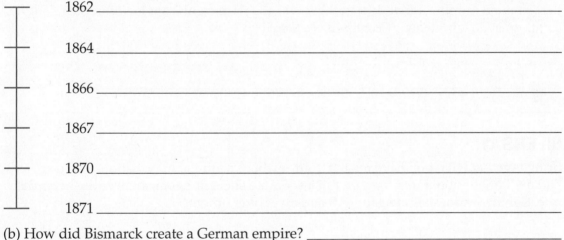

1862 _____

1864 _____

1866 _____

1867 _____

1870 _____

1871 _____

(b) How did Bismarck create a German empire? _____

_____

_____

11. Imperialism: How did European strategies of indirect rule, exploitation, trade, and treaties enable these powers to control their colonies? *(Chapter 12, Sections 1–5)*

_____

_____

_____

_____

Concept Connector Journal

12. WebQuest: Empire How has what you have learned about specific empires broadened your understanding of how a state gains or loses its power over others?

> **Transfer Your Knowledge**
> For: WebQuest **Web Code:** nbh-0808

_____
_____
_____
_____
_____

13. Decline of the Soviet Union: By the late 1800s, the Ottoman Empire was in a state of decline. Among the causes of the decline of the Ottoman Empire were nationalist revolts, economic problems, corruption, competition among European nations to expand their influence, and the efforts of some officials to reject reform and try to rebuild autocratic rule. How was the fall of the Soviet Union similar to and different from the fall of the Ottoman Empire? What do you think was the most significant factor in the fall of communist governments? *(Chapter 18, Section 5)*

_____
_____
_____

III. ESSAY

Bring together what you have read in your textbook with the information you have gathered online about this concept. **On a separate sheet of paper, answer the essential question: How does a state gain or lose power over others?**

Concept Connector Journal

Genocide

Essential Question: Why do people sometimes commit the crime of genocide?

I. WARM-UP

Crimes against humanity are committed by governments as well as by individuals. The most horrific of these crimes is called genocide.

1. You are most likely familiar with the word *homicide.* This word comes from two Latin words: *homo,* meaning "man," and *cide,* meaning "killing." So a homicide is the killing of a person. The word *genocide* comes from the Greek word *geno,* meaning "race or tribe," and the Latin word *cide.* Based on this information, write a definition on the chart below for the word *genocide.*

English Word	Word Parts	Greek or Latin Meanings	English Meaning
homicide	homo + cide	man + killing	killing of a person
genocide	geno + cide	race or tribe + killing	

2. How much of the meaning of *genocide* does your definition capture? What else would you say to explain what genocide is?

_____

_____

_____

II. EXPLORATION

The word *genocide* was not used before 1944, but such killings of entire populations had occurred at earlier times in history. During the Third Punic War between the Romans and the Carthaginians, the Romans killed or sold into slavery the entire population of Carthage in North Africa and poured salt on the land so that nothing could grow. As you complete the following journal entries, you will learn more about times in history when a stronger group has committed the crime of genocide against a weaker foe.

Concept Connector Journal

1. Native Americans: How did genocide occur among Native Americans after the arrival of the Europeans? *(Chapter 15, Section 1)*

_____

_____

_____

_____

2. Armenians: In the 1890s, tensions arose between Turkish nationalists in the Ottoman Empire and minority groups, like the Armenians, who sought their own states.

a. What political reason did Muslim Turks offer for killing Christian Armenians? *(Chapter 24, Section 3)*

_____

_____

b. How might the theory of Social Darwinism explain how Muslim Turks could justify the Armenian massacre? *(Chapter 21, Section 3)*

_____

_____

_____

3. WebQuest: Genocide How has what you have learned as you completed your WebQuest affected your view about why some people commit genocide?

> **Transfer Your Knowledge**
> **For:** WebQuest **Web Code:** nbh-2908

_____

_____

_____

_____

Concept Connector Journal

4. Holocaust: Complete the cause-and-effect chart to show some of the reasons that ordinary Germans and other Europeans failed to stand up to Hitler's Final Solution policies. *(Chapter 28, Sections 1 and 5; Chapter 29, Section 3)*

Acceptance of Hitler's Final Solution

5. Bosnia Civil War: What advantage did the dominant ethnic group in Bosnia hope to gain by ethnic cleansing? *(Chapter 32, Section 1)*

_____

_____

_____

_____

III. ESSAY

Bring together what you have read in your textbook with the information you have gathered online about this concept. **On a separate sheet of paper, answer the essential question: Why do people sometimes commit the crime of genocide?**

Concept Connector Journal

Geography's Impact

 Essential Question: How do geography and people affect one another?

I. WARM-UP

Geography is a part of your everyday life. The plants that grow in your community, the amount of rain your area gets, the type of clothes you wear each day, and even the route you take to school are all affected by geography.

1. Climate is one aspect of geography. Complete the cause-and-effect chart below to show one way that climate affects you.

Yesterday's Temperature	
Yesterday's Weather	**What You Wore as a Result**

2. How else does the climate in your region affect your life? How does it affect your community?

_____

_____

_____

_____

II. EXPLORATION

Geography has always played a role in history. As you complete the following journal entries, you will see how geography has influenced people's lives throughout time.

1. Early People: What was the most important difference between the way Old Stone Age people and New Stone Age people used their environment to get food?

Old Stone Age	New Stone Age
Hunted and gathered	Stayed in one place and farmed

Concept Connector Journal

Geography's Impact (continued)

2. First Civilizations: Early civilizations arose in river valleys for a number of reasons.

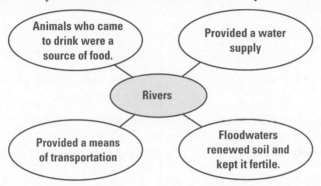

3. Tigris and Euphrates: a. Describe the location of the Tigris and Euphrates rivers.

The Tigris and Euphrates rivers arise in Asia Minor and flow southeast into the Persian

Gulf. They flow through the region named Mesepotamia, or "land between the rivers"

by the ancient Greeks.

b. How did the Tigris and Euphrates rivers affect the development of Mesopotamia?

The floodwaters of the rivers created rich soil for farming; the rivers provided a means

of transportation for traders. The region became a crossroads for people and ideas.

4. Aegean and Mediterranean Seas: a. Describe the location of the Aegean and
Mediterranean seas.

The Aegean Sea lies between Greece and Asia Minor, north of the Mediterranean Sea. The

Mediterranean Sea lies between Europe and Africa.

b. What was the impact of the Aegean and Mediterranean seas on Greek trade and
cultural diffusion?

The Greeks became skilled sailors and traded throughout the eastern Mediterranean. In

addition to cargo, they returned with ideas such as the Phoenician alphabet.

Concept Connector Journal

5. Farming in Mesoamerica: Complete the chart to show how the Maya and Aztecs solved farming problems.

Problem	Solution
After a few years, fields were no longer fertile.	The Maya let the fields lie fallow every few years to regain their nutrients.
Floodwaters from rivers could ruin crops.	The Maya built raised fields to protect their crops from floods.
There was limited land for crops in a lake environment.	The Aztecs made artificial islands on which to grow crops.

6. The Vikings: How did the Vikings' use of the seas affect trade and cultural diffusion?

They opened trade routes that connected northern Europe to lands in the Mediterranean. They also settled in different parts of Europe and Russia and mixed with the people there.

7. Impact of Rivers: Complete the chart with examples to compare how rivers affected the development of Russia with how they affected the development of Sumer in Mesopotamia.

How Rivers Affected Development	
Sumer in Mesopotamia	Russia
• trade: traded with Egypt and India	• trade: Kiev on the Dnieper River was at the heart of trade with Constantinople.
• migration: Akkadians and Babylonians arrive.	• migration: The Vikings or Varangians migrated south along the rivers.
• cultural diffusion: Akkadians, Babylonians, Assyrians adapt cuneiform to use with their own languages.	• cultural diffusion: They adopted the Cyrillic alphabet.

Concept Connector Journal

8. Africa's Geography: Compare and contrast the impact of geography on East Africa and West Africa. See the Venn diagram below.

East Africa

major
geographic feature:
Red Sea

goods traded:
ivory, spices,
precious stone,
animal hides

cultural links:
Christianity

Both

Mediterranean
Sea

Gold, cotton

New religions
introduced

West Africa

major
geographic feature:
Sahara Desert

goods traded:
leather, salt, kola nuts,
enslaved people

cultural links:
Islam

9. WebQuest: Geography's Impact How has what you have learned about the impact of geography broadened your understanding of the relationship between people and geography?

Transfer Your Knowledge
For: WebQuest **Web Code:** nbh-0608

_____

_____

_____

10. Latin America: Complete the timeline by listing an event and its significance for each date that linked the U.S. and Latin America between 1800 and 1914. (*Chapter 25, Section 4*)

1800s Ideas from American Revolution influence Latin American revolutionaries

1823 _____

_____

1848 _____

_____

1898 _____

_____

(*Continued*)

Concept Connector Journal

Geography's Impact (continued)

1904 _____

_____

1914 _____

_____

III. ESSAY

Bring together what you have read in your textbook with the information you have gathered online about this concept. **On a separate sheet of paper, answer the essential question: How do geography and people affect one another?**

Concept Connector Journal

Human Rights

 Essential Question: How are human rights won or lost?

I. WARM-UP

Human rights are a basic set of freedoms and protections that all people are entitled to. Protecting human rights begins with showing respect for others who are different from you. Suppose you are with some friends and one of them tells a joke that makes fun of someone of a different ethnic group. Check off what you would do.

_____ Repeat the joke to others.

_____ Join in the laughter, but not repeat the joke yourself.

_____ Not join in the laughter.

_____ Not join in the laughter and explain privately to your friend why you do not think he or she should tell that kind of joke.

_____ Not join in the laughter and tell your friend in front of others why you don't think he or she should tell that kind of joke.

How can refusing to listen to ethnic jokes be a step toward strengthening human rights?

_____

_____

II. EXPLORATION

Throughout history, people have struggled to gain human rights, a basic set of freedoms and protections to which all humans are entitled. As you complete the following journal entries, you will see how people have sometimes won their rights or sometimes lost them.

1. Spain: In the 1400s, under Muslim rule in Spain, Jews, Christians, and Muslims were allowed freedom of worship. In 1492, the Spanish monarchs Ferdinand and Isabella united Spain under Christian rule and forced religious conformity on everyone. Complete the chart below about the effects of Ferdinand and Isabella's denial of religious freedom to Jews and Muslims.

Cause
Ferdinand and Isabella decide to enforce Christianity as the only religion in Spain.

Effect	Effect	Effect
Church courts tried those accused of heresy and set punishments.	Hundreds of thousands of Jews and Muslims fled Spain or risked execution.	Spain lost many of its skilled people who had contributed to its economy and culture.

Concept Connector Journal

2. Totalitarian Rulers: a. How were culture, education, and propaganda used by Mussolini, Stalin, and Hitler to deprive their citizens of their human rights? List at least three ways. *(Chapter 16, Sections 3, 4, 5)*

Dictators	Culture	Education	Propaganda
Mussolini	• • •	• • •	• • •
Stalin	• • •	• • •	• • •
Hitler	• • •	• • •	• • •

b. How might these steps above be effective in depriving people of their human rights?

_____

_____

_____

3. Civil Rights Movement: As a result of the Atlantic slave trade that began in the 1600s and lasted to the 1800s, millions of enslaved Africans were transported to the Americas against their will. Even after they gained their freedom as a result of the Civil War and the 14th Amendment to the U.S. Constitution, former slaves and their descendents still were denied their human rights. How did the government and the people bring about changes in human rights following World War II? *(Chapter 18, Section 2)*

_____

_____

_____

_____

Concept Connector Journal

4. South Africa: When South Africa won its independence from Britain in 1910, the white minority government passed laws severely limiting the rights of the black majority. How did black South Africans finally win their human rights? *(Chapter 32, Section 2)*

a. Restrictions on black South Africans: _____

_____

b. African National Congress (ANC) response: _____

_____

c. Steps to ending apartheid: _____

_____

5. WebQuest: Human Rights How has what you have learned while completing your WebQuest influenced your understanding about the ways human rights are won and lost?

> **Transfer Your Knowledge**
> **For:** WebQuest **Web Code:** nbh-3408

_____

_____

_____

III. ESSAY

Bring together what you have read in your textbook with the information you have gathered online about this concept. **On a separate sheet of paper, answer the essential question: How are human rights won or lost?**

Name _____ Class _____ Date _____

Impact of the Individual

 Essential Question: How can an individual change the world?

I. WARM-UP

Many changes across the globe have been the result of one individual's actions. The chart shows five individuals whose actions changed the world.

Individual	Actions	Changes
Indian leader Mahatma Gandhi	Led a long, nonviolent struggle against British rule of India; set an example to gain support	Freed India from British rule; led to weakening and eventual collapse of the British Empire
Ecologist/writer Rachel Carson	Wrote of dangers of chemicals to the environment; founded the environmental movement	Made people aware of effects of pollution; spurred worldwide efforts to eliminate it
Medical scientist Jonas Salk	Developed the first successful vaccine against polio	Greatly reduced or wiped out polio around the world; furthered medical research
Computer engineer Tim Berners-Lee	Developed software systems; invented the World Wide Web; worked with others to promote its use	Revolution in communications that spread ideas and information across a global network
Theologian Martin Luther	Protested actions and teachings of the Catholic Church; urged others to reject Church authority	Caused the Protestant Reformation that split the Christian world; led to reforms in the Catholic Church

1. Choose one of the individuals and explain how their actions affect you.

_____

_____

2. Think of a situation in your school or community in which you would like to see some change. How could you go about helping to make that change?

_____

_____

_____

Concept Connector Journal

II. EXPLORATION

In the course of history, actions by many individuals have had a significant impact on the lives of people around the world. As you complete the following journal entries, you will see how an individual's efforts can bring about change.

1. Hammurabi and Confucius: Two individuals who have gained fame for their influence are Hammurabi and Confucius. About 1790 B.C. Hammurabi brought much of Mesopotamia under his control. He established Hammarabi's Code, the first major known attempt of a ruler to codify the laws of his state. He had the laws carved on pillars where everyone could see them. How did Confucius influence Chinese society?

Confucius was concerned with ensuring social order and good government. He taught

that everyone had duties and responsibilities. Superiors should care for inferiors and

lead by example. The best rulers consider the advice of educated men.

2. Muslim Leaders: Muslim leaders, such as Muhammad and Akbar the Great had a lasting impact on history.

Muslim Leader	Actions	Influence
Muhammad	Devoted his life to spreading Islam	Thousands of Arabs adopted Islam, which has spread around the world.
Akbar the Great	Was tolerant of Hindus, hired effective officials, modernized the army, introduced land reforms	Recognized India's diversity and strengthened its government

3. John Locke: What ideas of John Locke influenced Thomas Jefferson? *(Chapter 5, Section 1)*

_____

_____

_____

4. Leaders of the American Revolution: Of the leaders of the American Revolution, which individual's actions do you think had the greatest influence on the outcome of the war? *(Chapter 5, Section 3)*

Leader and actions _____

_____

Influence on outcome of the war _____

_____

Concept Connector Journal

5. WebQuest: Impact of the Individual How has what you have learned as you completed your WebQuest affected your view about the impact of any one individual?

> **Transfer Your Knowledge**
> **For:** WebQuest **Web Code:** nbh-1808

_____

_____

_____

6. Jiang Jeishi and Mao Zedong: a. Fill in the Venn Diagram below to show the goals of Jiang Jeishi and Mao Zedong.

Goals of Jiang Jeishi   Goals of Mao Zedong

Control China

b. How did Mao Zedong's success change the course of the history of China? *(Chapter 15, Section 4)*

_____

7. Nelson Mandela: How did Nelson Mandela help change the course of history in South Africa? *(Chapter 17, Section 2)*

_____

_____

_____

III. ESSAY

Bring together what you have read in your textbook with the information you have gathered online about this concept. **On a separate sheet of paper, answer the essential question: How can an individual change the world?**

Name _____ Class _____ Date _____

Migration

 Essential Question: Under what circumstances do people migrate?

I. WARM-UP

People have been moving from place to place on Earth since early times. Migration still goes on today.

1. Have you or members of your family ever moved? If so, what were the main reasons for moving?

_____

_____

_____

2. How does moving affect someone's life? Fill in the web below to show some of the ways.

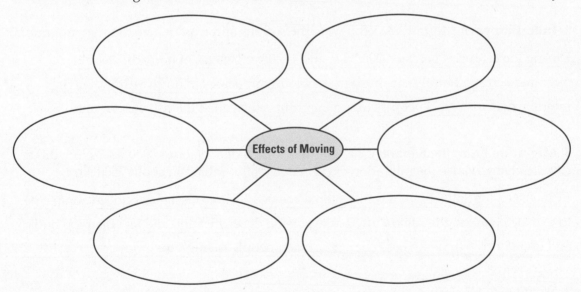

II. EXPLORATION

Migration occurs when large groups of people move from one place to another. As you complete the following journal entries, you will see how migration has played a role in world events.

Concept Connector Journal

1. Early People: Look at the chart below to see how different factors contributed to the migration of early people.

Contributing Factors	Examples
Food sources	Migration of animals led people to follow them.
Climate changes	Drought
Environmental events	Earthquake or flood
Competition with other groups	For land, resources, food

2. Indo-European Migrations: Who were the Aryans and from where did they migrate?

During the centuries between 2000 B.C. and 1500 B.C., waves of nomadic people

migrated across Central Asia through the mountain passes in northwest India. They

intermarried with local peoples to form a group who called themselves Aryans.

3. Migration From the Sahara: What was the Sahara like in about 2000 B.C.? How did a climate change cause the migration of people from the Sahara in about 2500 B.C.?

In 2000 B.C., the Sahara was a well-watered area with rich grasslands and savanna. Due

to climate changes, the Sahara dried out, causing desertification and leaving croplands

and grasslands parched. These changes caused people to migrate.

4. WebQuest: Migration How has what you have learned about migratory patterns broadened your understanding of why people migrate?

> **Transfer Your Knowledge**
> **For:** WebQuest **Web Code:** nbh-2308

_____

_____

_____

Concept Connector Journal

5. Irish and American Migration: Just as thousands of people in the past migrated in search of a better life, large numbers of people were on the move in the nineteenth century. Millions of Irish migrated to the United States, starting in the mid 1800s. At the same time, Americans began migrating westward across their continent. Complete the cause-and-effect charts to show why these migrations occurred and what happened to Native Americans as a result of the westward push. *(Chapter 11, Sections 2 and 4)*

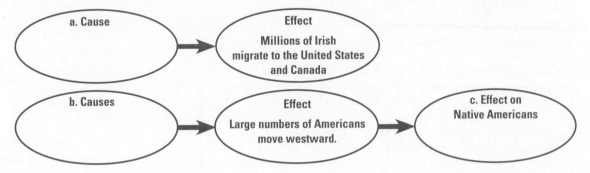

6. Westward Movement: How did the concept of Manifest Destiny affect the nation's boundaries? *(Chapter 11, Section 4)*

_____

_____

_____

III. ESSAY

Bring together what you have read in your textbook with the information you have gathered online about this concept. **On a separate sheet of paper, answer the essential question: Under what circumstances do people migrate?**

Concept Connector Journal

Nationalism

? **Essential Question:** How can nationalism be a unifying and a divisive force?

I. WARM-UP

1. Nationalism is a strong feeling of pride in and devotion to one's country. Each nation has symbols that help bring those feelings to mind.

Sketch below and identify three symbols that you associate with the United States.

How do these symbols help foster a feeling of unity in the nation?

_____

_____

_____

II. EXPLORATION

Nationalism can be an ideology, a feeling, or a social or political movement that focuses on the nation. As you complete the following journal entries, you will see how nationalism has been a unifying and divisive force in shaping the modern world.

1. French Revolution: Review the songs, symbols, and slogans associated with the French Revolution.

Songs	Symbols	Slogans
Marseillaise: "Forward children of the homeland / The day of glory has arrived / Against us, tyranny's bloody standard / Has been raised." **La Carmagnole:** "Let's dance the Carmagnole / Long live the canon's roar."	Tricolor flag Red cap of liberty Everyone called "citizen" Elaborate clothes abolished	"Liberty, Equality, Brotherhood, or Death" "Tremble, enemies of France"

Concept Connector Journal

How did these songs, symbols, and slogans foster nationalism? *(Chapter 6, Section 3)*

_____

_____

_____

_____

2. Balkan Nationalism: The breakup of the Ottoman Empire in the nineteenth century planted the seeds of further conflict in the region that stretched from Eastern Europe and the Balkans to North Africa and the Middle East. The unresolved problems of the late nineteenth century eventually spilled over into the late twentieth and early twenty-first centuries. Complete the chart of the effects of Balkan nationalism on the Empire and Europe in the late 1800s and early 1900s. *(Chapter 10, Section 4)*

Cause	Effects
Independence movements helped weaken the multinational Ottoman Empire, leaving it subject to attack by European powers.	• _____ • _____ • _____ • _____

3. WebQuest: Nationalism How has what you have learned as you completed your WebQuest affected your view about whether nationalism is a unifying or divisive force?

> **Transfer Your Knowledge**
> **For:** WebQuest **Web Code:** nbh-2208

_____

_____

_____

4. Imperialism: How did British imperialism spark nationalism in India and China? *(Chapter 12, Sections 4 and 5)*

_____

_____

_____

Concept Connector Journal

5. Latin America: During the 1920s and 1930s, Latin American nationalism was influenced by events around the world. How did these events unify or divide the nations of Latin America? *(Chapter 15, Section 1)*

a. World economy _____

_____

b. United States influence _____

_____

c. Types of governments that developed in Latin America _____

_____

6. India: In India, religion and the state are separate, but the Bharatiya Janata Party (BJP) has called for a government based on the principles of Hinduism. Would this be a unifying or a divisive force in India? Why? *(Chapter 19, Section 1)*

_____

_____

_____

III. ESSAY

Bring together what you have read in your textbook with the information you have gathered online about this concept. **On a separate sheet of paper, answer the essential question: How can nationalism be a unifying and divisive force?**

Concept Connector Journal

Political Systems

 Essential Question: How do political systems rise, develop, and decline?

I. WARM-UP

A political system, or government, is set up to make decisions for a society, and when necessary, defend it from attack. The Greeks identified three main kinds of political systems: rule by one, rule by a few, and rule by many.

1. Create an organization chart of your school government. An organization chart is a visual representation of levels of responsibility and relationships.

2. What responsibilities does your student government have? In what ways is it like and unlike a true political system?

_____

_____

_____

II. EXPLORATION

Throughout history, political systems have taken many forms, depending on circumstances. As you complete the following journal entries, you will see how political systems have affected the way civilizations have developed.

Concept Connector Journal

1. Zhou Dynasty: The rise and fall of the Zhou Dynasty was an example of the dynastic cycle. The Zhou overthrew the Shang and in turn were replaced by the Qing. How did feudal lords under the Zhou help China's economic growth? How did feudalism contribute to the end of the Zhou dynasty? Write your answers in the arrows below.

2. Political systems: How did each of these political systems develop in Greek city-states?

a. monarchy At first, the ruler of the polis was a king.

b. aristocracy Power shifted from the king to the aristocracy who were the only ones who could afford weapons. At first the aristocrats defended the king, then they won power for themselves.

c. oligarchy Wealthy middle class merchants, farmers, and artisans challenged the landowning nobles for power and began to dominate some city-states in an oligarchy.

3. Republic: List three ways plebeians made the Roman senate more democratic.

a. They gained the right to elect their own tribunes.

b. The tribunes could veto any laws that were unfavorable to plebeians.

c. They got the Laws of the Twelve Tables set up in the Forum so everyone could know what the laws were.

Concept Connector Journal

4. Aztecs and Incas: Well before Europeans reached the America, powerful civilizations developed in the Americas. Two of the longest lasting were the Aztecs in Mexico and the Incas in Peru. Identify the source of power and role of each of these civilizations' emperors.

a. Aztec Emperor: Elected by a council of nobles, priests, and military leaders; carried on continual warfare; had prisoners of war sacrificed to the gods.

b. Incan Emperor: Proclaimed himself emperor, claimed to be divine, laid claim to all the land, herds, mines, and people of his empire; demanded that everyone in the empire adopt the Incan language and religion; quickly put down any rebellions; passed his position on to his son.

5. End of Feudal System: The chart below shows how the Agricultural Revolution and the revival of trade and travel led to the decline of feudalism.

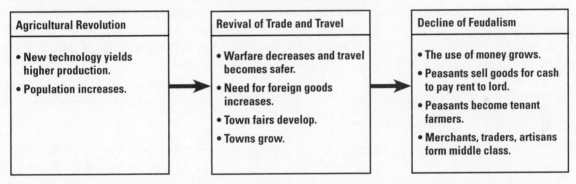

Agricultural Revolution	Revival of Trade and Travel	Decline of Feudalism
• New technology yields higher production. • Population increases.	• Warfare decreases and travel becomes safer. • Need for foreign goods increases. • Town fairs develop. • Towns grow.	• The use of money grows. • Peasants sell goods for cash to pay rent to lord. • Peasants become tenant farmers. • Merchants, traders, artisans form middle class.

6. WebQuest: Political Systems How has what you have learned while completing your WebQuest expanded your understanding of how political systems rise, develop, and decline?

Transfer Your Knowledge
For: WebQuest **Web Code:** nbh-1508

_____

_____

_____

Concept Connector Journal

7. Absolute Monarchs: Write a brief description of how each of the following rulers weakened his empire by using absolute power. *(Chapter 4, Sections 1, 2, 3, and 5)*

a. Philip II _____

_____

b. Louis XIV _____

_____

c. Charles I _____

_____

d. Peter the Great _____

_____

8. Federal Government: The United States government is a political system based on fundamental democratic principles. How is the federal government of the United States organized to ensure a system of checks and balances? What are the benefits of this system? *(Chapter 5, Section 3)*

_____

_____

_____

III. ESSAY

Bring together what you have read in your textbook with the information you have gathered online about this concept. **On a separate sheet of paper, answer the essential question: How do political systems rise, develop, and decline?**

Concept Connector Journal

Revolution

 Essential Question: Why do political revolutions occur?

I. WARM-UP

A revolution is associated with change. Often, advertisers or salespeople use the word "revolutionary" to draw consumer attention to a new and different product.

1. What do you think about when you hear that something is "revolutionary"? Write your ideas on the web below.

Revolution/
Revolutionary

2. Do you think a revolution always improves a society? Why or why not?

_____

_____

_____

_____

II. EXPLORATION

Numerous political revolutions have occurred over time in all parts of the world. As you complete the following journal entries, you will see how revolutions have changed the course of history in different ways.

1. Glorious Revolution: List three reasons that support the idea that the Glorious Revolution was a true revolution. *(Chapter 4, Section 3)*

a. _____

_____

b. _____

_____

c. _____

_____

Concept Connector Journal

2. French Revolution and Peasants' Revolt in Germany: Both the Peasants' Revolt in Germany in 1542 and the French Revolution in the late 1700s were started by suppressed people hoping to improve their living conditions and gain civil rights. Complete the chart to show how the outcome of the French Revolution differed from that of the Peasants' Revolt. *(Chapter 1, Section 3 and Chapter 6, Sections 2 and 3)*

Outcome of Peasants' Revolt	Outcome of French Revolution
• Peasants fail to get support of Martin Luther. • Nobles suppress revolt, killing tens of thousands.	• •

3. WebQuest: Revolution: How has what you have learned as you completed your WebQuest affected your view about why revolutions occur?

> **Transfer Your Knowledge**
> **For:** WebQuest **Web Code:** nbh-2008

_____

_____

_____

4. Latin American Revolutions: Why did the social structure of Latin America lead to revolt there? *(Chapter 8, Section 3)*

_____

_____

_____

_____

Concept Connector Journal

5. Revolution of 1905: Complete the cause-and-effect chain to show how one concession of the tsars was impacted by industrialization in the years leading up to the Revolution of 1905. *(Chapter 10, Section 5)*

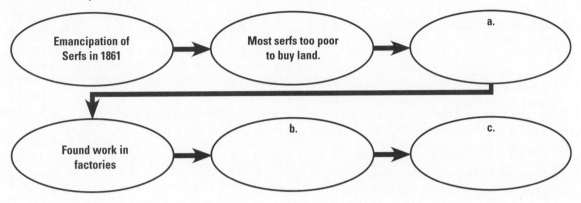

6. French and Russian Revolutions: Complete the chart to compare the Russian Revolution with the French Revolution. *(Chapter 14, Section 5)*

	French Revolution	Russian Revolution
Causes	Influenced by American Revolution; financial woes; class system; lack of social reform	
Duration/Phases	10 years; Commune, Reign of Terror, Directory	
Leaders	Lafayette; Robespierre	
World Reaction	Some countries threatened to intervene to protect monarchy	
Results	Overthrow of king; church under state control; social reform; nationalism; Declaration of the Rights of Man and the Citizen	

Concept Connector Journal

7. Independence movements: Compare the emergence of a new nation after World War II with the American Revolution, including how independence was achieved and the challenges facing the new nation. *(Chapter 19)*

_____

_____

_____

8. Revolution in Latin America: Review your response to Question 6 and compare the circumstances of a revolution in Latin America with these earlier revolutions. *(Chapter 21, Section 4)*

_____

_____

_____

III. ESSAY

Bring together what you have read in your textbook with the information you have gathered online about this concept. **On a separate sheet of paper, answer the essential question: Why do political revolutions occur?**

Name _____ Class _____ Date _____

Concept Connector Journal

Science and Technology

 Essential Question: What are the benefits and costs of science and technology?

I. WARM-UP

Science and technology have propelled civilizations forward throughout history. Even today, they play a very significant role in creating economic and social benefits. However, technological advances also have costs.

1. Complete the web below to show three ways you communicate with others.

2. What are the benefits and costs of these types of communication?

_____

_____

_____

II. EXPLORATION

Science and technology are responsible for enormous changes in the lives of humans and the development of civilizations. As you complete the following journal entries, you will see how science and technology have affected history.

Concept Connector Journal

1. Egypt and Mesopotamia: Name three technological advances made by Egyptians or the people of Mesopotamia and explain how those advances affected their civilization.

a. Cuneiform developed by Sumerians enabled people to record economic exchanges. As it improved, they could also record prayers, myth, laws and business contracts.

b. Extracting iron from ore enabled Hittites to make stronger tools and weapons, which gave them an advantage over other civilizations.

c. Mummification enabled Egyptians to learn more about the human body and disease. It enabled later historians to learn more about how Egyptians lived and died.

2. China and Greece: The Chinese and the Greeks both made advances in knowledge about astronomy and medicine. Imagine two people from these ancient civilizations bragging about their accomplishments. Complete the dialogue.

China

We measured the movement of stars and planets and improved calendars. Our doctors developed anesthetics, herbal remedies, and acupuncture.

Greece

We determined that the Earth was round, rotated on its axis, and orbited the sun. Hippocrates studied the cause of illnesses and looked for cures. He set ethical standards for doctors.

3. Movable Type: How did the development of movable type help spread Chinese learning and culture?

It's faster to print text with movable type; it meant Chinese text could be printed in greater quantities.

_____

Name _____ Class _____ Date _____

Concept Connector Journal

4. Gunpowder: What was the benefit of gunpowder to the Chinese? What was a possible cost?

Gunpowder provided the Chinese with a weapon that was more effective than hand
combat. The cost was the possibility of a greater loss of human life.

_____

5. Scientific Revolution: How did the scientific method differ from earlier approaches to science? How did it pave the way for scientific thinking today? *(Chapter 1, Section 5)*

_____
_____
_____

6. WebQuest: Science and Technology How has what you have learned while completing your WebQuest influenced your view about the benefits and costs of scientific and technological advances?

> **Transfer Your Knowledge**
> **For:** WebQuest **Web Code:** nbh-1308

_____
_____
_____

7. Compass: How did an improvement to the compass help lead the way to a global age? *(Chapter 2, Section 1)*

_____
_____
_____

Concept Connector Journal

8. Steam Engine: Just as the printing press changed how people shared information, the steam engine became key to the Industrial Revolution. Complete the chart to compare the impact of the two developments. *(Chapter 7, Section 2)*

	Printing Press	Steam Engine
a. Who benefited		
b. How same jobs were done before		
c. Why it was important		

9. Changing Lives: a. Choose a scientific discovery or advance from the Scientific Revolution and the Industrial Revolution. Explain how each discovery changed people's lives. *(Chapter 1, Section 5 and Chapter 9, Section 1)*

Scientific Revolution

Industrial Revolution

b. Choose one current scientific or technological development and describe how it is changing people's lives.

_____

_____

_____

_____

Name _____ Class _____ Date _____

Concept Connector Journal

Science and Technology (continued)

10. Technological Changes: One chart below shows the impact of a technological change in the High Middle Ages. Choose a technological advance in the Industrial Revolution and complete the second chart to show what effects it had on the economy and peoples' lives. *(Chapter 9, Sections 1 and 2)*

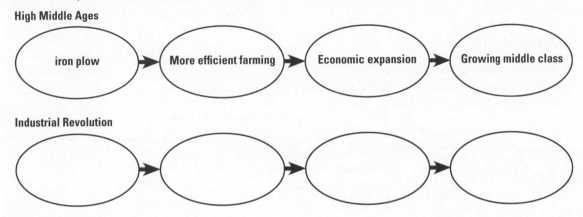

High Middle Ages

iron plow → More efficient farming → Economic expansion → Growing middle class

Industrial Revolution

11. Atomic Research: Describe a benefit and a cost resulting from the atomic research of Marie Curie and Albert Einstein. *(Chapter 16, Section 1)*

_____

_____

_____

III. ESSAY

Bring together what you have read in your textbook with the information you have gathered online about this concept. **On a separate sheet of paper, answer the essential question: What are the benefits and costs of science and technology?**

Concept Connector Journal

Trade

 Essential Question: What are the intended and unintended effects of trade?

I. WARM-UP

1. Trade is the voluntary exchange of goods or services, or both. Think of an occasion in which you have engaged in trading something for something else.

a. What did you trade? _____

b. What did you get in exchange? _____

c. Were you satisfied with the trade? Why or why not? _____

_____

d. What conditions have to be fulfilled for you to engage in trade? _____

_____

2. Why do nations trade?

_____

_____

II. EXPLORATION

From ancient times, individuals and groups have engaged in trade. It has had a major impact on economics and culture. As you complete the following journal entries, you will see the intended and unintended effects of that trade.

1. Phoenician Sea Traders: How did Phoenicians earn the title "carriers of civilization"?

The Phoenicians, who emerged as an independent people after the decline of the Egyptians, occupied land in the eastern Mediterranean region, now Lebanon and Syria. By trading with people and setting up colonies all around the Mediterranean Sea, they spread Middle Eastern civilization beyond its original borders.

Concept Connector Journal

2. Trade Networks: See the chart below for a comparison of China's Silk Road to the Phoenician trade network.

	PHOENICIAN TRADE	CHINA'S SILK ROAD
WHERE	From North Africa westward through the Mediterranean to the Atlantic Ocean	Silk Road stretched 4,000 miles from Western Asia to the Middle East
WITH WHOM	North Africa, Sicily, Spain, Britain	India, Rome, Persia, civilizations in Central Asia
WHAT GOODS	Glass, purple dye, tin	Fruits, furs, muslin cloth, glass, silk.
WHAT ELSE	Greeks adapted Phoenician alphabet	Chinese inventions, science, medicine spread to West

3. Trade in the Middle Ages: How was trade in the 1100s affected by each of the following factors?

a. population growth Traders began to crisscross Europe to meet the growing demand for goods that were caused by growing populations and demand by the wealthy for new goods.

b. decrease in foreign invasions Less turmoil allowed people to travel more extensively and trade more goods with local merchants.

c. merchant caravans Merchants banded together for protection and, as a result, revived old trade routes.

d. Hanseatic League This association of German towns protected traders interests and dominated trade in Northern Europe for more than 150 years.

e. banks As trade revived and the use of money increased, banks met the need for money for investment and provided a source of credit.

4. Russian Trade: Phoenicia was an early trading center along the coast of the Mediterranean Sea. In early Russia, the city of Kiev was established by Vikings and became a hub of trade.

a. Phoenicians sailed their ships around the Mediterranean to trade. Vikings traveled by longboats south from Scandinavia along rivers between the Baltic and Black seas and mixed their culture with that of the Slavs. Phoenicians established colonies throughout the Mediterranean. Vikings collected tribute from the Slavs and carried on a thriving trade with Constantinople.

Concept Connector Journal

b. How were Vikings affected by their trade with Constantinople?

Vikings founded Kiev and gave their name to Russia. Through trade with Byzantium, Kiev rulers eventually adopted much of Byzantine art and culture. Constantinople sent Christian missionaries to convert the Slavs. The missionaries adapted the Greek alphabet so they could translate the Bible into the Slavic tongue. This Cyrillic alphabet is still used in Russia.

5. Asia and East Africa: By the 600s, a flourishing trade existed between East Africa and Asia. The following diagram shows the exchange of goods and ideas.

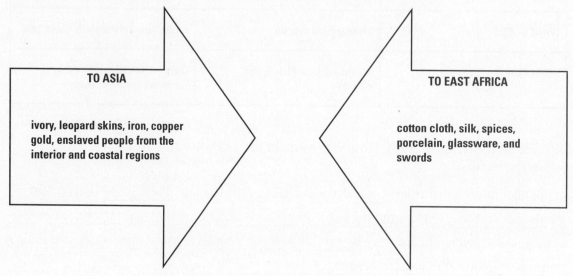

TO ASIA

ivory, leopard skins, iron, copper gold, enslaved people from the interior and coastal regions

TO EAST AFRICA

cotton cloth, silk, spices, porcelain, glassware, and swords

What was a major unintended consequence of this contact?

The development of the Swahili language and culture, which intermingled elements of African and Arab cultures

6. WebQuest: Trade How has what you have learned about free trade increased your understanding of the intended and unintended consequences of trade?

> **Transfer Your Knowledge**
> **For:** WebQuest **Web Code:** nbh-1208

_____

_____

_____

Concept Connector Journal

7. Dutch Trading Empire: How did the Dutch affect trade in Southeast Asia?
(Chapter 2, Section 3)

_____

_____

_____

8. Indian Trade in Southeast Asia: What was the result of French and English influence on the Mughal Empire? *(Chapter 2, Section 3)*

_____

_____

_____

9. A Global Age: The 1400s through the 1700s can be considered a global age. Curiosity and the desire for wealth drove Europeans to venture across the seas to the Americas, Africa, South Asia, and East Asia. For each region, write a brief description of the role trade played in this expanded contact. Think in terms of economics, politics, and society. *(Chapter 2)*

• Americas _____

_____

• Africa _____

_____

• South Asia _____

_____

• East Asia _____

_____

• Europe _____

_____

Concept Connector Journal

Trade (continued)

10. Slave Trade: a. Who benefited most from the transatlantic slave trade? Why?
(Chapter 3, Section 4)

_____

_____

_____

b. What were some unintended consequences of the slave trade for African states and societies?

_____

_____

_____

11. Japan: In 1853, the United States demanded that Japan open its doors to trade. Unable to defend itself from American threats to use military force, Japan agreed to give trading and other rights to the United States. How did Japan benefit? What were the costs? Use the graphic below to list three benefits and three costs. *(Chapter 13, Section 1)*

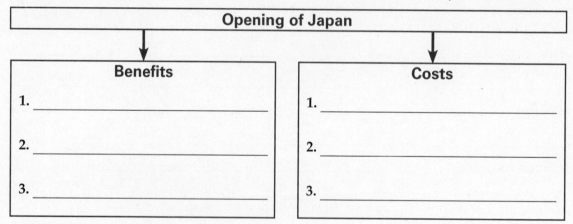

Opening of Japan

Benefits	**Costs**
1. _____	1. _____
2. _____	2. _____
3. _____	3. _____

III. ESSAY

Bring together what you have read in your textbook with the information you have gathered online about this concept. **On a separate sheet of paper, answer the essential question: What are the intended and unintended effects of trade?**